LOTUS 1-2-3®

Tutorial and Applications

Dr. Nancy Groneman

Emporia State University,
Emporia, Kansas

MW01518950

SOUTH-WESTERN PUBLISHING CO.

Credits:
Managing Editor: Robert E. First
Production Manager: Carol Sturzenberger
Production Editor: Karen E. Davis
Associate Director/Design: Darren K. Wright
Associate Photo Editor/Stylist: Linda Ellis
Marketing Manager: Brian Taylor
Consulting Editor: Minta Berry

Copyright © 1993

by SOUTH-WESTERN PUBLISHING CO.

Cincinnati, Ohio

ALL RIGHTS RESERVED

The text of this publication, or any part thereof, may not be reproduced or transmitted in any form or by any means, electronic or mechanical, including photocopying, recording, storage in an information retrieval system, or otherwise, without the prior written permission of the publisher.

ISBN: 0-538-61593-1

Library of Congress Catalog Card Number: 91-66313

2 3 4 5 6 H 97 96 95 94 93 92

Printed in the United States of America

Photo Credits:
Page 2 Courtesy of Software Publishing Corporation

PREFACE

Lotus® 1-2-3®[1] Tutorial and Applications is designed to teach the three basic components of Lotus 1-2-3: spreadsheets, database management, and graphics. Lotus 1-2-3 is a popular software package in businesses and schools.

This book is designed mainly for high school or post-secondary school students. It can also supplement the various manuals and materials available from Lotus Development Co. You must have a copy of the Lotus 1-2-3 software package before using this book. You should also have the template disk that accompanies the book.

Chapter 1 provides an introduction to the 1-2-3 software and covers start-up operations. Chapters 2-7 cover basic spreadsheet operations. You will learn the main elements of the spreadsheet. Chapters 8-12 cover advanced spreadsheet operations. Chapters 13-15 cover graphics, including how to create pie charts, bar charts, line graphs, and XY graphs. Chapters 14-18 cover database management operations. You will learn about creating and using databases to answer queries (questions). The final chapter, Chapter 19, introduces the exciting options available with WYSIWYG (What you see is what you get). Release 2.3 of the software is required to use WYSIWYG. WYSIWYG allows you to change the type size and style used on the spreadsheet, to display and print graphs with spreadsheets, and many other useful features.

The format of each chapter includes:

1. **Chapter objectives**   Specific objectives that will be covered in the chapter.

2. **Background information**   An explanation of various commands, their functions, and uses in the schools, business, or home environment..

3. **Tutorials**   Step-by-step instructions including each keystroke needed to complete an operation. Tutorial instructions are provided for each objective covered in a chapter.

4. **Activities**   Short exercises that provide you the opportunity to apply the skills you have learned in the tutorial instructions. An activity is provided for each major objective covered in a chapter. You will need the template disk that accompanies this book to complete the tutorials and activities.

5. **Theory Exercises**   Each chapter contains an end-of-chapter true/false quiz and a completion quiz related to the content of the chapter. Theory exercises can be used as self-tests or review.

6. **Final End-of-Chapter Activity**   A final activity at the end of each chapter is designed to make you think on your own and apply what you have learned in the chapter.

Some tutorial exercises and some activities will require you to create spreadsheet or databases on your own. For others, you will use files stored on the template disk to manipulate the data in the files. You will also complete template files containing only partial data.

---

[1]Lotus® 1-2-3® is a registered trademark of Lotus Development Corporation.

CONTENTS

Cycle 2 □ Advanced Spreadsheet Tutorials and Exercises

Cycle 3 ❑ Graphics Tutorials and Exercises

CHAPTER 1

OBJECTIVES

☐ Define the three functions of Lotus 1-2-3
☐ List the uses for Lotus 1-2-3
☐ Specify the minimum hardware requirements of Lotus 1-2-3
☐ Identify the hardware components of a personal computer
☐ Identify the parts of a keyboard

WHAT CAN LOTUS 1-2-3 DO?

Lotus 1-2-3 is an integrated software program, which means it contains more than one function. Lotus 1-2-3 includes three main functions—spreadsheets, database management, and graphics. Other software programs similar to 1-2-3 are called Lotus 1-2-3 clones. They look like and perform functions similar to Lotus 1-2-3, but their start-up procedures are somewhat different.

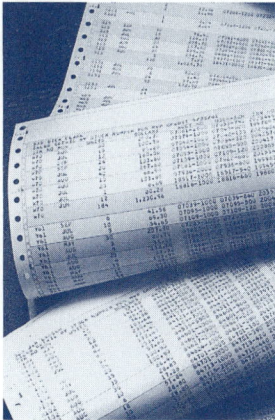

SPREADSHEETS

Spreadsheets are often considered financial planning tools. Spreadsheets make it easy to make calculations, prepare financial statements, plan budgets, and make financial decisions.

A spreadsheet printout

DATABASE MANAGEMENT

The database management function makes it easy to organize and locate information. Address lists, inventory information, and personnel records are often stored as databases. Information stored in a database can be located, sorted alphabetically and numerically, selected based on given criteria, and printed in a variety of report formats.

GRAPHICS

The graphics function allows pie charts, bar charts, and line graphs to be made. Graphs are often used within reports to highlight or clarify complicated numerical information. A graph will often get a point across much faster than a verbal explanation or a written report. Graphs can also be useful for presentations. In small groups, the graph can be shown directly on the computer monitor. Slides or transparencies of graphs can be prepared for use with large groups.

Graphs add visual interest to a presentation.

HOW IS LOTUS 1-2-3 USED?

Each of the three Lotus 1-2-3 functions can be used at home, at school, or on a future job. Lotus 1-2-3 is one of the most popular software programs in the United States, so it is likely you will use it even after you graduate.

Spreadsheet Uses

Spreadsheets can be used at home to handle personal finances. Records of monthly and yearly household expenses can be kept on a spreadsheet. Spreadsheets can be used to figure your or your parents' income taxes or to determine how much car or house payments will be. School principals often use spreadsheets to determine raises in teachers' salaries each year. Spreadsheets are also used to keep track of the expenses of each department in the school to determine how much is spent by the physical education department, science department, or business department.

Databases Uses

Database software can be used at home to keep records of your friends' and relatives' names, addresses, phone numbers, and birthdays. These lists can be useful to send birthday cards or mailings at various holidays. Database software is used in schools to keep records of students' attendance, grades, and class schedules. In businesses, databases are used frequently to keep inventory records and mailing lists.

Graphics Uses

Graphics software is likely to be used at home by students for school assignments such as term papers or special class presentations. In schools, administrators may use graphics software to create charts depicting budgets for various departments within the school. Line graphs may be created to show changes in school attendance from week to week or year to year. In businesses, graphics are used in stockholder's reports, advertising brochures, and financial reports.

WHAT COMPUTER HARDWARE AND SOFTWARE ARE NEEDED?

A computer has several components that operate together and create a computer system. Generally, a computer system includes a central processing unit (CPU), a monitor, keyboard, disk drives, and a printer. An IBM personal computer (PC) or IBM compatible computer is required to run Lotus 1-2-3.

Before using Lotus 1-2-3, you must go through an installation process, in which special instructions called drivers are selected and installed on the Lotus 1-2-3 System Disk. These drivers allow the program to use the specific type of monitor, keyboard, and printer you have.

Hardware Requirements

To use Lotus 1-2-3, Releases 2.0 or 2.1, you must have an IBM or IBM compatible personal computer with a minimum of 256K of random access memory (RAM). You should have two floppy disk drives or one floppy disk drive and a hard disk drive. If it is connected to a local area network, your computer should still have one floppy disk drive for your data disk.

To use Lotus 1-2-3, Release 2.2, you must have an IBM or IBM compatible personal computer with a minimum of 320K of RAM memory with at least two disk drives. This version must run under DOS 2.0 or higher releases of DOS.

To use Lotus 1-2-3, Release 2.3, you must have an IBM or IBM compatible personal computer. Your computer must have a minimum of 384K of RAM memory, DOS 2.1 or higher, and a hard disk.

To use Lotus 1-2-3, 3.0 or 3.1, you must have an IBM or IBM compatible personal computer. Your computer must have a minimum of 1MB (megabyte) of random access memory (RAM), an 80286 or higher microprocessor, DOS 3.0 or higher, and a hard disk. If you are using Release 3, make sure no other program such as a RAM resident program is using part of the 1MB of RAM memory.

A monochrome or color monitor can be used with Lotus 1-2-3. A color monitor will usually give higher resolution graphics. A graphics card or board is required to view graphs, but it is not required to use the spreadsheet or database functions.

A dot matrix or laser printer is recommended. A daisywheel printer will print spreadsheets and database reports but will not print graphs.

Software Requirements

The disk(s) on which the program is stored is called software. Software gives the computer instructions that make it perform the spreadsheet, database, and graphics functions.

Lotus Development Corp. has introduced a number of versions of Lotus 1-2-3 over the last few years. Each version has different computer requirements.

Lotus 1-2-3, Release 2.01. To use Lotus 1-2-3, Release 2.01, you will need:

- ❑ System Disk
- ❑ PrintGraph Disk
- ❑ 320K RAM memory
- ❑ Two floppy disk drives or one hard disk and one floppy disk
- ❑ DOS 2.0 or higher

The System Disk is the software program disk that allows you to create and store spreadsheets, databases, and graphs. It also lets you print spreadsheets and databases. The PrintGraph Disk is required to print graphs. A hard disk system is not required to run Lotus 1-2-3 Release 2.01.

Lotus 1-2-3, Release 2.2. To use Lotus 1-2-3, Release 2.2, you will need:

- ❑ System Disk
- ❑ Two floppy disk drives or one hard disk and one floppy disk
- ❑ 320K RAM memory
- ❑ DOS 2.0 or higher

Lotus 1-2-3, Release 2.3. To use Lotus 1-2-3, Release 2.3, you will need:

▢ System Disk
▢ One hard disk and one floppy disk
▢ 384K RAM memory (512K RAM for WYSIWYG display)
▢ DOS 2.1 or higher

Lotus 1-2-3, Release 3. To use Lotus 1-2-3, Release 3, you will need:

▢ System Disk
▢ One hard disk and one floppy disk
▢ 1MB RAM memory
▢ DOS 3.0 or higher

To store Lotus 1-2-3 on a hard disk drive, you will need to create a directory on the hard disk for the Lotus 1-2-3 program. It is recommended that you name the directory **Lotus.** Then, use the Install Disk to copy the other Lotus 1-2-3 disks into the Lotus directory on the hard disk as shown in Figure 1.1. The disks to be copied onto the hard disk include the System Disk, Drivers Disk 1, Drivers Disk 2, and Font Disk.

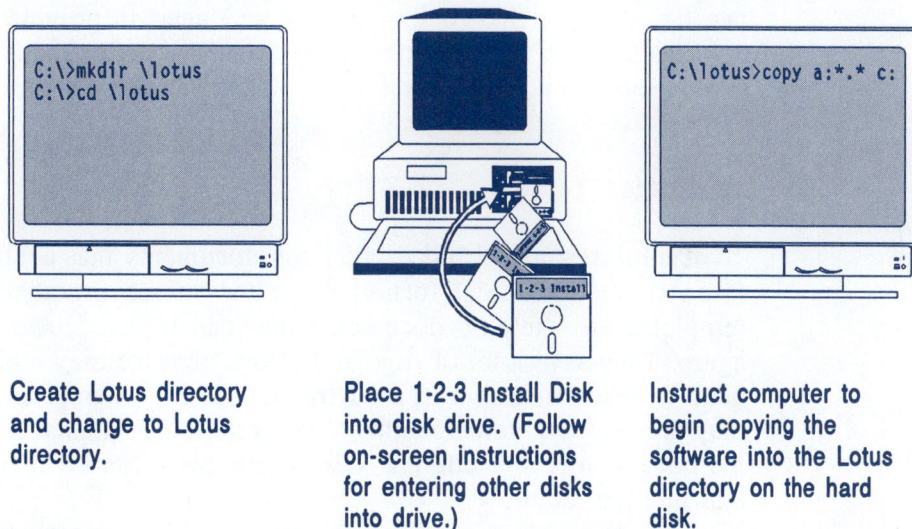

```
C:\>mkdir \lotus
C:\>cd \lotus
```

```
C:\lotus>copy a:*.* c:
```

Create Lotus directory and change to Lotus directory.

Place 1-2-3 Install Disk into disk drive. (Follow on-screen instructions for entering other disks into drive.)

Instruct computer to begin copying the software into the Lotus directory on the hard disk.

Figure 1.1 ▢ *Copy Lotus Disks to Lotus Directory*

Data Disks

To store spreadsheets, databases, and/or graphics, you should have a blank data disk. Although you may be using a computer with a hard disk, it is best in a classroom situation to store your own work on a floppy disk.

Data disks come in two sizes, either 5 1/4 inch or 3 1/2 inch. The size you will need depends on the size of the disk drives on your computer. Disks are made from a round plastic sheet coated with a magnetic surface. This plastic sheet is inserted in either a 5 1/4 inch plastic jacket or a 3 1/4 inch plastic cartridge.

There are two main differences between 5 1/4 inch and 3 1/2 inch disks. First, the 5 1/4 inch disks can store much less information than 3 1/2 inch disks. Second, the 5 1/4 inch disks can be damaged easily and should be handled very carefully, while the 3 1/2 inch disks are less susceptible to damage. However, both types of disks can be damaged, and the data stored on those disks can be permanently lost. So that the data you create is not destroyed, follow these rules:

- ❑ Keep disks at normal room temperatures.
- ❑ Do not bend diskettes.
- ❑ Do not spill liquids on diskettes, especially hot liquids.
- ❑ Do not place disks near magnets or telephones.
- ❑ Do not touch the exposed area of the disk.
- ❑ Keep the disk in its sleeve when not in use.

Formatting Disks

Before using a disk for the first time, you must format it. The formatting process creates sectors, much like pie slices, and tracks, much like grooves in a record. Once a disk is formatted, documents can be stored on it. Your instructor will need to provide you with a formatted disk that contains files you will use to complete Activities in this book. These files are called templates.

Templates

Templates are partial or skeleton documents that contain labels (words), mathematical formulas, and/or values (numbers). These templates are skeleton documents that can be used over and over again. They save a lot of time and effort, because they eliminate the need to rekey data that is used frequently. For example, a business may create a template document for its monthly balance sheet. Once the document is created, new values (numbers) can be entered at the end of each month.

Businesses often purchase template disks containing accounting or other financial documents that are designed especially for their types of business. For example, template disks can be purchased for the oil and gas industry, for manufacturing firms, and many other businesses.

You will be using a template disk. Your template disk contains some of the data for the Activities in this textbook. In some cases, entire documents are stored on the disk, and you are asked to revise the format or change the data. In other cases, the template disk contains only part of the Activity, and you must enter the remaining data. You may use the template disk as your data disk to store files you create on your own.

WHAT DO YOU NEED?

After Lotus 1-2-3 has been installed, you will need the following items:

☐ Textbook
☐ Lotus 1-2-3 System Disk on floppy disk or on hard disk
☐ Template disk that will be used as your data disk

DOS (DISK OPERATING SYSTEM)

Before a personal computer can run, it needs a specific set of instructions. These instructions are called **DOS** which stands for disk operating system. DOS instructions are stored on either a floppy disk or a hard disk. DOS instructions allow the computer to send information back and forth to the central processing unit, the monitor, the keyboard, and the printer. DOS also allows you to:

☐ Format disks
☐ Erase files
☐ Set up directories
☐ Prepare bootable disks for application programs such as Lotus 1-2-3
☐ Start up application programs

When turned on, the computer looks for DOS either on a hard disk or a floppy disk. Unless the computer can find the disk operating system (DOS) instructions and place those instructions in random access memory (RAM), the computer cannot run a program such as 1-2-3. The DOS instructions can be stored in one of two places, depending on the kind of disk drives you have. If you have a hard disk, DOS will be stored on the hard disk. If you have only floppy disk drives, DOS will be stored on a floppy disk.

HOW TO BOOT THE COMPUTER

Once DOS is located, the computer copies and stores the DOS instructions in RAM memory. Everything stored in RAM memory is erased as soon as you turn off the computer. Therefore, DOS must be placed in RAM memory each time you want to operate your computer. This procedure is referred to as **booting** the computer.

Lotus 1-2-3 releases prior to Release 2.0 allow you to store the 1-2-3 System Disk and DOS together on the same disk as shown in Figure 1.2. Once DOS and 1-2-3 are stored on the same floppy disk, you will have a **bootable System Disk.** If you have a hard disk system, you store both the software program and DOS on the hard disk. Your instructor should have prepared a bootable System Disk or have stored DOS and the software program on your hard disk for you.

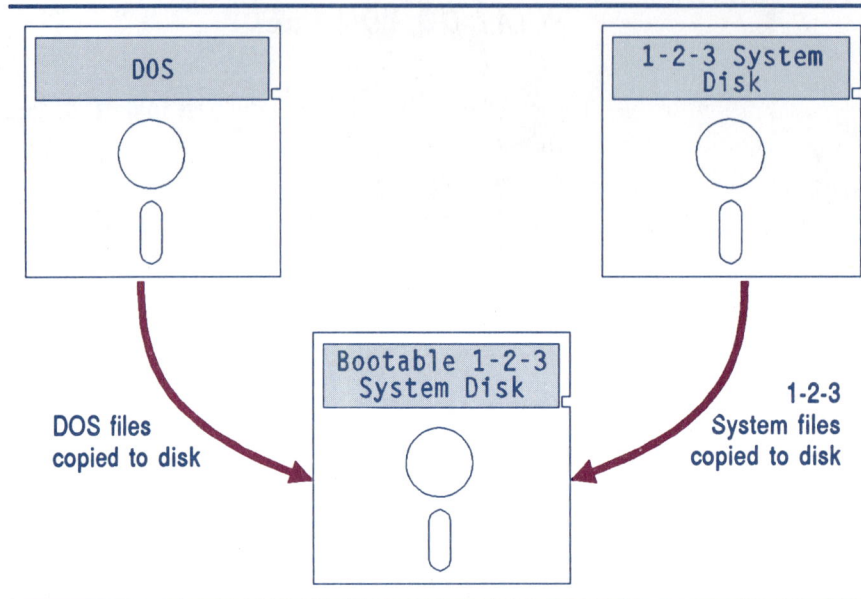

Figure 1.2 ❑   *DOS and Lotus 1-2-3 Stored on One Disk*

After DOS is transferred either to the hard disk or onto the Lotus 1-2-3 System Disk, you can start up the program. Separate instructions are given for floppy disk users and hard disk users.

Lotus 1-2-3 first loads the Lotus 1-2-3 Access System menu. From this menu, you select the Lotus 1-2-3 functions.

FOR FLOPPY DISK DRIVE USERS

1. Turn on the printer, if one is attached to the system.
2. Turn on the monitor.
3. Insert a bootable copy of the Lotus 1-2-3 System Disk in Drive A.

   a. Open the disk drive door for Drive A, if using a 5 1/4 inch disk drive. A 3 1/2 inch disk drive has no door.

   b. If using a 5 1/4 inch disk, hold the system disk so that the label is faceup and your thumb is on the label. If using a 3 1/2 inch disk, hold the disk so that the printing on the label is faceup. Insert the metal protector in the disk drive first.

   c. Insert the disk all the way into the disk drive. Never take the disk out while the disk drive's red light is on.

   d. With a 5 1/4 inch disk drive, close the latch on the disk drive by pushing it down. A 3 1/2 inch disk drive has no door.

4. Insert your template/data disk in Drive B.
5. Turn on the computer. The location of the power switch may vary from brand to brand, but it is usually on the right side or back of the central processing unit.

    a. The red light on Drive A will come on.

    b. The disk drive will make a humming sound.

    c. The monitor may show the amount of RAM memory in kilobytes (KB) at the top of the screen.

6. Current date information will appear at the top of the monitor, similar to the following:

```
Current date is Tue 1-01-1992
Enter new date (mm-dd-yy):
```

ENTER (today's date using a mm-dd-yy format)

PRESS ⏎ (⏎ is used as the symbol for the Enter or Return key)

7. Now the system will display the default time on the screen and ask you to enter the correct time. When prompted, enter the new time:

ENTER (the present time using the international time format, e.g., 8:10 for 8:10 a.m. or 13:30 for 1:30 p.m.)

PRESS ⏎ (Enter)

8. After you enter the date and time, information similar to the following should appear on the monitor:

```
        Current date is Tue 1-01-1992
        Enter new date (mm-dd-yy):  11-20-92
        Current time is  0:02:30.60p
        Enter new time:  10:30

The IBM Personal Computer DOS
Version 3.01 (C) Copyright IBM Corp. 1981, 1982, 1983, 1984

A>
```

Figure 1.3 ◻ *Enter Time and Date*

9. The A followed by the greater than symbol (>) is called the **A prompt.** It indicates that Drive A is the current drive or default drive. The current drive should be the drive in which the System Disk is located.

10. Now enter the command to use the program.

ENTER lotus

PRESS ⏎ (Enter)

You will now see the Access System menu on the monitor as shown in Figure 1.4.

```
1-2-3   PrintGraph   Install   Exit
Use 1-2-3


1-2-3 Access System
Copyright 1986, 1989
Lotus Development Corporation
All Rights Reserved
Release 2.2

The Access system lets you choose 1-2-3, PrintGraph, or the
Install program, from the menu at the top of this screen.  If
you're using a two-diskette system, the Access system may prompt you to
change disks.  Follow the instructions below to start a program.

* Use  →  or  ←  to move the menu pointer (the highlighted rectangle
  at the top of the screen) to the program you want to use.

* Press ENTER to start the program.

You can also start a program by typing the first character of its name.

Press HELP (F1) for more information.


                              Press NUM LOCK
```

Figure 1.4 ◻ *Lotus 1-2-3 Menu*

The instructions on the screen tell how to use this Access System. Presently, the characters 1-2-3 are highlighted with a rectangle. On the line below the highlighted block, is the message *Use 1-2-3*. This indicates that the Lotus 1-2-3 spreadsheet, graphics, and database program will be entered if the 1-2-3 option is selected.

11. Any item on the Access System menu can be highlighted by moving the Left and Right Arrow keys on the keyboard. To select the 1-2-3 option, highlight it and then:

PRESS   ↵ (Enter)

12. The next screen that appears will vary, depending on the release of Lotus 1-2-3 that you are using. With older versions of 1-2-3, the screen shown in Figure 1.5 will appear.

```
                              1-2-3
                      Copyright (C) 1982, 1983
                   Lotus Development Corporation
                        All Rights Reserved
                           Release 1A





                    (Press Any Key To Continue)
```

Figure 1.5 ◻ *Copyright Screen*

To view a blank worksheet:

PRESS   any key on the keyboard

13. With newer versions of 1-2-3, a blank worksheet like the one in Figure 1.6 will appear with no intervening copyright information.

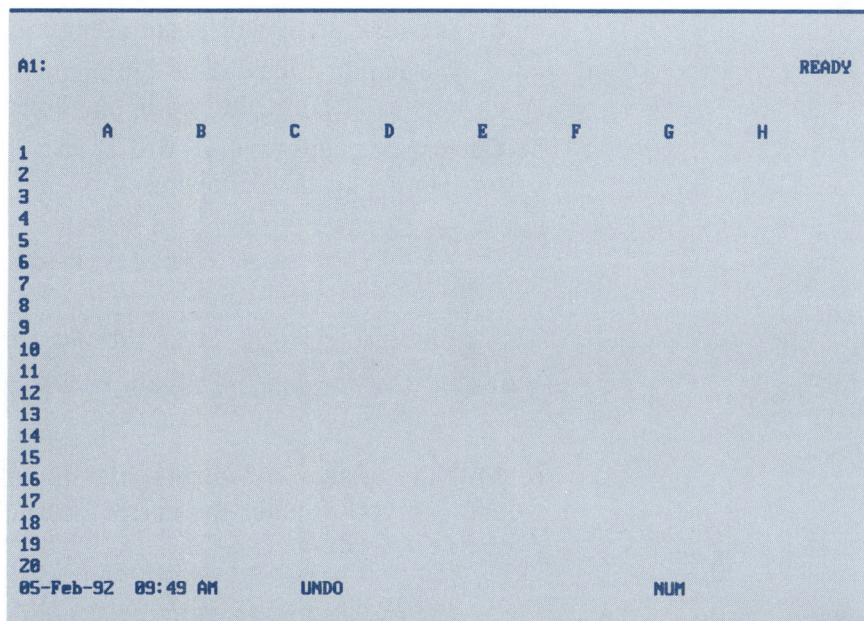

Figure 1.6 ▢ *Blank Worksheet*

At this point, you are ready to begin entering words and numbers onto the worksheet, but you will not do this until Chapter 2. Since you have not created any data yet, you can turn the computer components off and not destroy data or damage the program. With a floppy disk system, you may wish to pull your disks out of the disk drives before turning the computer system off.

FOR HARD DISK DRIVE USERS

1. Turn on the printer, if one is attached to the system.
2. Turn on the monitor.
3. Insert your template/data disk in Drive A.
   a. Open the disk drive door for Drive A if using a 5 1/4 inch disk drive. A 3 1/2 inch disk drive has no door.
   b. If using a 5 1/4 inch disk, hold the disk so that the label is face up and your thumb is on the label. If using a 3 1/2 inch disk, hold the disk so that the printing on the label is faceup. Insert the metal protector in the disk drive first.
   c. Insert the disk all the way into the disk drive. Never take the disk out while the disk drive's red light is on.
   d. With a 5 1/4 inch disk drive, close the latch on the disk drive by pushing it down. A 3 1/2 inch disk drive has no door.

4. Turn on the computer. The location of the power switch may vary from brand to brand, but it is usually on the right side or back of the central processing unit.

   a. The red light on Drive A will come on.

   b. The disk drive will make a humming sound.

   c. The monitor may show the amount of RAM memory in kilobytes (KB) at the top of the screen.

5. Current date information will appear at the top of the monitor, similar to the following:

   ```
   Current date is Tue 1-01-1992
   Enter new date (mm-dd-yy):
   ```

E N T E R   (today's date using a mm-dd-yy format)

P R E S S   ↵ (↵ is used as the symbol for the Enter or Return key)

6. Now the system will display the default time on the screen and ask you to enter the correct time. When prompted, enter the new time:

E N T E R   (the present time using the international time format, e.g., 8:10 for 8:10 a.m. or 13:30 for 1:30 p.m.)

P R E S S   ↵ (Enter)

7. After you enter the date and time, information similar to the following should appear on the monitor:

```
              Current date is Tue 1-01-1992
              Enter new date (mm-dd-yy):  11-20-92
              Current time is   0:02:30.60p
              Enter new time:   10:30


The IBM Personal Computer DOS
Version 3.01 (C) Copyright IBM Corp. 1981, 1982, 1983, 1984

C>
```

Figure 1.7 ◻ *Enter Time and Date*

8. The *C* followed by the greater than symbol (>) is called the **C prompt.** It indicates that Drive C, the hard disk, is the current drive or default drive. The current drive should be the drive on which the Lotus 1-2-3 software is located.

9. The current directory is probably the root directory for the hard drive. The root directory is indicated as a backslash (\ ) following the C prompt, *C:\ >.*

10. At this point, you must change the current directory to the one in which 1-2-3 is stored. If this directory has been named **Lotus,** enter the DOS command to change directories.

ENTER cd \lotus

PRESS ↵

11. If DOS is set up to display directories, the prompt will show *C:\lotus*. If DOS is not set up to display directory names, it will still show *C:* on the screen.

12. Now enter the password to use the system.

ENTER lotus

PRESS ↵

Now you will see the Access System menu on the monitor as shown in Figure 1.8.

```
1-2-3   PrintGraph   Install   Exit
Use 1-2-3 — Lotus Worksheet/Graphics/Database program


                    1-2-3 Access System
                     Copyright 1986
                 Lotus Development Corporation
                     All Rights Reserved
                       Release 2.01

The Access System lets you choose 1-2-3, PrintGraph, the Translate
utility, the Install program, and A View of 1-2-3 from the menu at
the top of this screen. If you're using a diskette system, the Access
System may prompt you to change disks.  Follow the instructions below
to start a program.

* Use → or ← to move the menu pointer (the highlighted rectangle
  at the top of the screen) to the program you want to use.

* Press [RETURN] to start the program.

You can also start a program by typing the first letter of the menu
choice.  Press HELP (F1) for more information.


                      Press NUM LOCK
```

Figure 1.8 □ *Lotus Menu*

13. At the top of the screen will be the words 1-2-3, Print-Graph, Translate, Install, View, and Exit. This is a one-line Access System menu. Notice that the instructions on the screen, tell you how to use this Access System. Presently, the characters 1-2-3 are highlighted with a rectangle. On the line below the highlighted block, is the message *Enter 1-2-3 — Lotus Worksheet/Graphics/Database program*. This indicates that the Lotus spreadsheet, graphics, and database program will be entered if the 1-2-3 option is selected.

Other items on the Access System menu can be highlighted by moving the Left and Right Arrow keys on the keyboard. To select the 1-2-3 option, use the Right and Left Arrow keys to move the menu pointer to 1-2-3, and then:

PRESS ↵ (Enter)

14. The next screen that appears will vary, depending on the release of Lotus 1-2-3 that you are using. With older versions of Lotus, the screen shown in Figure 1.9 may appear.

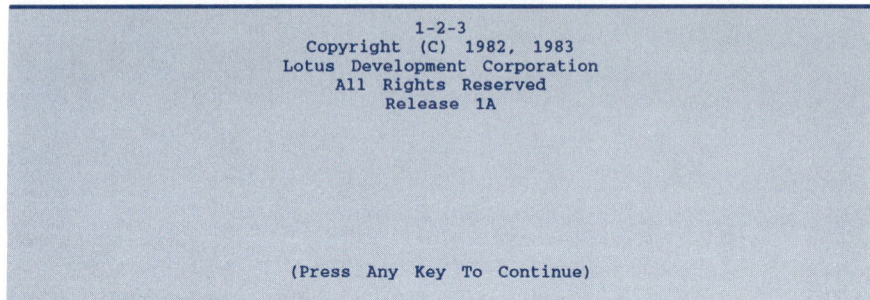

```
                          1-2-3
                Copyright (C) 1982, 1983
              Lotus Development Corporation
                   All Rights Reserved
                      Release  1A




                (Press Any Key To Continue)
```

Figure 1.9 ▢ *Copyright Screen*

Then, to view a blank worksheet:

PRESS   (any key on the keyboard)

15. With newer releases of 1-2-3, a blank worksheet like the one in Figure 1.10 will appear with no intervening copyright information.

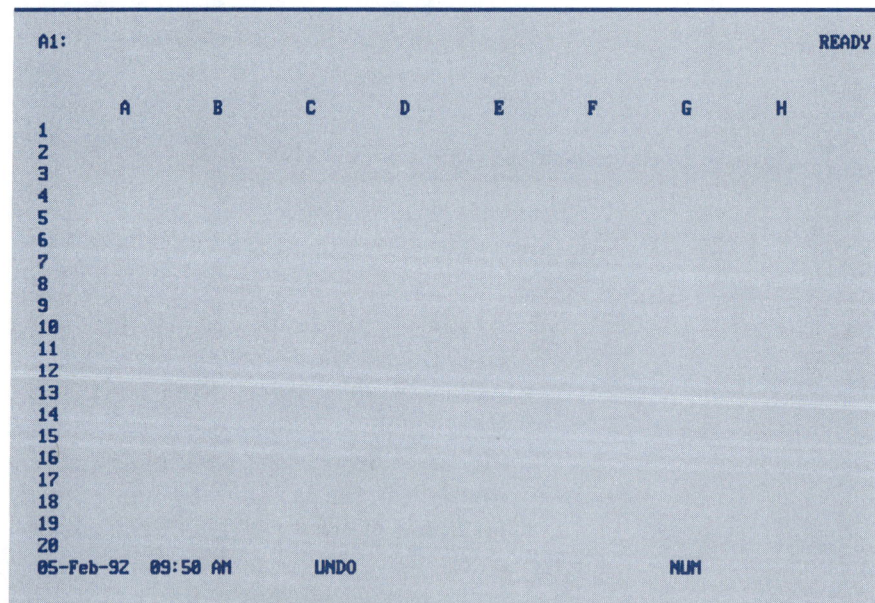

```
A1:                                                           READY

          A        B        C        D        E        F        G        H
    1
    2
    3
    4
    5
    6
    7
    8
    9
   10
   11
   12
   13
   14
   15
   16
   17
   18
   19
   20
05-Feb-92  09:50 AM       UNDO                           NUM
```

Figure 1.10 ▢ *Blank Worksheet*

At this point, you are ready to begin entering words and numbers onto the worksheet, but you will not do this until Chapter 2. Since you have not created any data yet, you can turn the computer components off and not destroy data or damage the program.

C H A P T E R   1   □   T H E O R Y   E X E R C I S E S

True/False |||||||||| Each of the following statements is either True or False. Indicate your choice by circling **T** for a true statement or **F** for a false statement.

1. Lotus 1-2-3 has only two functions—spreadsheets and graphics.   1.   T   F

2. Spreadsheets allow one to make mathematical calculations.   2.   T   F

3. Databases are used to organize and locate information easily.   3.   T   F

4. Lotus 1-2-3 allows one to create and view pie charts, line graphs, and bar charts but not print them.   4.   T   F

5. To use Lotus 1-2-3, Release 2.2, you must have an IBM or IBM compatible personal computer with a minimum of 320K of random access memory.   5.   T   F

6. To use Lotus 1-2-3, Release 3, you must have an IBM or IBM compatible personal computer with a minimum of 1 megabyte of random access memory and a hard disk.   6.   T   F

7. A graphics card or board is required to view graphs.   7.   T   F

8. A daisywheel printer can be used to print spreadsheets, database reports, and graphs.   8.   T   F

9. Software gives the computer instructions that make it perform specific functions such as spreadsheets, databases, and graphs.   9.   T   F

10. RAM is an abbreviation for random access memory.   10.   T   F

Completion ||||||||| For each item below fill in the word (or words) that completes the statement or answers the question.

1. List the types of printers that can be used to print spreadsheets, databases, and graphs.

   a. _____

   b. _____

2. Specify the recommended name for a directory to store the Lotus 1-2-3 software on a hard disk.

   _____

3. Why do businesses purchase template disks?

   _____

   _____

4. Name six rules to follow to keep floppy disks from being damaged.

_____

_____

_____

_____

_____

_____

5. List the functions of DOS.

_____

_____

_____

_____

_____

_____

6. Explain what a bootable Lotus 1-2-3 System disk is.

_____

_____

_____

7. List the steps needed to start a computer system.

_____

_____

_____

ACTIVITY 1.1 ☐ *Computer Configuration*

With the assistance of your instructor, identify the brands and types of computer hardware components you are using. Also identify the brand and version of software you are using.

1. Brand of computer _____

2. Type of microprocessor (8086, 8088, 80286, 80386) _____

3. Brand of monitor _____

4. Type of monitor (color, monochrome) _____

5. Type of graphics board _____

6. Number and types of disk drives (hard disk, 5 1/4 inch, or 3 1/2 inch disk drives)

   _____

7. Brand of printer _____

8. Type of printer (dot matrix, laser, daisywheel) _____

9. Name and version of software _____

ACTIVITY 1.2 ☐ *Starting Your Computer*

Locate the on and off switches for your central processing unit (CPU), monitor, and printer.

ACTIVITY 1.3 ☐ *Booting Lotus 1-2-3*

To complete this exercise, you must have computer hardware that is capable of running the version of software you plan to use.

Now, without looking at the instructions in this chapter, boot Lotus 1-2-3 on your computer. Also insert the template (data) disk in the appropriate disk drive. After you have a blank worksheet on the screen, you can turn off your computer and remove any diskettes from the disk drives.

CYCLE 1
Beginning Spreadsheet Tutorials and Exercises

CHAPTER 2

Getting Started with the Spreadsheet

O B J E C T I V E S

- ☐ Define spreadsheet terminology
- ☐ Move the cursor around a spreadsheet
- ☐ Use the menu structure
- ☐ Retrieve, edit, and save a file
- ☐ Exit from a spreadsheet

WHAT IS A SPREADSHEET?

A **spreadsheet** is software with columns and rows in which you can enter data and make calculations. It is an electronic replacement for an accountant's columnar ledger, pencil, and calculator. Figure 2.1 shows an example of a spreadsheet.

```
A1: 'April                                                    READY


        A         B         C         D         E         F         G         H
1   April     $100
2   May       $200
3   June      $400
4   Total     $700
5
6
7
8
9
10
11
12
13
14
15
16
17
18
19
20
04-Feb-92  08:46 PM        UNDO                                    NUM
```

Figure 2.1 ☐ *Creation of a Spreadsheet From a Ledger*

The file or document created with spreadsheet software is called either a worksheet or a spreadsheet, depending on the software being used. In this text-workbook the term spreadsheet will be used.

In order to save each file created, you must give a file a name of eight or fewer characters. A filename should describe the document. For example, the filename BUDGET90 might be the name of the 1990 budget. Some software programs add to the filename a period and a three-character filename extension. With some software programs, the filename extension **wk1** or **wks** is added automatically to every worksheet created; for example, BUDGET90.WK1 or BUDGET90.WKS.

The Spreadsheet Screen

Figure 2.2 shows an example of the initial spreadsheet screen before any data is entered. The following section will describe each of the different parts of the spreadsheet.

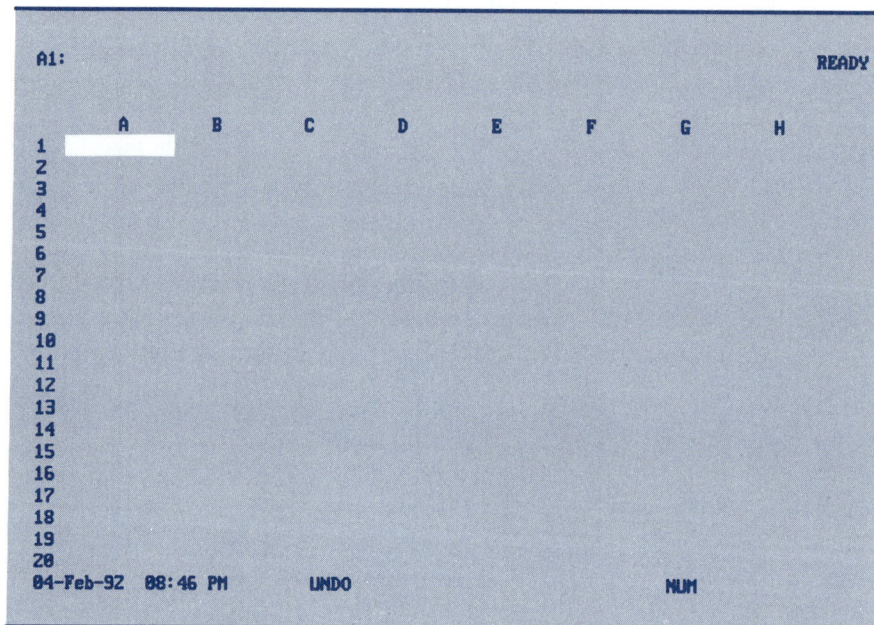

```
A1:                                                              READY

          A         B         C         D         E         F         G         H
  1
  2
  3
  4
  5
  6
  7
  8
  9
 10
 11
 12
 13
 14
 15
 16
 17
 18
 19
 20
04-Feb-92  08:46 PM        UNDO                          NUM
```

Figure 2.2 □ *Spreadsheet Screen*

Columns

Across the top of the spreadsheet are letters of the alphabet. These letters represent columns that run vertically down the screen. Usually, only eight columns are seen on the screen at once, but many more columns are available for you to use. These columns run from A to Z, AA to AZ, BA to BZ, and so forth. At this time, all 1-2-3 releases have 256 columns.

Rows

On the left side of the screen is a set of numbers called **row numbers.** Rows run horizontally across the screen. The number of rows in the spreadsheet has varied from 2,048 rows, included in 1-2-3, Release 1.0, to 8,192 with most new 1-2-3 releases.

Cells

A **cell** is an area on the spreadsheet where a row and column intersect. Words, numbers, and formulas are stored in cells. Usually, each cell can contain 9 characters. This is the standard column width, called the **default width.**

Cell Addresses.   Each cell has a **cell address** consisting of the column letter and row number. For example, A3 is for the intersection of column A and row 3, or F199 is for the intersection of column F and row 199.

Cell Pointer or Cursor.   When keyed in, data is entered on the screen in the cell highlighted by the cell pointer. Notice in Figure 2.3 that cell C6 is highlighted. This indicates that the **cell pointer (cursor)** is at cell C6. The location of the cell pointer is shown at the top of the screen along with the data contained in the cell.

```
C6: 12                                                                        READY

          A         B         C         D         E         F         G         H
 1    PERSONAL EXPENSES
 2                  May       June
 3    Clothes        25        20
 4    Snacks          6         8
 5    Lunch          20         0
 6    Movies          6        12
 7    TOTAL          57        40
 8
 9
10
11
12
13
14
15
16
17
18
19
20
04-Feb-92  08:47 PM            UNDO                              NUM
```

Figure 2.3 ❑ Cell Pointer at C6

Control Panel

The three top lines on the screen are called the **control panel.** The top line shows the cell address of the cell pointer, the contents of that cell, and the mode of operation. Examples of modes include Ready, Menu, and Wait. The screen shown below indicates the software is in the READY mode.

```
A1: 'PERSONAL EXPENSES                                                    READY

          A       B       C       D       E       F       G       H
```

The second line of the control panel contains one of three types of information.

1. When you create or edit a cell, the second line displays the current cell data as shown:

```
A3: 'Clothes                                                              LABEL
 Clothes

          A       B       C       D       E       F       G       H
```

2. As shown below, the second line may display a main menu or a submenu.

Main Menu →
```
A1: 'PERSONAL EXPENSES                                                     MENU
Worksheet  Range  Copy  Move  File  Print  Graph  Data  System  Add-In  Quit
Global  Insert  Delete  Column  Erase  Titles  Window  Status  Page  Learn
          A       B       C       D       E       F       G       H
1    PERSONAL EXPENSES
2                May     June
3    Clothes      25      20
4    Snacks        6       8
5    Lunch        20       0
6    Movies        6      12
7    TOTAL        57      40
```

3. If you select certain commands, the second line will display the prompt or message related to that command.

The third line of the control panel can display a submenu as shown below.

Submenu →
```
A1: 'PERSONAL EXPENSES                                                     MENU
Worksheet  Range  Copy  Move  File  Print  Graph  Data  System  Add-In  Quit
Global  Insert  Delete  Column  Erase  Titles  Window  Status  Page  Learn
          A       B       C       D       E       F       G       H
1    PERSONAL EXPENSES
2                May     June
3    Clothes      25      20
4    Snacks        6       8
5    Lunch        20       0
6    Movies        6      12
```

Or the third line can list instructions for a command. As shown below, the second line has the command **C**opy highlighted, and the third line gives a description of the Copy command.

```
A1: 'PERSONAL EXPENSES                                                    MENU
Worksheet  Range  Copy  Move  File  Print  Graph  Data  System  Add-In  Quit
Copy a cell or range of cells
         A       B        C         D       E      F       G        H
1    PERSONAL EXPENSES
2                May      June
3    Clothes      25       20
4    Snacks        6        8
5    Lunch        20        0
6    Movies        6       12
7    TOTAL        57       40
8
9
10
11
```

Description of Command

Status Indicators

The status indicators identify the condition of certain keys or when certain operations are performed. For example, when using the Caps Lock key, CAPS appears in the right corner of the worksheet.

Date and Time Indicators

The last line on the screen may show the name of the file and the current date and time as shown below.

```
18
19
20
04-Feb-92  08:49 PM                                                      NUM
```

Labels

Usually, **labels** are words entered into a cell, but labels can be any alphabetic or numeric data that will not be part of a computation. For example, labels for a city, state, and ZIP Code might be: Hutchinson, KS 67501.

Values

Values are numbers that can be used for computations. Any negative or positive number and 0 can be used for calculations. Commas should not be entered manually within numbers. The software will allow 7000, but not 7,000, to be entered. Dollar signs ($) cannot be entered before a dollar figure either.

Ranges

A **range** is a group of one or more cells arranged in a rectangle as Figure 2.4 shows. One cell is the smallest possible range. A range may be part of a column or row or may span several rows and columns. A range may be referred to by using its beginning and ending cell addresses such as A1 to B20.

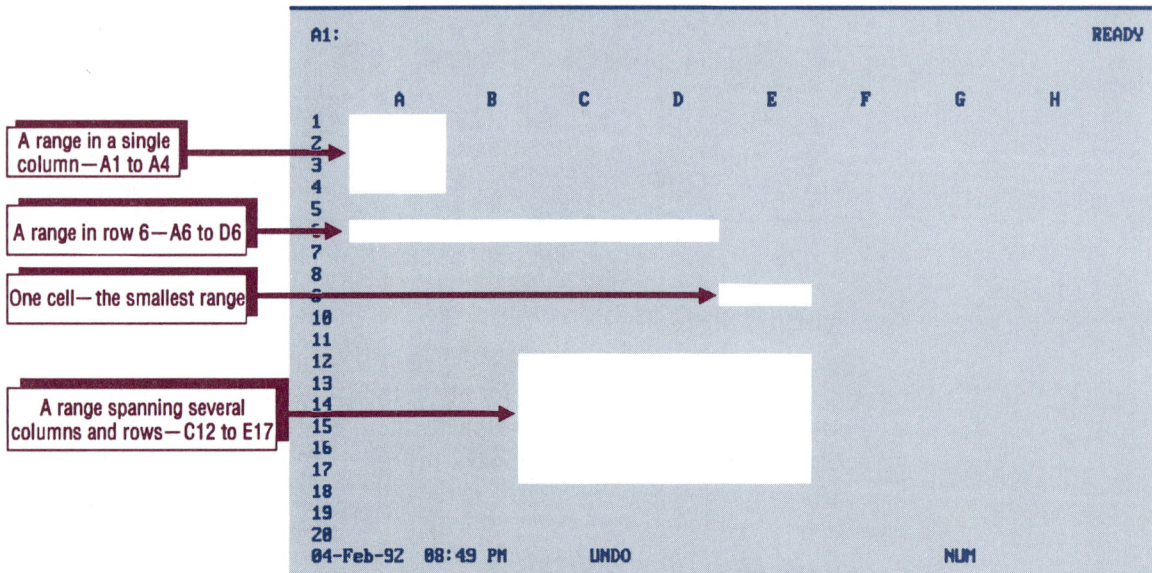

Figure 2.4 □ *Examples of Ranges*

HOW TO GET AROUND IN THE SPREADSHEET

A number of techniques can be used to move the cell pointer around the screen. In this section, those techniques are explained.

Arrow Keys

The arrow keys are the most used method to move the cell pointer around the screen. These keys are placed either on the numeric keypad, or they may be in a separate location. When you press the Right Arrow key (→) once, the cell pointer moves one cell to the right. When you press the Left Arrow key (←), the pointer moves one cell to the left. The Down Arrow key (↓) moves the cell pointer down one cell, and the Up Arrow key (↑) moves it up one cell.

Home Key

The Home key moves the cell pointer to cell address A1. If you ever become confused about your position on the spreadsheet, you can always press the Home key to return to cell A1. That is the only function of the Home key.

Movement keys are found on the right side of most keyboards.

Page Down Key

The Page Down key (PgDn) moves the cell pointer 20 lines (one screen) down at a time. If the cell pointer is at A1 and you press the Page Down key, the cell pointer will move to A21.

Page Up Key

The Page Up key (PgUp) moves the cell pointer 20 lines (one screen) up at a time. If the cell pointer is at A21 and you press the Page Up key, the cell pointer will move to A1.

End Key

The End key is used in conjunction with arrow keys. Pressing End and the Up Arrow key or the Down Arrow key, the cell pointer moves up or down the current column to the next cell that contains data.

When the End key is used with the Right Arrow key or the Left Arrow key, the cell pointer moves right or left in the current row to the next cell in the row that contains data.

Tab Key

The cell pointer can be moved to the right one screen at a time by using the Tab key. If the cell pointer is at A1 and you press the Tab key, the cell pointer will move to I1.

The cell pointer can be moved to the left one screen at a time by holding down the Shift key and pressing the Tab key. If the cell pointer is at I1 and you press the Shift and Tab keys, the cell pointer will move to A1.

Go To Key

To move quickly to any cell on the worksheet, you can use the Go To key. The Go To key is the F5 function key. If the cell pointer is at A1 and you press the F5 key, the prompt *Enter address to go to: A1* will appear in the control panel. To move the cell pointer to R15, you would need to enter the cell address R15 and press the Enter key.

The function key (F5) is used to go to a specific location on the spreadsheet.

ACTIVITY 2.1 ☐ Getting Around in the Spreadsheet

In this activity, you will learn to move the cell pointer around the spreadsheet.

1. Boot the software and bring an empty spreadsheet onto the screen.
2. Press the Right Arrow key once.
3. Hold down the Right Arrow key for several seconds. Move the cell pointer to the farthest column to the right.
4. Move the cell pointer to the left several cells.
5. Use the Down Arrow key to move the cell pointer to row 40.
6. Move the cell pointer up several cells.
7. Move the cell pointer to the home position, A1, with one keystroke using the Home key.
8. Use the Tab key to move the cell pointer two screens to the right.

9. Move the cell pointer two screens to the left.

10. Move the cell pointer one screen or 20 lines down with the Page Down key.

11. Move the cell pointer one screen or 20 lines up.

12. Move the cell pointer to D10 by pressing the Go To key, F5, entering the cell address, D10, and pressing the Enter key.

13. Move the cell pointer to Y20 using the Go To key.

14. Move the cell pointer to A150.

15. Move the cell pointer back to A1 using one key only.

HOW TO USE THE LOTUS 1-2-3 MENU STRUCTURE

To display the Lotus 1-2-3 menu, you must press the Slash (/) key. The menu will appear on the second line of the control panel.

PRESS   / (Command key)

The Worksheet option will be highlighted as illustrated below. The submenu for the Worksheet option, the highlighted option, will appear on the third line of the control panel.

```
A1:                                                                    MENU
Worksheet  Range  Copy  Move  File  Print  Graph  Data  System  Add-In  Quit
Global     Insert Delete Column Erase Titles Window Status Page  Learn
           A        B       C      D     E      F      G     H
```

HOW TO RETRIEVE A FILE

To select an item from the menu, you can use one of two methods. The first method is using the Right or Left Arrow keys to highlight the command you wish to select and then to press the Enter key. For example, to select the option related to saving or retrieving files (File), you could do the following:

PRESS   → → → → (to File)
PRESS   ↵ (Enter)

However, the faster and preferred method of selecting commands from menus is by entering the first character of the command itself. You can use either upper- or lowercase letters. For example, to select the File option, you could:

E N T E R   f (File)

This second method will be used in this text workbook.

  After you select **File** from the main menu, a submenu appears on the second line. An explanation of the highlighted command will be shown in the third line of the control panel. The explanation for the Erase command is shown on the top of the next page in the third line of the control panel.

```
A1:                                                           MENU
Global  Insert  Delete  Column  Erase  Titles  Window  Status  Page  Learn
Erase the entire worksheet from memory
        A         B        C        D        E       F       G       H
```

To bring a file up on the screen, you will do the following:

E N T E R   r (Retrieve)

Now the menus will be replaced with the prompt *Enter name of file to be retrieved:* on the second line of the control panel. The third line will list names of files stored on your data disk.

  Use the Right Arrow key (→) to highlight the name of the file you wish to retrieve to the screen. To see more filenames than the eight that appear on the screen originally, keep pressing the Right Arrow key to scroll through the rest of the filenames. The filenames are listed in alphabetical order.

  Two techniques can be used to indicate the filename you want to retrieve. One technique is to type the filename. The other is to use the arrow keys to highlight the filename and then press the Enter key. Use the following technique to retrieve the file named SALES:

P R E S S   → (Right Arrow key to locate the file)
P R E S S   ↵

The SALES file appearing on the screen should be similar to Figure 2.5. The file that you see on the screen is a copy. The original file is still stored on your disk.

HOW TO CHANGE DATA IN CELLS

  Once a file has been retrieved onto the screen, several techniques can be used to change or edit data in cells. One technique is to move the cell pointer to the cell you want to change and enter new data. The previous data will disappear after the Enter key has been pressed.

  Using the SALES file, move the cell pointer to B4 and change the number in that cell to 200.

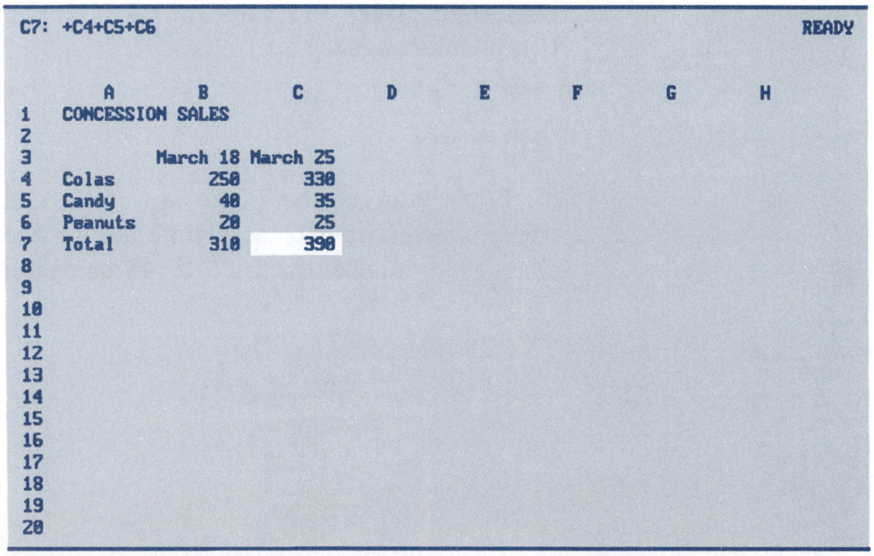

```
C7: +C4+C5+C6                                                    READY

        A       B       C       D       E       F       G       H
 1  CONCESSION SALES
 2
 3             March 18 March 25
 4  Colas        250     330
 5  Candy         40      35
 6  Peanuts       20      25
 7  Total        310     390
 8
 9
10
11
12
13
14
15
16
17
18
19
20
```

Figure 2.5 ☐ *Sales File*

PRESS F5 (Go To key)

ENTER B4

PRESS ↵

ENTER 200

PRESS ↵

As you key new data, it appears in the control panel; but it is not permanently entered in the cell until the Enter key is pressed. When the value in B4 is changed, the total for column B is also changed.

Edit Key

Another technique to change data in a cell is to use the Edit key, the F2 key. First, you must move the cell pointer to the cell to be edited. Then, you press the F2 key. To delete one character at a time from the right side to the left side, use the Backspace key. To delete one character within a number, move the flashing cursor to the appropriate character using the arrow keys and press the Delete (Del) key.

Move the cell pointer to cell C4 in the SALES file and change 330 to 335.

PRESS F2 (Edit key)

PRESS ← (Backspace key)

ENTER 5

PRESS ↵

Notice that when the value in C4 is changed, the total for column C is also changed.

Delete Key

When you use the F2 key to edit a cell, the Del key will erase one character of data at a time. Move the cell pointer to C6 and change the number from 25 to 45 using the Delete key.

PRESS	F2 (Edit key)
PRESS	← ←
PRESS	Del key
ENTER	4
PRESS	↵

Insert Feature

To insert new data in a cell, move the cell pointer to the character position where new data should be entered, key in the new data, and press the Enter key. When the F2 key is used, Lotus 1-2-3 is in insert mode automatically.

Move the cell pointer to A1 and add the word Stand between Concession and Sales. Notice that when you use the Caps Lock key, CAPS appears in the lower part of the screen.

PRESS	F2 (Edit key)
PRESS	← ← ← ← ←
PRESS	Caps Lock
ENTER	STAND
PRESS	Spacebar once
PRESS	Caps Lock
PRESS	↵

When a label is too long to fit in one cell, it carries over to the adjacent empty cells but is stored in a single cell.

HOW TO DELETE ALL DATA FROM CELLS

To delete all of the information in a cell, you can use the **R**ange and **E**rase commands. Move the cell pointer to A7 and erase Total.

PRESS	/ (Command key)

PRESS r (Range)

PRESS e (Erase)

Notice that *Enter range to erase: A7..A7* appears in the second line of the control panel. Accept this cell range as the one you want to erase by pressing the Enter key.

PRESS ↵

Now enter the word TOTAL in all capital letters.

PRESS Caps Lock

ENTER TOTAL

PRESS Caps Lock

PRESS ↵

A large range of cells can be erased using the **/ R**ange **E**rase command. This method will be shown in a future chapter.

HOW TO SAVE A FILE

To save a file on disk, you must use the slash (/) key to show the main menu in the control panel. Before a file can be saved, it must be given a name that is 1 to 8 characters long. Depending on the software version you are using, a three-character filename extension, **wk1** or **wks**, may be added automatically when a file is saved.

After pressing **/ F**ile **S**ave, you will notice that the name of the file shown on the screen, SALES, will appear. To save the file under that name, merely press the Enter key. To change the filename, enter characters over the top of the name. Save the revised SALES file that you were working with under a new name, SALESREV.

PRESS / (Command key)

ENTER f (File)

ENTER s (Save)

ENTER salesrev

PRESS ↵

PRESS r (Replace to replace the file with a revised file)

The last menu in the **F**ile **S**ave command allows you to select Cancel, leaving the existing file intact, or to select Replace, allowing you to replace the original file with a revised version.

The letter of the disk drive on which you store your data files may have appeared before the filename. The complete path statement including the drive letter, the directory name, and the filename may also have appeared, depending on the version of 1-2-3 you are using. An example is shown below:

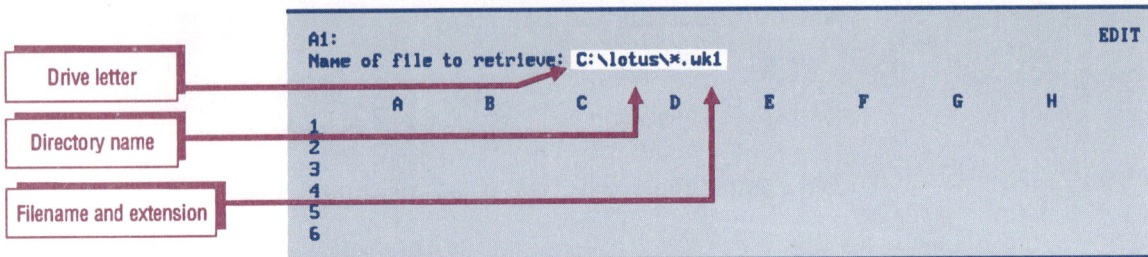

```
A1:                                                                    EDIT
Name of file to retrieve: C:\lotus\*.wk1

              A       B       C       D       E       F       G       H
         1
         2
         3
         4
         5
         6
```

Drive letter

Directory name

Filename and extension

After you enter **/ File Save** to store a newly created file, *.wk1 may appear where the filename is to be entered. The *.wk1 will be replaced by the exact filename once you key in a name.

Filenames do not have to be entered in all capital letters as 1-2-3 automatically converts the name to capital letters. If you enter **sales** or **Sales** as the filename, 1-2-3 will store it as **SALES**. You can save time and effort by entering the filename in small characters.

HOW OFTEN SHOULD A FILE BE SAVED?

Spreadsheet users should save their partially created spreadsheets every 15-20 minutes. This way, if there is a power outage, less than 20 minutes worth of work would be lost.

HOW TO ESCAPE FROM THE MENU STRUCTURE

The Escape (Esc) key can be used any time when you have menus on the screen. When you press the Escape key, it will move you from a submenu to a higher level menu or from the main menu out of the menus. Now practice using the Escape key.

PRESS	/ (Command key)
ENTER	f (File)
ENTER	r (Retrieve)
PRESS	Esc
PRESS	Esc
PRESS	Esc

Any time you want to get out of the menu structure, press the Escape key.

HOW TO QUIT USING LOTUS

To stop using 1-2-3, the **Quit**, **Yes**, and **Exit** commands are selected from the menus.

PRESS   / (Command key)

PRESS   q (Quit)

PRESS   y (Yes)

PRESS   e (Exit)

Note: The final **Exit** prompt will not appear with newer releases of Lotus 1-2-3.

You should now have a DOS prompt on the screen. This is the preferred method to exit Lotus 1-2-3, although you can quit 1-2-3 by turning off the computer. By using the **Quit** and **Exit** commands, you will be able to continue working at the computer and use other software programs without turning off the computer.

ACTIVITY 2.2 □ Using the Menu Structure and Locating Data

In this activity, you will retrieve a file and locate various data.

1. Retrieve the file named EXPENSES.
2. Locate and write down the entire cell contents using the following instructions.

   a. Use the Tab key to locate the rent expense for August.   _____

   b. Use the Shift Tab key to locate January's Phone expense.   _____

   c. Use the Go To key to find the cell contents of I6.   _____

   d. Use the Go To key to find the cell contents of B8.   _____

   e. Locate the total amount spent on rent during the year.   _____

   f. Locate the total expenses for March.   _____

3. Save the file under its present name.

ACTIVITY 2.3 ☐ *Retrieving, Editing, and Saving a File*

1. Retrieve the file named ACT2-3.
2. Use the **R**ange **E**rase commands to delete the label in A2.
3. Use the Edit key and change the label in A1 to YEARLY EXPENSES.
4. Correct the spelling of June.
5. In A1, enter OF RONALD JONES after the word EXPENSES.
6. Change the February food expense to 225.
7. Change the September phone expense to 33.
8. Change Total to TOTAL using the Backspace key to edit.
9. Use the **R**ange **E**rase command to delete the January Clothing expense.
10. Enter 38 as the January clothing expense.
11. Save the revised file under the name JONESEXP.

ACTIVITY 2.4 ☐ *Command Review*

To help you review the keystrokes used in this chapter, list the keystrokes in the blanks provided for the operations listed on the left.

Operation	Keystrokes
1. Move the cell pointer one cell down.	_____
2. Move the cell pointer one cell to the right.	_____
3. Move the cell pointer one cell up.	_____
4. Move the cell pointer one cell to the left.	_____
5. Move the cell pointer to A1 immediately.	_____
6. Move the cell pointer one screen down.	_____
7. Move the cell pointer one screen up.	_____
8. Move the cell pointer one screen to the right.	_____
9. Move the cell pointer one screen to the left.	_____
10. Retrieve a file.	_____
11. Save a file.	_____
12. Delete the contents of a cell.	_____
13. Edit a cell.	_____
14. Move to a higher level menu or out of the main menu.	_____

C H A P T E R   2 □ T H E O R Y   E X E R C I S E S

True/False ‖‖‖‖‖‖   Each of the following statements is either True or False. Indicate your choice by circling **T** for a true statement or **F** for a false statement.

1. A spreadsheet is a document with columns and rows.   1. T   F

2. The file or document created with spreadsheet software is called either a worksheet or a spreadsheet, depending on the software being used.   2. T   F

3. A filename must have ten characters or less.   3. T   F

4. With some software versions, the file name extension WKS or WK1 may be added automatically to every worksheet created.   4. T   F

5. Columns run horizontally across the screen.   5. T   F

6. On the left side of the screen is a set of numbers called row numbers.   6. T   F

7. A cell is an area on the spreadsheet where a row and column intersect.   7. T   F

8. The three top lines on the screen are called the status lines.   8. T   F

9. The top line in the control panel shows the cell address, the contents of the cell, and the mode of operation.   9. T   F

10. The status indicators will indicate when the Caps Lock key is down.   10. T   F

11. Labels are words or numbers that will not be part of a computation.   11. T   F

12. A range is a group of one or more cells arranged in a rectangle.   12. T   F

13. The smallest range must include two cells.   13. T   F

14. The cell addresses A1 to B20 refer to a range of cells.   14. T   F

15. The Page Down key moves the cell pointer 10 lines down at a time.   15. T   F

16. The Tab key moves the cell pointer to the right one screen at a time.   16. T   F

17. The cell pointer can be moved to the left one screen at a time by holding down the Control key and pressing the Tab key.   17. T   F

18. The Go To key is the F4 function key.   18. T   F

19. To display the Lotus 1-2-3 menu, the Slash key (/) must be pressed.   19. T   F

20. After the Slash key (/) is pressed, the menu will appear on the second line from the bottom of the screen.   20. T   F

21. The fastest method to select commands from menus is by entering the first character of the command itself.   21. T   F

22. A technique to change data in a cell is to use the F2 key.   22. T   F

23. To delete all of the information in a cell, the **R**ange and **R**emove commands can be used.   23. T   F

24. To save a file, press **/ F**ile **S**ave and enter the filename.   24. T   F

25. The Escape key can be used to move from a submenu to a higher level menu or from the main menu out of the menus.   25. T   F

26. To stop using 1-2-3, press Escape.   26. T   F

Completion ||||||||| For each item below fill in the word (or words) that completes the statement or answers the question.

1. Explain what columns are. _____

   _____

   _____

2. Explain what rows are. _____

   _____

   _____

3. List one use for spreadsheets for each of the following situations:

   a. In businesses: _____

   b. In schools: _____

   c. In homes: _____

4. Give two examples of labels. _____

   _____

5. Give two examples of values. _____

   _____

6. List the keystrokes to be used for the following cell pointer movements.

   a. To the next cell down _____

   b. To the next cell to the left _____

   c. To the next cell to the right _____

    d. One screen to the right _____

    e. One screen to the left _____

    f. Down 20 lines _____

    g. Up 20 lines _____

7. List the keystroke used for the Go To command. _____

8. The name of a document is called a _____

9. In BUDGET.WK1, the filename extension is _____

10. To display menus in the control panel, the _____ key must be pressed.

11. When the main menu is displayed in the second line of the control panel, the third line of the panel will contain a _____ or _____.

12. The mode of operation is located on the screen in the _____.

13. The word READY on the screen is an example of a _____.

14. The default or standard number of characters in a cell is _____.

15. The word Sales has been entered in C4 of a spreadsheet, but no data should be there. The fastest method to delete Sales is to _____

 _____.

16. The value 1,299,486 has been entered in a cell, but the value should be 1,599,486. The best method to change the value is to _____

 _____

 _____

17. An operator has keyed in the value 1,200, but 1-2-3 will not accept it because

 _____

 _____

ACTIVITY 2.5 □ *Retrieving, Editing, and Saving a File*

1. Retrieve the file named ASPEN.
2. Use the **R**ange **E**rase commands to delete the label in A1.
3. Enter MOUNTAINSIDE BICYCLE SHOP in A1.
4. Use the **R**ange **E**rase commands to delete the label in A2.
5. Enter PROFIT FOR THE SECOND QUARTER in A2.
6. Use the Edit key to insert an R in April.
7. Change the June costs to 2,940.
8. Save the file under the name ASPENREV.

CHAPTER 3

Planning and Creating a Spreadsheet

OBJECTIVES

- ☐ Apply spreadsheet design rules
- ☐ Enter labels
- ☐ Correct errors
- ☐ Enter values
- ☐ Enter formulas

HOW SHOULD A SPREADSHEET BE DESIGNED?

A spreadsheet is a document used to analyze data and make decisions in businesses, schools, and homes. To make them easy to understand and analyze, spreadsheets should be designed by certain rules. Try to use the following rules when designing a spreadsheet.

A spreadsheet designer uses several rules when designing a new spreadsheet.

Rule No. 1

Since it is difficult to center headings above a table, place main
spreadsheet headings at the top left side of a spreadsheet, as in Figure 3.1. Main headings are often keyed in capital letters to make
them stand out.

```
A1: 'PROJECTED                                                      READY


        A       B       C       D       E       F       G       H
 1  PROJECTED
 2  DEPARTMENTAL BUDGET
 3
 4           1990    1991 Change
 5  Salaries  95000   92500    -2500
 6  Travel     6000    4600    -1400
 7
 8
 9
10
11
12
13
14
15
```

Figure 3.1 ☐ *Main Headings*

Rule No. 2

Use appropriate column headings such as months of the year
(January - December) as shown in Figure 3.2.

```
B3: [W9] "JANUARY                                                   READY


            A               B       C       D       E       F
 1  PROJECTED
 2  CASH FLOW 19--
 3                       JANUARY FEBRUARY   MARCH   APRIL     MAY
 4  CASH INFLOW:
 5
 6  STUDENT FEES          7,250   4,250   4,250
 7  STATE APPROPRIATIONS  5,741   5,741   5,741   5,741   5,741
 8  HOSPITAL SERVICES    10,542  10,542  10,542  10,542  10,542
 9  STUDENT AID           2,173   4,100   2,173   2,173   2,173
10
11
12
13
14
15
```

Figure 3.2 ☐ *Months as Column Headings*

Rule No. 3

Label rows to describe appropriately the data in the row. The
labels Income, Expenses, Profit, Loss, and Revenue describe the data
in the corresponding rows in Figure 3.3.

```
A6: [W20] '    Sales                                              READY


         A              B              C              D              E
1  NORTH BRIDGE NETWORKS, INC.
2  INCOME STATEMENT
3  FOR YEAR ENDED JUNE 30, 19--
4
5  Revenue:
6     Sales                          $11,906,276
7
8  Cost of Goods Sold                5,520,823
9     Gross Profit                   6,385,453
10
11 Expenses:
12    Advertising                    $16,510
13    Computer Services              113,239
14    Fringe Benefits                249,216
15
16
```

Figure 3.3 ☐ *Examples of Row Headings*

Rule No. 4

Although values and labels can be entered in any order, certain techniques save time and effort. First, enter the main heading(s). Then enter all the data for column A, then column B, then column C, and so forth as shown in Figure 3.4. Formulas are not always entered in this same order as will be shown in Chapter 6.

```
C5: [W12] 600                                                    READY


         A              B              C              D      E      F
1  HALE'S CARD SHOP SALES
2
3                     November      December
4  Cups               200.00        100.00
5  Calendars          500.00        600.00
6  Notepads           100.00
7  Mugs               200.00
8  TOTAL              1000.00
9
10
11
12
13
14
15
```

Figure 3.4 ☐ *Data Entered One Column at a Time*

This technique lets you use the Down Arrow key to enter data, rather than using two keystrokes—pressing the Enter key first and then the Down Arrow key. By using the Down Arrow key to enter data, you save time and decrease the number of keystrokes needed.

Rule No. 5

Use a blank row between the main heading and the data to improve the spreadsheet's appearance.

Rule No. 6

Place variable information used to make what-if decisions in a separate cell. Place a description (a label) next to the variable itself. This makes it easy for people, other than the creator of the spreadsheet, to see and understand the values being manipulated. This is a better technique than hiding variables within formulas. Formulas will not be seen on the final printout.

What-if analysis is used frequently by school administrators. A school administrator may create several spreadsheets showing how much it would cost if teachers receive a 5 percent versus a 10 percent salary increase next year.

The what-if models in Figure 3.5 illustrate Rule No. 6. They show a variable and the description of the variable in separate cells. The variable is 0.05 in the model on the left and 0.10 in the model on the right. The description of the variable is % of Increase.

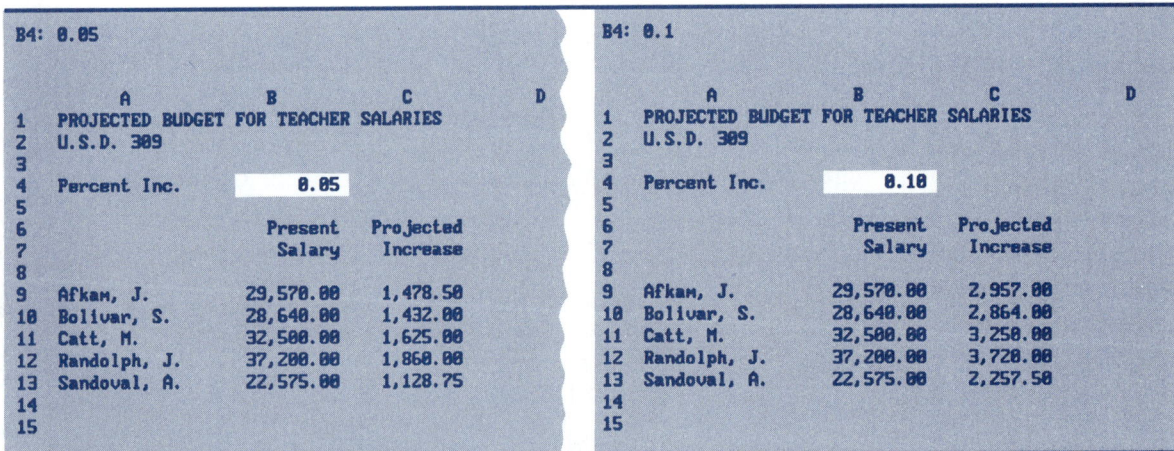

B4: 0.05					B4: 0.1			
	A	B	C	D		A	B	C	D
1	PROJECTED BUDGET FOR TEACHER SALARIES				1	PROJECTED BUDGET FOR TEACHER SALARIES			
2	U.S.D. 309				2	U.S.D. 309			
3					3				
4	Percent Inc.	0.05			4	Percent Inc.	0.10		
5					5				
6		Present	Projected		6		Present	Projected	
7		Salary	Increase		7		Salary	Increase	
8					8				
9	Afkam, J.	29,570.00	1,478.50		9	Afkam, J.	29,570.00	2,957.00	
10	Bolivar, S.	28,640.00	1,432.00		10	Bolivar, S.	28,640.00	2,864.00	
11	Catt, M.	32,500.00	1,625.00		11	Catt, M.	32,500.00	3,250.00	
12	Randolph, J.	37,200.00	1,860.00		12	Randolph, J.	37,200.00	3,720.00	
13	Sandoval, A.	22,575.00	1,128.75		13	Sandoval, A.	22,575.00	2,257.50	
14					14				
15					15				

Figure 3.5 □ *Spreadsheets with Variables*

WHAT SHOULD A SPREADSHEET BE NAMED?

It is important to use a logical filenaming system for spreadsheets so they can be located days or weeks later. A filename should describe the data in it, if possible. The date and the type of data in the spreadsheet are often included in the filename as shown below:

FILE DESCRIPTION	FILENAME
January expenses	JANEXP
February sales	FEBSAL

If similar spreadsheets are created annually, the year can be incorporated into the filename. Examples of using the year in the name are shown below:

FILE DESCRIPTION	FILENAME
1994 expenses	94EXP
1995 expenses	95EXP
1994 January expenses	94JANEXP
1994 February expenses	94FEBEXP

Many spreadsheet operators abbreviate words such as budget, income, and revenue in filenames.

FILE TOPIC	ABBREVIATION
Budget	BGT
Income	INC
Revenue	REV

Some people create a multitude of spreadsheets on a daily and/or weekly basis. They do not want to use the same name twice, so they create a coding system using numbers. The filename S25 may be a spreadsheet analyzing a business' profits for the year. The number, S25, is recorded in a book along with a description of the data stored in this file. This record book is used to locate files at a later date.

Now, use the tips for spreadsheet design and filenaming in the following activity.

ACTIVITY 3.1   ▢   *Planning a Spreadsheet*

Jesse Gaston is the owner of a T-shirt shop, called T-Time, Inc. He wants to analyze and compare the number of units of t-shirts, sweatshirts, and sweaters sold during each of the past three years, not including this year. He also wants to know the total sales for each year and the total sales of each type of merchandise for all three years.

1. Write two filenames that could be used.

   a. _____

   b. _____

2. Write a main heading that should be at the top of the spreadsheet.

   _____

3. Write the column headings to be used.

   _____

4. Write the row labels to be used.

   _____

HOW TO CREATE A SPREADSHEET

Labels, values, and formulas can be entered in cells in two different ways. One way is to key in the data. As you key data, it will appear in the second line of the control panel. To enter data in a cell, press either the Enter (↵) key or one of the arrow keys (→, ←, ↑, ↓). Whenever possible, enter an entire column of data at a time and use the Down Arrow key.

To enter the data shown in Figure 3.6, you should begin by entering GROSS SALES in A1, press the Down Arrow key twice, enter T-SHIRTS in A3, press the Down Arrow key, enter SWEATSHIRTS, press the Down Arrow key, enter SWEATERS, press the Down Arrow key, enter TOTAL and press the Enter key. Then enter the values in column B, beginning with 18500 in B3. By using the arrow keys to enter data in cells, you can save many keystrokes.

```
B5: 10500                                                               READY

          A            B         C         D         E         F         G
 1    GROSS SALES
 2
 3    T-shirts       18500
 4    Sweatshirts    12400
 5    Sweaters       10500
 6    Total
 7
 8
 9
10
11
12
13
```

Figure 3.6 □ *Enter Data Column by Column*

Turn your computer on and boot Lotus 1-2-3. A blank spreadsheet screen should appear. Begin with the cell pointer at A1.

ENTER   GROSS SALES

PRESS   ↓ (Down Arrow key twice)

ENTER   T-shirts

PRESS   ↓ (Down Arrow key)

ENTER   Sweatshirts

PRESS   ↓ (Down Arrow key)

ENTER   Sweaters

PRESS   ↓ (Down Arrow key)

ENTER   Total

PRESS   ↵ (Enter key)

Move the cell pointer to B3.

E N T E R	18500
P R E S S	↓ (Down Arrow key)
E N T E R	12400
P R E S S	↓ (Down Arrow key)
E N T E R	10500
P R E S S	↵ (Enter key)

Save the spreadsheet under the filename T-TIME.

P R E S S	/ (Main Menu)
P R E S S	f (File)
P R E S S	s (Save)
E N T E R	t-time
P R E S S	↵ (Enter)

The default setting for cell width is 9 characters. If a value takes more than 9 characters, the entire cell will be filled with asterisks. To view the correct value, the cell width will need to be increased.

Labels

If a label takes more than 9 characters, it flows into the next cell on its right if no data is stored there. For example, the heading QUARTERLY SALES REPORT may begin in A1 but carry over into A2 and A3. When data is entered in cells A2 and A3, only the first nine characters in cell A1 will be shown; however, the rest will be stored in A1's memory.

In Figure 3.7, the label Electricity has been entered in cell A2. As can be seen, when the cell pointer is on A2, the control panel shows that the entire word, Electricity, is stored in that cell. In A4, Heating Oil takes more than 9 characters; therefore, some characters are shown in B4. In a future chapter, you will be shown how to increase a column width and allow an entire label to be shown.

```
A2: 'Electricity                                                    READY


          A        B        C        D        E        F        G        H
   1    Phone      28.45
   2    Electrici  85.49
   3    Rent      450.00
   4    Heating oil
   5
   6
   7
   8
   9
  10
  11
```

Figure 3.7 ❐ Default Cell Width

Formulas

A **formula** is a cell entry that performs a calculation such as addition, subtraction, multiplication, or division. The ability to use formulas to make calculations is the most important feature of a spreadsheet. A cell that contains a formula will store both the formula and the value derived from the formula.

Formulas are written in algebraic form. They may contain numbers and/or cell addresses. They can be used to add, subtract, multiply, and divide. Numbers (20+30), cell addresses (+C2+C3), or a combination (+C5+30) can be entered in a formula. The addition sign (+) is inserted in front of the first cell in a formula to indicate that it is a formula, rather than a label. Within formulas, the following symbols are used to represent different mathematical functions:

+	Addition
-	Subtraction
*	Multiplication
/	Division

In the example shown in Figure 3.8, the total could be found by using the formula +100+200+400. However, there is a better way to find the total. Instead of telling the spreadsheet which numbers to add, tell it where the numbers are: +B2+B3+B4. After the formula is entered in cell B4 and the Enter key is pressed, the total will appear immediately in cell B4.

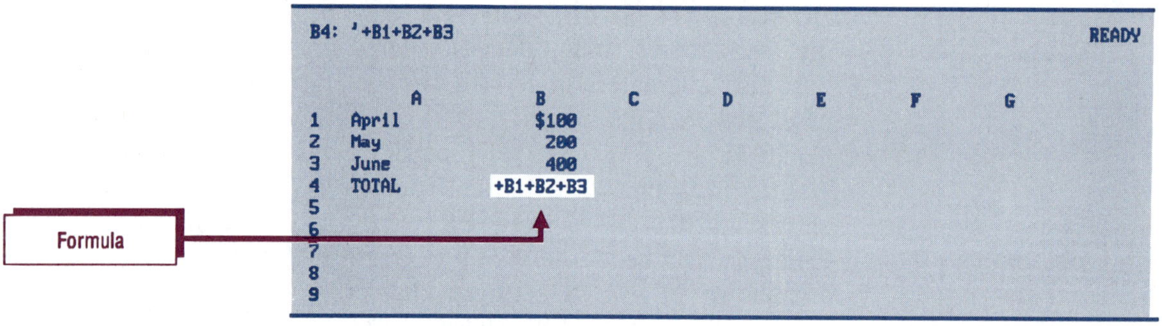

Figure 3.8 ◻ *Using a Formula*

If your computer is not already on, turn it on and boot up with Lotus 1-2-3. Retrieve the file named T-TIME.

Move the cell pointer to B6.

E N T E R   +B3+B4+B5
P R E S S   ⏎ (Enter)

The total will appear in B6, and the formula will appear in the top line of the control panel.

Move the cell pointer to Al. Notice that when the cell pointer is not located on the cell with the formula, the formula will not appear in the control panel.

HOW TO SAVE A REVISED SPREADSHEET

The command to save a revised spreadsheet is similar to the command to save a newly created spreadsheet.

Saving a Revision

Save the revised spreadsheet that you have been working on under the same name, T-TIME.

PRESS   / (Main Menu)

PRESS   f (File)

PRESS   s (Save)

The previous name, T-TIME, will appear in the control panel. Accept that name by pressing the Enter key.

PRESS   ↵ (Enter)

The words Cancel and Replace will appear in the control panel. Cancel will be highlighted. Select Replace by pressing the R key.

PRESS   r (Replace)

The revised document will now be saved.

Alignment of Labels

A **label prefix** is a special character added at the beginning of a label that tells the program how to display it—left aligned, centered, or right aligned. As shown in Figure 3.9, an apostrophe is used for left alignment in a cell, quotations marks for right alignment, and a carat for centering.

TYPE OF ALIGNMENT	SYMBOL	DESCRIPTION
Left	'	Apostrophe
Center	^	Carat
Right	"	Quotation mark

Figure 3.9 ☐ *Special Characters for Label Alignment*

Within a cell, Lotus 1-2-3 automatically left aligns labels that are words and right aligns values. Sometimes a worksheet is easier to read when labels used as column headings are centered or right aligned in a cell. When numbers such as 1991 and 1992 are used as labels, they may need to be left aligned or centered. Examples of the alignment procedures follow:

PROCEDURE	TYPE OF ALIGNMENT
E N T E R '1991	Left align the label 1991 (number can only be used as a label)
E N T E R ^1991	Center the label 1991 (number can only be used as a label)
E N T E R 1991	Right align 1991 (number can be used as a value)
E N T E R Sales	Left align the label Sales
E N T E R ^Sales	Center the label Sales
E N T E R "Sales	Right align the label Sales

As can be seen, when the number 1991 is entered, it is right aligned automatically because 1-2-3 recognizes all numbers as values and right aligns them. When Sales is entered, it is left aligned automatically because 1-2-3 recognizes all alphabetic characters as labels and left aligns labels.

To change the alignment for a label, delete the special alignment character and insert the appropriate character.

Turn your computer on and boot Lotus 1-2-3. A blank spreadsheet screen should appear. Retrieve the file named ATTEND.

Move the cell pointer to A3, center the word SCHOOL.

E N T E R ^ School
P R E S S ↵ (Enter)

Use the Edit key, the F2 key, to right align the labels DAY 1, DAY 2, DAY 3, DAY 4, and DAY 5 located in row 3. Begin in cell B3.

P R E S S F2

Move the cell pointer to the '.

P R E S S Del (Delete key)
E N T E R "
P R E S S ↵ (Enter)

Right align the labels in cells C3, D3, E3, and F3 using the previous instructions.

Center the word TOTAL in A8.

ENTER ^ TOTAL

PRESS ↵ (Enter)

ACTIVITY 3.2 ◻ *Creating and Saving a Spreadsheet*

In this activity, you will create and save a spreadsheet that uses labels, values, and formulas. You will create a speadsheet like the one shown.

```
A1: 'YOGURT DELIGHT                                              READY


        A        B        C        D        E       F       G       H
 1  YOGURT DELIGHT
 2  QUARTERLY SALES
 3
 4  Item     January February    March     Total
 5  Revenue     4500     4275     4856
 6  Costs       3575     4500     3425
 7  Profit
 8
 9
10
11
```

1. Boot Lotus 1-2-3 and have a blank spreadsheet on the screen.

2. Enter the two-line heading, starting with YOGURT DELIGHT in A1, and QUARTERLY SALES in A2.

3. Enter the other labels for column A as shown. Enter ITEM, REVENUE, COSTS, and PROFIT.

4. Right align the labels JANUARY, FEBRUARY, MARCH, and TOTAL in row 4 beginning with January in B4.

5. Enter the appropriate values in column B. Do not enter commas in the values.

6. Move the cell pointer to B7 and enter the formula to determine the profit for January, +B5+B6.

7. Enter the appropriate values in column C.

8. Move the cell pointer to C7 and enter the formula to determine the profit for February.

9. Enter the appropriate values in column D.

10. Move the cell pointer to D7 and enter the formula to determine the profit for March.

11. Move the cell pointer to E5.

12. Enter the formula to determine the total revenue for the quarter — +B5+C5+D5. Press the Down Arrow key.

13. Enter the formula to determine the total costs in E6. Press the Down Arrow key.

14. Enter the formula to determine the total profit for the quarter in E7. Press the Enter key.

15. Save the spreadsheet using the filename YOGURT.

ACTIVITY 3.3 ▢ *Creating and Saving a Spreadsheet*

In this activity, you will create a spreadsheet, right align column headings, use formulas, and save it as ECONTEST.

```
A1: [W14] 'CONSUMER ECONOMICS                                           READY

           A           B         C         D         E         F         G
 1  CONSUMER ECONOMICS
 2  TEST SCORES
 3
 4  Name          Test 1    Test 2    Test 3    Total
 5
 6  Brian             29        25        35
 7  Michael           19         8        22
 8  Jesse             32        30        35
 9  Afkam             26        27        30
10  Li                33        24        30
11
```

1. Boot Lotus 1-2-3 and have a blank spreadsheet on the screen.

2. Enter the two-line heading in all capital letters in cells A1 and A2 as shown.

3. Enter all the labels in column A as shown.

4. Right align the column headings, TEST 1, TEST 2, TEST 3, and TOTAL in row 4.

5. Enter all the values in column B. Use the Down Arrow key to enter them.

6. Enter the values in column C.

7. Enter the values in column D.

8. Find the total test points scored by Brian. In E6, enter a formula that will add the values in cells B6, C6, and D6.

9. Enter formulas to find the total scores for the other students and enter them in the Total column.

10. Save the spreadsheet under the name ECONTEST.

CHAPTER 3 □ THEORY EXERCISES

True/False ‖‖‖‖‖‖‖ Each of the following statements is either True or False. Indicate your choice by circling **T** for a true statement or **F** for a false statement.

1. It is easiest to place main spreadsheet headings at the top left side of a spreadsheet.   1. T   F

2. When comparing sales figures for five products in 1990, 1991, and 1992, it is best to use the years as row labels in column A.   2. T   F

3. It is best to use Revenue, Expenses, and Profit as column headings, rather than as row headings.   3. T   F

4. When designing a monthly budget for 12 months for yourself, it is best to use the months as row labels in column A.   4. T   F

5. The fastest technique to enter a column of values is to enter the first value and press the Down Arrow key.   5. T   F

6. The two techniques to enter labels or values in cells are (1) by pressing the Enter key or (2) by pressing any of the arrow keys.   6. T   F

7. If a cell has a width of 9 characters and the label SALES REPORT is entered in A1, the label will carry over into A2 until data is entered in A2.   7. T   F

8. The default cell width is 12 characters per cell.   8. T   F

9. A cell that contains a formula will store both the formula and the value derived from the formula.   9. T   F

10. The formula to add the value in B3 to the value in B4 is +B3+B4.   10. T   F

11. The formula to subtract 30 from the value in C5 is C5-30.   11. T   F

12. The formula to multiply .05 times the value in B8 is +.05*B8.   12. T   F

13. The formula to divide the value in D5 by 12 is +D5/12.   13. T   F

14. The formula to divide the value in C8 by the value in D8 is +D8/C8.   14. T   F

15. If the number in cell B2 is changed in a spreadsheet, the value in the cell containing the formula +B2-B3 will change when the spreadsheet is recalculated.   15. T   F

16. The command to save a file begins with /File Save.   16. T   F

17. To center the label 1990 in a cell, you would enter ^1990.   17. T   F

18. To right align the label April in a cell, you would enter 'April.   18. T   F

19. To left align the label 1991 in a cell, you would enter '1991.   19. T   F

20. To right align the value 2000 in a cell, you would enter "2000.   20. T   F

Completion IIIIIIIII For each item below fill in the word (or words) that completes the statement or answers the question.

1. Give two examples of column headings. _____

_____

2. Give two examples of row labels. _____

3. The Lotus 1-2-3 default alignment for labels is _____

4. The Lotus 1-2-3 default alignment for values is _____

5. The symbol _____ is entered at the beginning of a formula.

6. Answer each of the questions based on the following spreadsheet.

```
A1: [W14]                                                          READY

              A          B          C         D          E         F
1      [        ]     January   February   March      Total
2      Sales            500        525       540
3      Expenses         128        137       169
4      Net Profit
5
6
```

a. The labels January, February, and March have what type of alignment? _____

_____

b. To center the label January, you need to enter it as _____ .

c. To left align the label January, you need to enter it as _____ .

d. To right align the label January, you need to enter it as _____ .

e. The best type of alignment for January, February, and March is _____ .

f. To determine Net Profit, Expenses needs to be subtracted from the Sales figure. To determine the Net Profit for February, you would need to enter the formula in cell _____ .

g. The formula to determine the Net Profit for February should be

_____ .

h. The formula to determine the total sales for January, February, and March should be entered in cell _____ .

    i. The formula to determine the net profit for January, February, and March should be entered in cell _____ .

7. The default setting for cell width is _____ characters.

8. The formula to multiply the value in C5 by .04 is _____.

9. The formula to add cells C5, C6, and C7 is _____.

10. The formula to divide cell C8 by C9 is _____.

11. The formula to multiply cell G9 by H15 is _____.

12. The formula to subtract cell C15 from C7 is _____.

13. If you enter a value that has more characters than the cell width, the cell will be filled with _____.

14. When a label is too large for a cell, the label will _____

_____.

15. The default cell width setting is being used, and the label January has been entered in B1. When you enter the label Name of School in A1, the following will happen

_____.

ACTIVITY 3.4 ☐ *Creating an Inventory Spreadsheet*

In this activity, you are asked to set up a spreadsheet that will show the value of the current inventory for a pet store.

```
A1: 'ART'S PET STORE                                          READY


         A        B        C        D        E        F        G
 1  ART'S PET STORE
 2  CURRENT INVENTORY
 3
 4  Inventory          Unit of  Stock        Units   Cost per  Total
 5  Item               Count    No.        On Hand      Unit   Value
 6
 7  Collars            Each     B5             15      2.85
 8  Leashes            Each     B6             12      3.75
 9  Dog food           Sack     A15            87      8.95
10  Dog carriers       Each     A25             4     54.90
11  Dog snacks         Box      B19            65      0.78
12  Water dish         Each     A39            12      2.98
13  Black Labrador     Each                     2     75.95
14  Black Poodle       Each                     1     45.95
15  Australian Sheph.  Each                     2     65.95
16
17
```

1. Boot Lotus 1-2-3 and have a blank spreadsheet on the screen.

2. Enter the heading in cells A1 and A2 as shown.

3. Enter the label INVENTORY in A4 and ITEM in A5.

4. Use both columns A and B and enter each of the inventory items.

5. Left align the column headings, UNIT OF COUNT and STOCK NO., in rows 4 and 5.

6. Right align the column headings UNITS ON HAND, COST PER UNIT, and TOTAL VALUE in rows 4 and 5, respectively.

7. Enter all the data in columns C and D in rows 7-15.

8. Enter all the values in columns E and F. Be sure to enter decimal points as periods.

9. Determine the Total Value of each inventory item to enter in column G. Multiply the Units on Hand by the Cost per Unit using appropriate cell addresses in the formulas.

10. Save the spreadsheet under the filename INVENTORY.

CHAPTER 4

OBJECTIVES

- ❏ Change the column width
- ❏ Use global format
- ❏ Use range format
- ❏ Use the Help key
- ❏ Use the Escape key
- ❏ Use @SUM Formula
- ❏ Use automatic recalculation
- ❏ Save and replace a file

HOW CAN COLUMN WIDTHS BE CHANGED?

Many times the 9-character default cell width is not adequate for the length of the label or value to be entered. Labels that are over 9 characters carry over into the next cell to the right when there is no data in that cell, or they are cut off after 9 characters if there is data in the next cell to the right. Values that are too large for a cell are not shown. Instead, a series of asterisks (*********) fill the cell. To view those values, you must increase the cell width.

Cell width can be changed in two ways. The **Worksheet Global Column-Width** command allows you to change the width of every column on a spreadsheet. **Worksheet Column** commands let you change the width of individual columns. Global commands take precedence over individual column commands; therefore, global commands should be used before individual column commands.

In planning a spreadsheet, you should decide on the column width needed for the majority of columns on the spreadsheet. Use the **Worksheet Global Column-Width** command to set this column width. Then use the **Worksheet Column** command to change the width of individual columns.

For example, column A contains long labels that require up to 15 characters, but the other columns only need 12 characters in each. For this situation, global commands would be used first to set the column width at 12. Then, the width of column A would be changed to 15 characters using the individual column command.

To experiment with the column-width command, retrieve the file named JONESEXP. You will change the global column width to 10 characters. To retrieve a file:

PRESS /

PRESS f (File)

PRESS r (Retrieve)

PRESS → (until the name JONESEXP is highlighted)

PRESS ↵

To change the global column width to 10 characters:

PRESS /

PRESS w (Worksheet)

The control panel will display the following:

```
A1: 'YEARLY EXPENSES OF RONALD JONES                                      MENU
Global  Insert  Delete  Column  Erase  Titles  Window  Status  Page  Learn
Format  Label-Prefix  Column-Width  Recalculation  Protection  Default  Zero
        A           B           C           D           E           F           G
```

The first command highlighted is **Global**. The **Global** command means that the entire worksheet will be changed.

PRESS g (Global)

PRESS c (Column-width)

The control panel will display the following:

```
A1: 'YEARLY EXPENSES OF RONALD JONES                                      EDIT
Enter global column width (1..240): 9

        A           B           C           D           E           F           G
```

This means that the column width can be from 1 to 240 characters and that the present width is 9. To change the 9 to 10, merely key in 10 over the 9.

ENTER 10

The control panel will display the following:

```
A1: 'YEARLY EXPENSES OF RONALD JONES                                      EDIT
Enter global column width (1..240): 10

        A          B          C          D          E          F          G
```

PRESS ↵

Notice that all the columns now have 10 characters.

Now change the width of column A to 15 characters. Begin by moving the cell pointer to the column that needs to be changed—column A. Use the Home key to move the cell pointer to column A, if necessary.

PRESS   Home (Home key)

PRESS   /

PRESS   w (Worksheet)

PRESS   c (Column)

The control panel will display the following:

```
A1: 'YEARLY EXPENSES OF RONALD JONES                                      MENU
Set-Width  Reset-Width  Hide  Display  Column-Range
Specify width for current column
        A          B          C          D          E          F          G
```

This message asks you to set a new width, reset a width used previously, hide the width and not display it in the control panel, or display it.

PRESS   s (Set-width)

The control panel will display the following:

```
A1: [W10] 'YEARLY EXPENSES OF RONALD JONES                                POINT
Enter column width (1..240): 10

        A          B          C          D          E          F          G
```

ENTER   15

PRESS   ↵

Now Column A will have a width of 15 characters, while the other columns will have a width of 10 characters as shown in Figure 4.1.

```
A1: [W15] 'YEARLY EXPENSES OF RONALD JONES                            READY


          A         B         C         D         E         F
 1  YEARLY EXPENSES OF RONALD JONES
 2
 3
 4              January  February  March     April     May
 5  Rent          $425      $425      $425      $425      $425
 6  Phone          $20       $22       $24       $20       $21
 7  Clothes        $30       $30       $50       $40       $45
 8  Food          $200      $225      $170      $180      $200
 9  Car Insurance  $60       $60       $60       $60       $60
10  TOTAL
11
12
13
14
15
16
17
18
19
20
08-Feb-92  09:09 AM      UNDO                       NUM
```

Figure 4.1 □ *Changing Column Widths*

Note the *[W15]* in the control panel indicates that the cell width in column A is 15 characters. The first line of the control panel will display the column width, if the width is different from the global column width.

Now that you have increased the width of column A, edit the label CAR INSUR in column A and change it to CAR INSURANCE.

PRESS F5 (Go To key)
ENTER A9
PRESS ↵
PRESS F2 (Edit key)
ENTER ance
PRESS ↵

Save the file under the same name—JONESEXP.

PRESS /
PRESS f (File)
PRESS s (Save)
PRESS r (Replace)

ACTIVITY 4.1   □   *Changing the Global Column Width*

In this activity, you will retrieve a file used in Chapter 2 and change all column widths to 12 characters.

1. Retrieve the file ASPENREV.
2. Use the Global Column-width command to change all columns to a 12-character width.
3. Save the file under the same name, ASPENREV.

ACTIVITY 4.2   □   *Changing the Width of One Column*

In this activity, you will retrieve a file created in Chapter 3, change column A to 20 characters, and edit data in the file.

1. Retrieve the file ECONTEST.
2. Change the width of column A only to 20 characters.
3. Add last names to the labels in A6 through A10 as shown.
4. Save the file as ACT4-2.

```
A1: [W20] 'CONSUMER ECONOMICS                                            READY


                  A           B          C          D          E          F
 1   CONSUMER ECONOMICS
 2   TEST SCORES
 3
 4   Name                 Test 1     Test 2     Test 3     Total
 5
 6   Hobson, Brian            29         25         35         89
 7   Jenks, Michael           19          8         22         49
 8   Lantz, Jesse             32         30         35         97
 9   Hussein, Afkam           26         27         30         83
10   Wu, Li                   33         24         30         87
11
12
13
14
15
16
```

HOW CAN VALUE FORMATS BE CHANGED?

The format command is used to change the appearance or format of values on a spreadsheet. Nine different formats are available. The General format is the global default format and displays numbers with no commas, no $ signs (e.g. 4000), and no trailing zeros after the decimal point. The general format shows decimal places if they are keyed. For example 2.345 is displayed with three decimal places.

The format of an entire spreadsheet can be changed using the / Worksheet Global Format command. Individual cells or ranges of cells can be changed to a different format using the / Range Format command. In planning a spreadsheet, you should decide on the format needed for the majority of columns on the spreadsheet. Use the Worksheet Global Format command to set this format. Individual cell formats and range formats can be changed to a different format using the / Range Format command.

You can choose from the following formats:

Fixed displays numbers with a specified number of decimal places (e.g. 3.455).

Scientific displays numbers in exponential form with a specified number of decimal places (e.g., 4.00E+01).

Currency displays numbers with a $, commas, and a specified number of decimal places (e.g., $1,200.00).

, (comma) displays numbers with commas and a specified number of decimal places (e.g., 3,450.00).

General displays values with no dollar signs or commas and no trailing zeros after the decimal point. (e.g., 4500, 456.785).

+/- displays positive numbers as plus signs and negative numbers as minus signs (e.g., 3 as + + + ; -3 as - - -).

Percent displays numbers as percents with a specified number of decimal places (e.g., 3.5%)

Date displays numbers as a date (e.g., 1 as 01-Jan-1900).

Text displays formulas in the cells as they were entered on the screen. It displays numbers in General format, and a printout of the spreadsheet will show cell formulas.

Global Currency Format

Retrieve the file JONESEXP. Change the entire spreadsheet to Fixed format with 2 decimal places.

P R E S S /

P R E S S w (Worksheet)

P R E S S g (Global)

P R E S S f (Format)

P R E S S f (Fixed)

The control panel will display the following:

```
A1: [W15] 'YEARLY EXPENSES OF RONALD JONES                          EDIT
Enter number of decimal places (0..15): 2
```

Select 2 decimal places by pressing the Enter key.

PRESS ↵

The entire spreadsheet should now be in Fixed format with 2 decimal places.

For practice, change the format for the entire spreadsheet to the Currency format with zero decimal places.

PRESS /
PRESS w (Worksheet)
PRESS g (Global)
PRESS f (Format)
PRESS c (Currency)
ENTER 0
PRESS ↵

Now all the values in the spreadsheet should have dollar signs but no decimal places. Save the revised file as JONESEXP.

Dollar signs ($) should not be entered manually at the beginning of values. If dollar signs are needed, use the Currency Format command.

Range Format

A range of cells, rather than an entire spreadsheet can be formatted in a particular way. You may not want an entire spreadsheet to be in Currency format. Instead, you can format individual rows or columns in Currency format.

Retrieve the file named WICHITA. Format the values in the TO-TALS row for currency with 0 decimal places.

PRESS Home (Home key)
PRESS /
PRESS r (Range)
PRESS f (Format)
PRESS c (Currency)
ENTER 0 (0 decimal places)

The second line of the control panel will display the following:

```
A1: 'SALES IN WICHITA PLANT                                          POINT
Enter range to format: A1..A1
```

The range shown, *A1..A1,* is the present location of the cell pointer.

Define a Range

A range of cells can be one cell or any rectangular block of cells, including a row, several rows, a column, or several columns.

Two methods can be used to define a range. One method involves keying in the beginning and ending cell addresses in the range. The other one, which will be explained later in this chapter, is the pointing method.

In some cases, the format for a range is set before values and/or formulas are entered in that range. Key in the range B8 through D8 by entering the beginning cell address in the range, B8, a period, and the ending cell address in the range, D8.

ENTER B8.D8

PRESS ↵

The totals should be in currency format now.

Values above 1,000 are often easier to read if they have commas in them. Format the values in rows 5, 6, and 7 using the , (comma) format with 0 decimals. This time, select the range by using the pointing method.

Press the Home key so that your screen will display the range: A1..A1.

PRESS Home (Home key)

PRESS /

PRESS r (Range)

PRESS f (Format)

PRESS , (comma format)

ENTER 0 (0 decimal places)

PRESS ↵

The screen will now display the following:

```
A1: 'SALES IN WICHITA PLANT                                          POINT
Enter range to format: A1..A1
```

The range shown is the present location of the cell pointer. Press the Backspace key to change this range and allow the cell pointer to move.

P R E S S   Backspace key

Use the arrow keys to move the cell pointer to B5, the upper left corner of the range to be formatted.

P R E S S   ↓ (4 times)
P R E S S   → (1 time)

Cell B5 should be highlighted.

P R E S S   . (Period key to anchor the cell pointer)

Now use the arrow keys to move the cell pointer to the lower right corner, cell D7, of the range to be formatted.

P R E S S   ↓ (2 times)
P R E S S   → (2 times)

Now the entire range that needs to be formatted should be highlighted on the screen as shown in Figure 4.2.

```
D7: (,0) Z334                                                      POINT
Enter range to format: B5..D7

          A        B        C        D        E      F      G      H
 1   SALES IN WICHITA PLANT
 2   FROM 1993-95
 3
 4               1993     1994     1995
 5   Pipes      23,400   24,500   26,800
 6   Rings      13,400   14,788   15,688
 7   Sealers     4,560    3,665    2,334
 8   TOTALS    $41,360  $42,945  $44,822
 9
10
11
12
```

Figure 4.2 □ A Formatting Range is Defined

P R E S S   ↵

The spreadsheet should now be in two different formats—the , (comma) format for rows 5-7 and Currency format in row 8.
Save the file as WICHITA.

HOW CAN A SPREADSHEET BE ERASED FROM THE SCREEN?

Each spreadsheet created should be assigned a filename and stored on disk. When a file is retrieved onto the screen, the image on the screen is a copy of the file stored on disk. You may have noticed that after you save a spreadsheet on disk, the spreadsheet still appears on the screen. If you want to begin creating a new spreadsheet, you must erase the one on the screen. The command to erase this image on the screen is **/ Worksheet Erase Yes**.

You should be very careful before using this command. Be sure the spreadsheet on the screen is stored on disk if you want to use it in the future. Generally, you should use the **File Save** command immediately before you remove the image from the screen.

You should now have the file WICHITA on the screen. If you do not, retrieve the WICHITA file at this time. Then erase the spreadsheet from the screen.

P R E S S **/**

P R E S S w (Worksheet)

P R E S S e (Erase)

P R E S S y (Yes)

The spreadsheet screen should be clear and ready for you to enter data. The file named WICHITA is still stored on your disk.

ACTIVITY 4.3 ☐ *Formatting a Spreadsheet*

Create the spreadsheet shown at the top of the next page, using the appropriate label alignment, column widths, and value formats.

1. Enter the main headings in A1 and A2 in capital letters.
2. Center and capitalize the column labels in row 4.
3. Enter the labels in A6 through A9.
4. Change the entire spreadsheet to 12 characters per column.
5. Format the range B6 through B9 using the , (comma) format with 0 decimal places.
6. Format the range D6 through D9 in Currency format with 2 decimal places.
7. Enter the values in columns B and C.
8. Move the cell pointer to D6 and enter the formula to multiply the sales for L. Bach by the commission rate — +B6*C6.

```
A1: 'DOLE INVESTMENTS                                                    READY


           A            B            C            D            E            F
   1   DOLE INVESTMENTS
   2   WEEKLY COMMISSION REPORT
   3
   4     BROKER        SALES      COMMISSION   COMMISSION
   5                                 RATE
   6   L. Bach         15,488        0.03       $464.64
   7   R. Edwards      33,789        0.04     $1,351.56
   8   A. Lambert      18,450        0.03       $553.50
   9   K. Drexel        9,231        0.02       $184.62
  10
  11
  12
  13
  14
  15
  16
  17
  18
  19
  20
```

9. Enter formulas in column D to determine the commissions earned by the other three brokers.

10. Save the spreadsheet as DOLECOMM.

11. Erase the spreadsheet from the screen.

HOW IS THE HELP KEY USED?

Each of the function keys (F keys) has been programmed to perform a specific operation within Lotus 1-2-3. The F1 key, the Help key, allows you to access an on-line help manual. Any time you have forgotten a command, you can press F1 to obtain information about it.

When you press F1, your spreadsheet is replaced temporarily by a menu showing the topics you may choose from. To get help on a specific topic, you may have to make a selection from a main menu and from a submenu of topics at the bottom of the screen.

Now practice using the on-line Help manual.

PRESS F1 (Help key)

A help screen like the one shown in Figure 4.3 should appear.

```
A1: 'DOLE INVESTMENTS                                              HELP


1-2-3 Help Index

About 1-2-3 Help          Linking Files              1-2-3 Main Menu
Cell Formats              Macro Basics               /Add-In
Cell/Range References     Macro Command Index        /Copy
Column Widths             Macro Key Names            /Data
Control Panel             Mode Indicators            /File
Entering Data             Operators                  /Graph
Error Message Index       Range Basics               /Move
Formulas                  Recalculation              /Print
@Function Index           Specifying Ranges          /Quit
Function Keys             Status Indicators          /Range
Keyboard Index            Task Index                 /System
Learn Feature             Undo Feature               /Worksheet


To select a topic, press a pointer-movement key to highlight the topic and then
press ENTER.  To return to a previous Help screen, press BACKSPACE.  To leave
Help and return to the worksheet, press ESC.
```

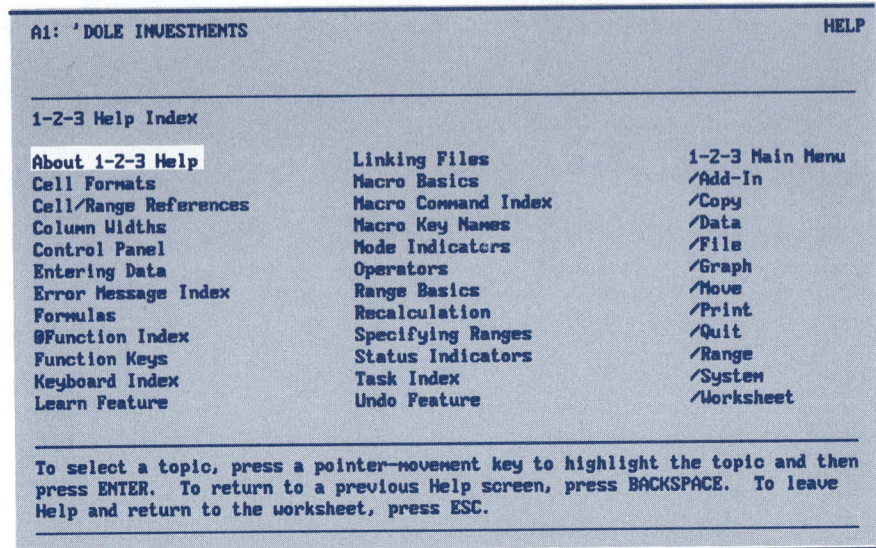

Figure 4.3 □ *A Help Screen*

To select a topic, press an arrow key to highlight the topic and then press the Enter key. To return to a previous Help screen, press the Backspace key. To exit the Help and return to the spreadsheet, press the Esc key.

On your own, practice selecting one or more topics and then return to the spreadsheet.

The Help manual can be used at any time. It can be used when you are in the middle of a command or while you enter keystrokes. For example, if you are in the middle of a global format command but are not sure what global means, you can press the Help key and obtain a definition of global. To use this Help function:

PRESS /

PRESS w (Worksheet)

PRESS g (Global)

PRESS F1 (Help)

The Help screen that appears will explain the purpose of the Worksheet Global command.

WHEN IS THE ESCAPE KEY USED?

The Escape (Esc) key is used for two purposes. One is to get out of the Help menus. The other is to get out of a command or go to a higher level command menu when you change your mind or make a mistake.

Press the Escape key to view the spreadsheet and escape from the command line.

P R E S S   Esc (2 times)

Now practice using the Escape key. Begin by entering the command to change the global column width to 15.

P R E S S   /

P R E S S   w (Worksheet)

P R E S S   g (Global)

Now you decide you don't want to use the Global command; you only want to change the width of column A.

P R E S S   Esc

P R E S S   c (Column-width)

At this point, you decide you don't want to change any of the column widths, so you exit from the command line by pressing the Escape key several times.

P R E S S   Esc (3 times)

To exit from the middle of a command or from the Help manual, press the Escape key one or more times.

HOW ARE @ FUNCTIONS USED?

One feature of Lotus 1-2-3 that increases productivity and saves time is the use of @ functions, also called **shortcut formulas.** Many functions allow you to enter a range of cells, rather than individual cell addresses.

Instead of using a formula such as +B2+B3+B4+B5+B6 to find the total of a column of numbers, an @SUM function could be used. The formula will include the name of the function (@SUM), the beginning cell address in the range to be added (B2), a period, and the ending cell address in the range (B6).

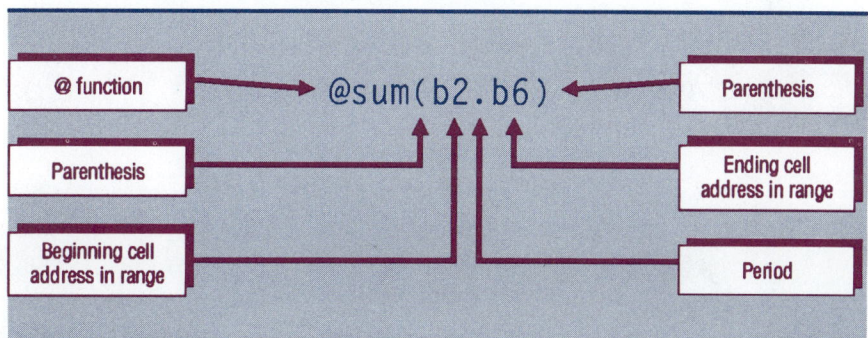

Numerous @ functions are available, but the ones used most frequently are:

@SUM To find the total of a range of values

@AVG To find the average of a range of values

@MIN To locate the smallest value in a range

@MAX To locate the largest value in a range

@COUNT To count the number of cells in a range that are not blank

@IF To produce a value based on whether a logical condition is true or false

Retrieve the file named WICHITA. Change the formulas in row 8 to @sum formulas as shown in Figure 4.4.

```
B8: (T) @SUM(B5..B7)                                                READY


        A        B        C        D        E        F        G        H
1    SALES IN WICHITA PLANT
2    FROM 1993-95
3
4                1993     1994     1995
5    Pipes      23,400   24,500   26,800
6    Rings      13,400   14,780   15,688
7    Sealers     4,560    3,665    2,334
8    TOTALS   @SUM(B5. @SUM(C5. @SUM(D5.
9
10
11
12
13
14
15
16
```

Figure 4.4 ☐ *Using the @SUM Function*

Move the cell pointer to B8.

ENTER   @sum(b5.b7)

PRESS   ↵

Move the cell pointer to C8.

ENTER   @sum(c5.c7)

PRESS   ↵

Move the cell pointer to D8.

ENTER   @sum(d5.d7)

PRESS   ↵

Now move the cell pointer to B5 and change the value.

ENTER 35000

PRESS ↵

Save the file as WICHITA.

WHAT IS AUTOMATIC RECALCULATION?

Did you notice in the last tutorial that the total for 1993 sales changed automatically when 23400 was changed to 35000? This is because Lotus 1-2-3 defaults are set for Automatic Recalculation.

Lotus 1-2-3 recalculates all formulas in a spreadsheet automatically when data is changed. In lengthy spreadsheets containing many formulas, this process can take from several seconds to several minutes.

ACTIVITY 4.4 ☐ Using the @SUM Function and the Help Manual

In this activity, you will retrieve the file named CARDSHOP, enter two @sum formulas, and use the Help screens.

```
A1: 'HALE'S CARD SHOP SALES                                          READY


        A        B        C        D        E        F        G        H
1   HALE'S CARD SHOP SALES
2
3            November December
4   Cups        200.00   100.00
5   Calendars   500.00   600.00
6   Notepads    100.00   200.00
7   Mugs        200.00   200.00
8   Total
9
10
11
12
13
14
15
```

1. Retrieve the file named CARDSHOP.
2. Move the cell pointer to B8.
3. Enter the formula @SUM(B4.B7) in B8.

4. Move the cell pointer to C8, enter @SUM and press the F1 key, the Help key.

5. On the Help screen, press the appropriate arrow keys to highlight *Using "@" Functions in Formulas.* Then press the Enter key. Read the information about @ functions.

6. Press the Escape key to view the spreadsheet again.

7. Enter the rest of the @sum formula, (C4.C7) in C8.

8. Save the spreadsheet as ACT4-4.

CHAPTER 4 □ THEORY EXERCISES

True/False IIIIIIIII Each of the following statements is either True or False. Indicate your choice by circling **T** for a true statement or **F** for a false statement.

1. The default setting is 12 characters per cell.   1.   T   F

2. Global column width commands change the width of every column on a spreadsheet.   2.   T   F

3. The command **/ Worksheet Column Set-Width 15** will change the column width of only one column to 15 characters.   3.   T   F

4. If column A needs to have a width of 20 characters and all the other columns need 12 characters, the **Global Column-Width** command should be used first to set all columns at 12 characters.   4.   T   F

5. To change the width of column B only, you must move the cell pointer in column A before invoking the command to change the column width.   5.   T   F

6. The **Currency** format requires that you use three decimal places.   6.   T   F

7. To change the format of an entire spreadsheet, you must use the **/ Range Format** command.   7.   T   F

8. The General format displays commas in values.   8.   T   F

9. The format of individual columns can be changed but not the format of individual cells.   9.   T   F

10. The Percent format will display numbers with % signs after them.   10.   T   F

11. The number 3,500.75 is shown in comma format with two decimal places.   11.   T   F

12. To erase a worksheet displayed on a screen, use the command **/ Worksheet Erase Yes.**   12.   T   F

13. The key that accesses the Help facility is F3.   13.   T   F

14. The Help key should only be used when you are not in the middle of a command.   14.   T   F

15. To exit from the Help screens, press the Backspace key.   15.   T   F

16. The shortcut function to find the average of a range of values is @avg.   16.   T   F

17. The shortcut formula to find the total of a series of values in cells E2, E3, E4, and E5 is @sumE2.E5.   17.   T   F

18. To find the largest number in a range, you should use the @min function.   18.   T   F

19. Lotus 1-2-3 recalculates a spreadsheet automatically when data is changed.   19.   T   F

20. In lengthy spreadsheets with many formulas, the recalculation of
    formulas may take from several seconds to several minutes.   20. T   F

21. To find the total of a column of numbers located in the range B2
    through B8, you should use the shortcut formula @sumB2.B8.   21. T   F

22. The formula @avg(c4.c7) will find the average of the numbers lo-
    cated in cells C4, C5, C6, and C7.   22. T   F

Completion ‖‖‖‖‖‖‖ For each item below fill in the word (or words) that completes the
statement or answers the question.

1. To increase the width of only one column, enter the command _____.

2. To increase the width of all columns in a spreadsheet to 15 characters, enter the

   command _____ .

3. When the first line of the control panel shows B6 [W12]: 250, it means that

   _____

   _____ .

4. Column A needs to have a width of 20 and the other columns need a width of 15.

   To set all columns to a width of 15 characters, enter the command _____ .

5. To change the format of all the values in a spreadsheet at once, use the command

   _____ .

6. To change the format of a range of cells, use the command _____.

7. To display the value 3500.5, use the _____ format and select _____
   decimal place(s).

8. To display the value $500.25, use the _____ format and select _____
   decimal place(s).

9. To display 86.8 as 86.8%, use the _____ format and select _____
   decimal place(s).

10. To display 1500 as 1,500, use the _____ format.

11. The default format setting is the _____ format.

12. A range of cells can be defined (highlighted) by moving the cell pointer to the be-

    ginning cell in the range, pressing the _____ key, using the arrow keys to

    move the cell pointer to the ending cell address in the range, and pressing the

    _____ key.

13. The command to erase a spreadsheet displayed on the screen is / Worksheet
    _____ Yes.

14. The command to erase a spreadsheet displayed on the screen (does/does not)
    _____ erase the spreadsheet file stored on disk.

15. To access the Help facility, press the _____ key.

16. After accessing the Help screens, press the _____ key to return your
    spreadsheet to the screen.

17. The _____ function can be used in a formula to find the total of a
    column or row of numbers.

18. To find the total of a range of values located in D6 through D12, you should enter
    the formula _____ .

19. To find the average of a range of values located in B2 through B7, you should enter
    the formula _____ .

20. When data is changed in a spreadsheet, Lotus 1-2-3 recalculates all formulas
    _____ .

ACTIVITY 4.5 ◻ *Setting Column Widths and Formats*

In this activity, you will use the template file SPORTS. This spreadsheet is designed to show departmental and quarterly sales for a retail store that sells sporting goods and sports clothing. You will change the column widths and formats and enter formulas to determine the departmental sales and quarterly sales.

1. Retrieve the template file named SPORTS.
2. Set the global column width at 13.
3. Set the column width for column A at 18.
4. Set the Global format to **,** (comma) format with 2 decimal places.
5. Set the format for the range B15 through E15 to Currency format with 2 decimals.
6. Change the label in A4 to DEPARTMENT.
7. Enter appropriate formulas in row 15 to determine the total sales for each month (October, November, and December) and the Total Sales for the quarter.
8. Enter the appropriate formulas in column D to determine the Total Quarterly Sales for each department.
9. Save the file under the name ACT 4-5.

CHAPTER 5

Inserting Rows and Columns
❑ *Inserting Underlines* ❑
Printing a Spreadsheet

OBJECTIVES

❑ Insert rows
❑ Insert columns
❑ Use underlines
❑ Use double underlines
❑ Use hyphenated lines
❑ Print a spreadsheet

HOW CAN BLANK ROWS BE INSERTED IN A SPREADSHEET?

Occasionally, you may find that the appearance of the spreadsheet could be improved if an extra row or column were added to it. In other cases, you may have forgotten to enter a row or column. Lotus 1-2-3 allows you to add one or more blank rows or columns anywhere in a spreadsheet at any time.

Use the / **Worksheet Insert** command to insert blank rows or columns. Before beginning the command, locate the cell pointer in the row or column where a blank one needs to be inserted. When new rows or columns are inserted, cell references in formulas are adjusted automatically.

Retrieve the file named WICHITA and insert two blank rows and a blank column for the 1992 sales figures.

Begin by inserting a blank row 5 to separate the column headings 1993, 1994, and 1995 from the values in those columns. Move the cell pointer to a location in row 5.

PRESS	F5 (go to key)
ENTER	A5
PRESS	↵
PRESS	/
PRESS	w (Worksheet)

P R E S S   i (Insert)

P R E S S   r (Row)

The control panel will now display the following:

```
A5: 'Pipes                                              POINT
Enter row insert range: A5..A5

      A       B      C       D      E       F       G       H
```

Since row 5 is the location for the blank row, select the range shown in the control panel.

P R E S S   ↵

Move the cell pointer to cells B9, C9, and D9. Notice that the ranges in the cell formulas have changed.

   Now insert a blank row above the TOTALS row. Move the cell pointer to any location in the TOTALS row.

P R E S S   /

P R E S S   w (Worksheet)

P R E S S   i (Insert)

P R E S S   r (Row)

Select the range shown in the control panel.

P R E S S   ↵

Insert a blank column where column B is located. Move the cell pointer to any location in column B.

P R E S S   /

P R E S S   w (Worksheet)

P R E S S   i (Insert)

P R E S S   c (Column)

P R E S S   ↵

Use the data in Figure 5.1 to enter the column heading 1992, the values, and the appropriate formula in column B. Also edit the main heading in cell A2, changing 1993 to 1992.

   Enter a formula to determine the total 1992 sales.

   Format B6 through B8 in , (comma) format with 0 decimals. Format the total 1992 sales in Currency with 0 decimals.

	1992
Pipes	20575
Rings	12935
Sealers	3788

Figure 5.1 ☐ *1992 Sales Figures*

Save the file as WICHITA.

ACTIVITY 5.1 ☐ *Inserting Rows and Columns*

Retrieve the file named ACT4-4 and insert two new rows. Insert one row so that the words FOR THE 4TH QUARTER can be added. Insert a blank row to separate the Total row from the other rows. Finally, insert a new column and enter October sales figures in that column.

```
A1: 'HALE'S CARD SHOP SALES                                          READY


         A        B        C        D        E        F        G        H
1   HALE'S CARD SHOP SALES
2   FOR THE 4TH QUARTER
3
4            October  November December
5   Cups      160.00   200.00   100.00
6   Calendars 425.00   500.00   600.00
7   Notepads  150.00   100.00   200.00
8   Mugs      170.00   200.00   200.00
9
10  Total     905.00  1000.00  1100.00
11
12
```

1. Retrieve the file ACT4-4 created in the previous chapter.
2. Insert a blank row 2.
3. In A2, enter the main heading FOR THE 4TH QUARTER.
4. Insert a blank row to separate the Total row from the other rows.
5. Insert a blank column B.
6. Add the column heading OCTOBER, the sales figures, and an appropriate formula in column B.
7. Save the file as ACT5-1.

HOW ARE UNDERSCORES, DOUBLE UNDERSCORES AND HYPHENATED LINES CREATED?

Underscores, double underscores, and hyphenated lines are often used to improve the appearance of a spreadsheet. They may be used to separate column headings from the values in a spreadsheet. Underscores are often used to separate values in a column from the total values. Double underscores are used frequently below a row titled Totals or Gross Profits.

The first technique you will use allows an entire cell width to be filled with underscores, double underscores, or a hyphenated line. To fill a cell with hyphens, enter a backslash followed by a hyphen (\−) as shown below.

```
A1:                                                                          LABEL
\-

         A        B        C        D        E        F        G        H
```

To create underscores, enter a backslash followed by an underscore (_). For double underscores, enter \=. With this technique, the cell will remain completely filled with an underscore, double underscore, or hyphenated line even if cell widths are increased at a later time.

The other technique involves entering the underscores or hyphens manually as you would on a typewriter. These underscores or hyphenated lines will not fill the entire cell width if the cell width is increased.

Retrieve the file named WICHITA. You will insert a blank row, double underscores, and hyphens as shown in Figure 5.2.

```
A1: 'SALES IN WICHITA PLANT                                                  READY

        A        B        C        D        E        F        G        H
 1   SALES IN WICHITA PLANT
 2   FROM 1993-95
 3   =================================================
 4                     1993     1994     1995
 5
 6   Pipes            23,400   24,500   26,800
 7   Rings            13,400   14,780   15,688
 8   Sealers           4,560    3,665    2,334
 9                    -------  -------  -------
10   TOTALS          $41,360  $42,945  $44,822
11   =================================================
12
13
14
15
16
17
18
19
20
```

Figure 5.2 □ *Creating Double Underscores*

Move the cell pointer to A3.

ENTER \ (Backslash, not a slash)

ENTER = (Equals sign)

PRESS ↵

Now cell A3 will be filled with double underscores.

Move the cell pointer to B3 and enter a double underscore in this cell.

ENTER \ (Backslash, not a slash)

ENTER = (Equals sign)

PRESS ↵

Repeat the procedure for cells C3, D3, and E3.

Now create a double underscore in the row below the TOTALS row. Move the cell pointer to A11.

ENTER \ (Backslash, not a slash)

ENTER = (Equals sign)

PRESS ↵

Repeat this same command to create double underscores in cells B11, C11, D11, and E11.

This is a time-consuming technique to create lines. In a future chapter, you will learn how the copy command can help you create underlines and hyphenated lines more quickly.

Now use the manual technique for entering lines. Manually enter hyphenated lines to separate the values in rows 6, 7, and 8 from the TOTALS in row 10. Move the cell pointer to B9.

PRESS Spacebar (once)

ENTER –––––––– (8 hyphens)

PRESS ↵

The space before the hyphen is needed so that a space separates the hyphens in each cell in this row. The space indicates that the hyphens are to be treated as labels and not as part of a formula. If no space was intended, an apostrophe (') would be required before the hyphens so that the hyphens would be treated as labels.

Move the cell pointer to C9.

PRESS Spacebar (once)

ENTER --------- (8 hyphens)

PRESS ↵

Repeat this same command to create hyphens in cells D9 and E9. Save the file as WICHITA.

ACTIVITY 5.2 □ *Using Hyphenated Lines and Double Underscores*

In this activity, you will insert a row and add hyphenated lines and double underscores in a spreadsheet.

```
A1: 'MOUNTAINSIDE BICYCLE SHOP                                          READY


         A         B         C         D        E        F        G        H
1   MOUNTAINSIDE BICYCLE SHOP
2   PROFIT FOR THE SECOND QUARTER
3
4              APRIL     MAY        JUNE
5
6   Revenue     5500      6380       6800
7   Costs       2500      2750       2940
8              ------------------------
9   Profit      3000      3630       3860
10             ========================
11
12
13
14
15
16
17
18
19
20
```

1. Retrieve the file named ASPENREV.
2. Insert a blank row in row 8.
3. Enter a hyphenated line in cells B8, C8, and D8 using the \\– command.
4. Enter a double underscore in cells B10, C10, and D10.
5. Save the file as ACT5-2.

HOW IS A SPREADSHEET PRINTED?

The command to print a spreadsheet is **/ Print Printer Range Align Go**. The first part of the command, **/ Print Printer**, brings the print menu into the control panel as shown below.

```
A1:                                                              MENU
Range Line Page Options Clear Align Go Quit
Specify a range to print
```

The first time a spreadsheet is printed, the range to be printed must be selected. The **Range** command is used to tell 1-2-3 the portion of the spreadsheet that is to be printed. After you press R to select the range, the control panel will display the following:

```
A1:                                                             POINT
Enter print range: A1
```

If the current range shown is not the location where you want to begin printing, change the range. Press the backspace key, move the cell pointer to the upper left corner of the range to be printed. To anchor the beginning of the range, press the Period key. To complete the range, move the cell pointer to the lower left corner of the range to be printed, and press the Enter key. When a previously defined range is not the one you wish to print, begin by pressing the Backspace key to allow the cell pointer to move and to allow you to define a different range.

The next step is to select **Align**. This command ensures that page breaks will be in the correct spot when you print the range.

```
A1:                                                              MENU
Range Line Page Options Clear  Align  Go Quit
Reset to top of page (after adjusting paper)
```

The final command to print is **Go**.

```
A1:                                                              MENU
Range Line Page Options Clear Align  Go  Quit
Print the specified range
```

After a spreadsheet has been printed, the **Page** command can be used to move the paper to the top of the next page. Entering the **Page** command a second time moves the printed spreadsheet out of the printer. If you want to print several spreadsheets, do not press the **Page** command until after the last spreadsheet has been printed. If individual sheets of paper are used in the printer rather than continuous form paper, the **Page** command is not needed.

The final command to exit the print menu is **Quit**.

Put paper in the printer and turn it on. For non-laser printers, roll paper in the printer and align the top of the page with the top of the printer cartridge.

Retrieve the file WICHITA.

PRESS	Home (home key)
PRESS	/
PRESS	p (Print)
PRESS	p (Printer)
PRESS	r (Range)
PRESS	. (period)
PRESS	↓ (10 times)
PRESS	→ (4 times)
PRESS	↵
PRESS	a (align)
PRESS	g (go)

The spreadsheet should now begin to be printed.

If a spreadsheet does not print, check to see if the printer is turned on and is online, if there is an Online indicator. Repeat the steps above to try the printing command again. If the spreadsheet still does not print, ask your instructor for assistance.

Use the **Page** command to cause the paper to move to the top of the next page. This command is usually not needed when using a laser printer. Consult with the instructor if you are not sure if it is needed.

PRESS	p (Page)

Exit the **Print** command menus by using the **Quit** command.

PRESS	q (Quit)

To save the print range for use at a later date, save the file.

PRESS	/
PRESS	f (File)
PRESS	s (Save)
ENTER	↵

Use the **/ W**orksheet **E**rase command to remove the spreadsheet from the screen.

ACTIVITY 5.3 ☐ *Printing a Spreadsheet*

In this activity, you will retrieve a spreadsheet, select the range, and print the spreadsheet.

1. Retrieve the file named ACT5-2.
2. Place paper in the printer in the correct position.
3. Press the Home key so that when the range is defined, it begins at A1.
4. Enter the command to print the range A1.D11.
5. Select **A**lign and **G**o to print the spreadsheet.
6. If needed, use the **P**age command to eject the page from the printer.
7. Select **Q**uit to exit the print menus.
8. Save the file as ACT5-3.
9. Clear the spreadsheet from the screen.

Print a Section of a Spreadsheet

To print a section of a spreadsheet, use the **R**ange command and enter only the range that needs to be printed. For example, to print the first two columns in a spreadsheet, you might select A1.B23.

Once you select a range, Lotus 1-2-3 will remember that range the next time you print. However, you can easily change the range by entering new beginning and ending cell addresses.

In the following tutorial, you will print the entire spreadsheet first and then print a section of the spreadsheet.

Retrieve the file named ACT5-3.

P R E S S	Home (Home key)
P R E S S	/
P R E S S	p (Print)
P R E S S	p (Printer)
P R E S S	r (Range)
P R E S S	. (period)
P R E S S	↓ (9 times)
P R E S S	→ (3 times)
P R E S S	↵
P R E S S	a (align)
P R E S S	g (go)

The spreadsheet should now print. Do not remove the printout from the printer.

Now identify a print range including only columns A, B, and C.

P R E S S   r (Range)

P R E S S   Backspace key

P R E S S   . (period to anchor the cell pointer)

P R E S S   ↓   (9 times)

P R E S S   →   (2 times)

P R E S S   ↵

P R E S S   g (Go)

P R E S S   q (Quit)

If needed for your printer, use the **Page** command to eject the paper from the printer.

P R E S S   p (Page to eject the paper)

P R E S S   q (Quit)

Printing Options

Several other print options are available. The option used most frequently is the Margins option. This is used to set left, right, top, and bottom margins or to clear all margin settings. Lotus 1-2-3 uses the default margins shown in Figure 5.3.

MARGIN	SETTING
Left	4 characters on the left side of the page
Right	76 characters
Bottom	2 lines at the bottom of the page
Top	2 lines at the top of the page

Figure 5.3 ▢ *Default Margin Settings*

In this tutorial, you will change the left and right margin options and print a range of the spreadsheet.

Retrieve the file named JONESEXP.

P R E S S   Home

P R E S S   /

P R E S S   p (Print)

P R E S S   p (Printer)

P R E S S   r (Range)

E N T E R   A1.H10

PRESS ⏎

PRESS o (Options)

PRESS m (Margins)

PRESS l (Left)

ENTER 2

PRESS ⏎

PRESS m (Margins)

PRESS r (Right)

ENTER 81

PRESS ⏎

PRESS q (Quit)

PRESS a (Align)

PRESS g (Go)

After printing the spreadsheet, change the margin settings back to the default settings.

PRESS o (Options)

PRESS m (Margins)

PRESS l (Left)

ENTER 4

PRESS ⏎

PRESS m (Margins)

PRESS r (Right)

ENTER 76

PRESS ⏎

PRESS q (Quit)

PRESS q (Quit)

Besides margins, several other printing options are available. They include printing headers, footers, and borders, changing the page length, and setting up printer attributes.

CHAPTER 5 □ THEORY EXERCISES

True/False IIIIIIIII Each of the following statements is either True or False. Indicate your choice by circling **T** for a true statement or **F** for a false statement.

1. The **/ Range Insert** command is used to insert rows or columns. 1. T F

2. Before you can insert a blank column, the cell pointer must be located in the column where a blank one needs to be inserted. 2. T F

3. When a new row is inserted, cell references in the formulas must be changed manually. 3. T F

4. To fill a cell with hyphens, you must enter the command \– in that cell. 4. T F

5. To fill a cell with double underscores, you must enter the command \=. 5. T F

6. When underscores are entered in a cell without using the \– procedure and the cell width is later increased, the underscores will no longer fill the entire width of the cell. 6. T F

7. The basic command to print a spreadsheet for the first time is **/ Print Printer Align Go**. 7. T F

8. The **Align** command is used to ensure that page breaks will be in the correct spot when a range is printed. 8. T F

9. A print range can include the entire spreadsheet or a portion of a spreadsheet. 9. T F

10. The final command to make the printer begin printing is **Go**. 10. T F

11. The **Page** command is used to print an entire page of the spreadsheet. 11. T F

12. To exit the print menu, use the **Escape** command. 12. T F

13. To print 85 characters on a line, use the **/ Print Printer Options Margins Left**. 13. T F

Completion IIIIIIIII For each item below fill in the word (or words) that completes the statement or answers the question.

1. The command to insert a blank row is _____ .

2. The command to insert a blank column is _____ .

3. Before you can enter the command to insert a blank row in row 8 of a spreadsheet, the cell pointer should be located in _____ .

4. List the keystrokes to be used to fill a cell with underscores.

_____

5. List the keystrokes to be used to fill a cell with hyphens.

_____

6. List the keystrokes to be used to fill a cell with double underscores.

_____

7. List the keystrokes to be used to select the range a1 through d15 for printing.

_____

8. List the final command required to print. _____

_____

9. List the command to eject a page from the printer. _____

_____

10. List the command to exit from the print command menus. _____

_____

11. To set the left, right, top, or bottom margins, you must use the printer option

_____ .

ACTIVITY 5.4 ☐ *Printing an Entire Spreadsheet*

Retrieve file ACT5-2. Define the range to be printed as the entire spreadsheet. Use the appropriate command to print the spreadsheet.

CHAPTER 6

OBJECTIVES

□ Use the Copy command
□ Delete rows
□ Delete columns

HOW IS THE COPY COMMAND USED?

By using the / Copy command, you can copy formulas from one cell to a range of cells. This command can also be used to copy labels, values, and formulas from one location on a spreadsheet to another location. The Copy command is one of the most useful of all the Lotus 1-2-3 commands because it saves the operator so much time.

Copying Formulas Across a Row

When a formula is copied across a row, the column letters in the formula will change automatically in each cell. When a formula is copied down a column, the row numbers in the newly created formulas change automatically.

Retrieve the file DEDEXP.

This file lists monthly and yearly expenses that may be used as deductible expenses on a federal income tax form. In the next tutorial, you will enter the formula in B18 to determine the total January expenses. When entering the range in an @sum formula, you can include blank cells in the range. When summing a column of numbers, 1-2-3 treats a blank cell as zero.

Move the cell pointer to B18.

ENTER @sum(b5.b17)
PRESS ↵

With the cell pointer at B18, copy the formula in B18 to the range C18 through N18.

PRESS /

PRESS c (Copy)

The instructions in the control panel will show the following:

```
B18: @SUM(B5..B17)                                                    POINT
Enter range to copy FROM: B18..B18

               A                B       C       D       E       F
```

Accept the range, B18, shown in the control panel as the range to copy from.

PRESS ↵

The instructions in the control panel will show the following:

```
B18: @SUM(B5..B17)                                                    POINT
Enter range to copy TO: B18

               A                B       C       D       E       F
```

Since you do not want to copy from and to the same cell address, move the cell pointer one cell to the right to the beginning of the range to be copied to.

PRESS →

Define the range the formula should be copied to, C18 through N18.

PRESS . (Period key)

After the period key is pressed, two periods will appear on the screen followed by C18.

PRESS → (11 times)

The range C18 through N18 will be highlighted and be displayed in the control panel as shown in Figure 6.1.

PRESS ↵

```
N18:                                                              POINT
Enter range to copy TO: C18..N18

            G        H        I        J        K        L        M        N
1
2
3          June     July    August September October November December Totals
4
5           35       35      185       35       35       35       35
6                     3
7          226
8                             40                                   20
9          451      451      451      451      451      451      451
10         169      169      169      169      169      169      169
11          85      113      380       44       28       55      296
12
13
14         333               25       15       79
15          32       34       22       15       32       22       41
16           4        3        8        2        7        5        4
17         156      156      156      156      156      156      156
18
19
20
```

Figure 6.1 ☐ *Range Highlighted During Copy Process*

Now the formula has been copied across row 18. Notice that the formula @sum(b5..b17) was updated to @sum(c5..c17) when it was copied to cell C18. As you can see, Lotus 1-2-3 copies the formulas but alters the cell references in them.

Save the file as DEDEXP.

Copy Formulas Down a Column

The / Copy command can also be used to copy formulas down a column. When a formula is copied down a column, the row numbers in the new formulas will change automatically.

Retrieve the file DEDEXP, if it is not on the screen.

Enter the formula to determine the total Charitable Contributions for January through December. Move the cell pointer to N5.

ENTER @sum(b5.m5)

PRESS ↵

Copy the formula in N5 to the range N6 through N18.

PRESS /

PRESS c (Copy)

The control panel will display the following:

```
N5: @SUM(B5..M5)                                                 POINT
Enter range to copy FROM: N5..N5

            G        H        I        J        K        L        M        N
```

Accept the Copy From range shown in the control panel.

PRESS ↵

The instructions in the control panel will be as follows:

```
N5: @SUM(B5..M5)                                              POINT
Enter range to copy TO: N5

         G      H      I      J      K      L      M      N
```

So that you do not copy from and to the same cell address, move the cell pointer to the beginning cell address in the range you want to copy to. Then define the range to be copied to, N6 through N17.

PRESS ↓

PRESS . (Period key)

PRESS ↓ (11 times)

The control panel should show the following:

```
N17: @SUM(B17..M17)                                          POINT
Enter range to copy TO: N6..N17

         G      H      I      J      K      L      M      N
```

PRESS ↵

Move the cell pointer up and down column N to see how the row numbers in each formula have been changed.

Save the file as DEDEXP.

Creating Lines

Any label or symbol can be copied by using the Copy command. Lines separating headings from the values in a spreadsheet can be created very quickly by using the Copy command. Underscores and double underscores can also be created this way.

If the file DEDEXP is not on the screen, retrieve that file.

Create a hyphenated line above the Totals row. Begin by inserting a blank row above the Totals row.

Move the cell pointer anywhere in row 18.

PRESS /

PRESS w (Worksheet)

PRESS i (Insert)

PRESS r (Row)

PRESS ↵

Move the cell pointer to A18.

PRESS \ (Backslash)

PRESS - (Hyphen)

PRESS ↵

Now use the Copy command to copy the hyphens in cell A18 to the range B18 through N18. Begin with the cell pointer at A18.

PRESS /

PRESS c (Copy)

PRESS ↵

PRESS →

PRESS . (Period key)

PRESS → (12 times)

PRESS ↵

A row of hyphens will appear in cells A18 through N18.
Save the file as DEDEXP.

ACTIVITY 6.1 □ Using the Copy Command

In this activity, you will enter a formula to find the total concession stand sales and copy that formula to other cells.

```
A1: [W14] 'CONCESSION STAND SALES                                    READY

         A              B        C        D        E        F        G
 1   CONCESSION STAND SALES
 2
 3
 4   Dates          Sodas    Candy   Popcorn    Total
 5
 6   Feb. 1-7        1018      95      685
 7   Feb. 8-14       1286     125      769
 8   Feb. 15-21       987     113      802
 9   Feb. 22-28       725      88      672
10      Totals
11
```

1. Retrieve the file CONCESS.
2. Create a row of equals signs in row 3. Enter \= in A3 and copy it to the range B3 through E3.
3. Create another row of equals signs in row 11 using the same technique.
4. In B10, enter the formula to determine the total sales of sodas for February.
5. Copy the formula in B10 to C10 through E10.
6. In E6, enter a formula to determine the total sales for the first week in February.
7. Copy the formula from E6 to the other appropriate cells in column E.
8. Save the file as ACT6-1.
9. Print the file.

Copying a Range of Labels

Labels can be copied using the same command used to copy formulas and lines. Previously, you copied from one cell to many cells; but you can also copy from a range of cells.

Retrieve the file DEDEXP, if it is not already on the screen.

This spreadsheet shows expenses for 1992, January through December. Lotus 1-2-3 provides many columns and rows that allow one to record tax deductible expenses for many years in the same file.

To keep records on tax deductible expenses in 1993, you can copy the labels used for 1992 to a new location below the 1992 expenses. The 1993 expenses can be entered month by month in 1993.

In the following tutorial, you will copy all the labels in column A to a new location below the original spreadsheet.

Move the cell pointer to the beginning of the range to be copied—A1.

PRESS /

PRESS c (Copy)

The control panel will indicate the beginning cell in the range. Define the range to copy from as A1 through A19.

PRESS ↓ (18 times)

PRESS ↵

The control panel will ask you to enter the range to copy to. Move the cell pointer to cell A22. Only the cell in the upper left corner of the new range needs to be identified.

PRESS ↵

The labels in column A have been copied. Move the cell pointer down to A22 to view them.

When the cell pointer is at A22, enter the year 1993.

ENTER '1993 TAX DEDUCTIBLE EXPENSE
PRESS ↵

Copy the labels in row 3 (January, February, etc.) to row 24. Move the cell pointer to B3.

PRESS /
PRESS c (Copy)

The control panel will indicate the beginning cell in the range, B3. Define the range as B3 through N3.

PRESS → (12 times)
PRESS ↵

The control panel will ask you to enter the range to copy to. Move the cell pointer to cell B24.

PRESS ↵

The new form created is a template or skeleton form that includes labels only.

Save the file as DEDEXP.

Copying a Range of Formulas

A range of formulas can be copied just like a range of labels. In fact, any adjacent rows or columns can be copied whether they contain labels, values, or formulas.

Retrieve the file DEDEXP, if it is not already on the screen.

Copy the hyphenated line in row 18 and the formulas in row 19. Begin with the cell pointer at B18.

PRESS /
PRESS c (Copy)

In the control panel, enter the range to copy from as B18 through N19.

PRESS ↓
PRESS → (12 times)
PRESS ↵

The control panel will ask for the range to be copied to. Move the cell pointer to cell B39.

PRESS ↵

Use the Page Down key and arrow keys to view the new formulas.
The formulas in column N can also be copied to the 1993 Tax Deductible Expense template.
Move the cell pointer to N5.

PRESS F5 (Go To key)
ENTER N5
PRESS ↵
PRESS /
PRESS c (Copy)

The control panel will indicate the beginning cell in the range. Define the range N5 through N19.

PRESS . (Period)
PRESS ↓ (12 times)
PRESS ↵

The control panel will ask for the range to be copied to. Move the cell pointer to cell N26.

PRESS ↵

Enter the following January expenses for 1993.

Charitable Contributions	35
Credit Card Interest	2
Insurance—Rental House	0
Medical Expenses	18
Mortgage Int—Home	451
Mortgage Int—Rental	169
Employee Expenses	12
Real Estate Tax—Home	0

continued

Real Estate Tax—Rental   795
Rental House—Repairs   125
Sales Taxes—Large Items 18
Sales Taxes—Misc.   3
State Income Taxes   156

As you can see on the screen, the January expenses are automatically updated as the new expenses are entered. 1-2-3 automatically recalculates formulas when new values are entered.

Save the file as DEDEXP.

The completed template includes both labels and formulas. When you use spreadsheet designs over and over again, you save time by creating a template or skeleton document. Templates are very easy to create if you use the Copy command.

ACTIVITY 6.2 ☐ Copying Labels and Ranges of Formulas

In this activity, you will create a template using labels and formulas from a spreadsheet created previously.

```
E11: \=                                                           READY


          A             B        C        D         E        F        G
 1  CONCESSION STAND SALES
 2
 3  ========================================================
 4  Dates           Sodas    Candy    Popcorn    Total
 5
 6  Feb. 1-7        1018       95      685       1798
 7  Feb. 8-14       1286      125      769       2180
 8  Feb. 15-21       987      113      802       1902
 9  Feb. 22-28       725       88      672       1485
10      Totals      4016      421     2928       7365
11  ========================================================
12
13
14  CONCESSION STAND SALES
15
16  ========================================================
17  Dates           Sodas    Candy  Popcorn    Total
18
19                                               0
20                                               0
```

1. Retrieve the file created in the previous activity, ACT6-1.

2. Create a template below the original spreadsheet. This template will be used to record the Concession Stand Sales for the next month—March.

3. Move the cell pointer to A1. Use the **Copy** command to copy rows 1, 2, 3, and 4 to a location beginning at cell A14. These will be the headings for the template.

4. Copy rows 10 and 11 to rows 23 and 24 in the template.

5. Copy the formulas in column E to the appropriate location in the template.

6. Save the file as ACT6-2.

7. Print the file.

HOW CAN COLUMNS BE DELETED?

By using the **/ Worksheet Delete Column** command, you can delete columns. However, before using this command, you must locate the cell pointer somewhere in the column that will be deleted.

Be very cautious when using the **Worksheet Delete Column** command since you can accidentally erase or delete a column of information. Some spreadsheet operators save the spreadsheet on disk prior to using this command. This way they have a backup copy that can be retrieved in case important data is deleted.

The difference between the **Delete** command and the **Erase** command is that the **Delete** command removes a column or row and the data in it. The **Erase** command removes only the data and leaves the column or row empty.

Retrieve the file named TAXDED.

This file lists monthly and yearly expenses that may be used as deductible expenses on a federal income tax form. As shown in Figure 6.2, only the expenses for a few months of the year can be seen on the screen at any one time.

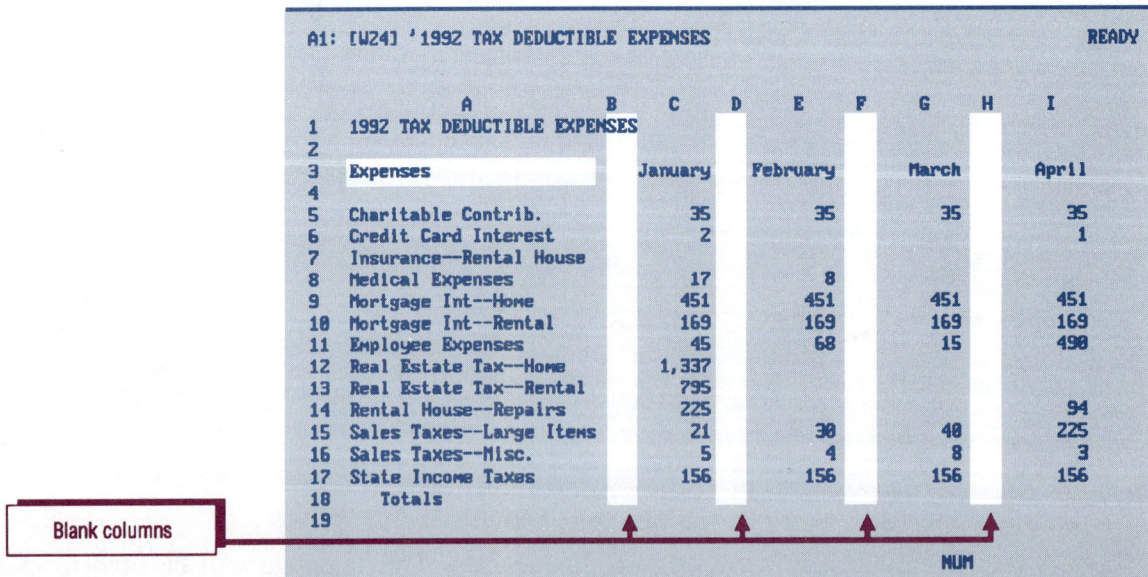

A1: [W24] '1992 TAX DEDUCTIBLE EXPENSES   READY

	A	B	C	D	E	F	G	H	I
1	1992 TAX DEDUCTIBLE EXPENSES								
2									
3	Expenses		January		February		March		April
4									
5	Charitable Contrib.		35		35		35		35
6	Credit Card Interest		2						1
7	Insurance--Rental House								
8	Medical Expenses		17		8				
9	Mortgage Int--Home		451		451		451		451
10	Mortgage Int--Rental		169		169		169		169
11	Employee Expenses		45		68		15		490
12	Real Estate Tax--Home		1,337						
13	Real Estate Tax--Rental		795						
14	Rental House--Repairs		225						94
15	Sales Taxes--Large Items		21		30		40		225
16	Sales Taxes--Misc.		5		4		8		3
17	State Income Taxes		156		156		156		156
18	Totals								
19									

Blank columns

NUM

Figure 6.2 □ *Spreadsheet with Blank Columns*

When the spreadsheet was created, blank columns were allowed between each monthly expense. This extra space between columns can make a spreadsheet easier to read. However, in this case, the spreadsheet is extremely wide, making it difficult to scroll from the left to the right side of the spreadsheet quickly.

Decrease the width of the spreadsheet by deleting each of the blank columns between the months of the year. Begin with the cell pointer anywhere in column B.

PRESS   /

PRESS   w (Worksheet)

PRESS   d (Delete)

PRESS   c (Column)

The control panel will indicate the location of the cell pointer. Since only one column needs to be deleted, accept the range shown. Two or more columns can be deleted at this point by identifying a larger range than the one shown in the control panel. To identify a range, use the same technique described in previous instructions for defining a range.

PRESS   ↵

After completing this command, Lotus 1-2-3 will close up the spreadsheet, and the blank column will no longer exist as shown in Figure 6.3.

```
B3: "January                                                          READY


             A                B    C    D    E    F    G    H    I
    1   1992 TAX DEDUCTIBLE EXPENSES
    2
    3   Expenses                January    February      March      April
    4
    5   Charitable Contrib.         35         35         35         35
    6   Credit Card Interest         2                                1
    7   Insurance--Rental House
    8   Medical Expenses            17          8
    9   Mortgage Int--Home         451        451        451        451
   10   Mortgage Int--Rental       169        169        169        169
   11   Employee Expenses           45         68         15        490
   12   Real Estate Tax--Home    1,337
   13   Real Estate Tax--Rental    795
   14   Rental House--Repairs      225                               94
   15   Sales Taxes--Large Items    21         30         40        225
   16   Sales Taxes--Misc.           5          4          8          3
   17   State Income Taxes         156        156        156        156
   18      Totals
   19
   20
```

Figure 6.3   ❐   *Spreadsheet with Blank Column Removed*

Move the cell pointer to the next blank column—column C. Delete column C.

P R E S S /

P R E S S w (Worksheet)

P R E S S d (Delete)

P R E S S c (Column)

P R E S S ↵

Now delete all the other blank columns within the spreadsheet using the same procedure.

When you have completed the deletions, save the spreadsheet as TAXDED.

ACTIVITY 6.3 ☐ *Deleting Multiple Columns*

In this activity, you will delete three columns within a spreadsheet. This spreadsheet shows a monthly budget for the first two quarters of the year. You are asked to delete the January, February, and March columns but to keep the April, May, and June columns.

```
A2: [W17] 'FOR JEFF ATKINSON                                          READY


         A          B         C         D         E         F         G
 1  PERSONAL BUDGET
 2  FOR JEFF ATKINSON
 3
 4              January February    March     April       May      June
 5
 6  Income
 7     Wages        1800      1800      1800      1800      1800      1800
 8     Dividends       0         0        50         0         0        50
 9     Total Income 1800      1800      1850      1800      1800      1850
10
11  Expenses
12     Clothing       70        60        60        80        60        60
13     Food          180       180       180       180       180       180
14     Insurance     115       115       115       115       115       115
15     Rent          450       450       450       450       450       450
16     Utilities      80        80        80        80        80        80
17     Misc.          90        90        90        90        90        90
18     Total Expenses 985      975       975       995       975       975
19
20  Savings          815       825       875       805       825       875
```

1. Retrieve the file ACT6-3.
2. Move the cell pointer anywhere in column B, the January column.
3. Delete columns B, C, and D using a single **Delete** command. Begin by entering the command **/ Worksheet Delete Column**. When the control panel indicates a single cell as the range, press the Period key once and the Right Arrow key twice to highlight a range including columns B, C, and D.
4. Press the Enter key.
5. Save the file as ACT6-3.
6. Print the file.

HOW CAN ROWS BE DELETED?

Occasionally, rows may need to be deleted. By using the **/ Worksheet Delete Row** command, you can delete one or more rows. The **/ Worksheet Delete Row** command not only erases the data in a row, but it also closes up the spreadsheet where the data was located.

More than one adjacent row can be deleted by defining a range larger than one row. As mentioned before, be very careful when using the **Delete** command to prevent the accidental deletion of important data.

Retrieve the file named TAXDED.

This spreadsheet lists monthly expenses that may be used as deductions on federal income tax forms. It includes two expenses that can no longer be used as deductions—Credit Card Interest and Sales Taxes.

Delete the rows for Credit Card Interest and Sales Taxes. Begin by moving the cell pointer to any cell in the Credit Card Interest row (row 6).

PRESS /

PRESS w (Worksheet)

PRESS d (Delete)

PRESS r (Row)

The control panel will display a range to be deleted. Accept the range shown.

PRESS ↵

Now you will delete the Sales Taxes—Large Items row and the Sales Taxes—Misc. row. Move the cell pointer to any cell in the row showing expenses for Sales Taxes—Large Items.

PRESS /
PRESS w (Worksheet)
PRESS d (Delete)
PRESS r (Row)

Define a range that includes Sales Taxes—Large Items (row 14), and Sales Taxes—Misc. (row 15).

PRESS ↓
PRESS ↵

The **Delete Row** command not only erases data in a row, but it also closes up the spreadsheet, as shown in Figure 6.4.

```
A15: [W24] 'State Income Taxes                                        READY

            A            B     C     D     E     F     G     H     I
 1   1992 TAX DEDUCTIBLE EXPENSES
 2
 3   Expenses                  January    February      March      April
 4
 5   Charitable Contrib.           35          35         35         35
 6   Credit Card Interest           2                                 1
 7   Insurance--Rental House
 8   Medical Expenses              17           8
 9   Mortgage Int--Home           451         451        451        451
10   Mortgage Int--Rental         169         169        169        169
11   Employee Expenses             45          68         15        490
12   Real Estate Tax--Home      1,337
13   Real Estate Tax--Rental      795
14   Rental House--Repairs        225                                94
15   State Income Taxes           156         156        156        156
16      Totals
17
18
19
20
```

Figure 6.4 ☐ *Spreadsheet with Two Rows Deleted*

Save the spreadsheet as TAXDED.

ACTIVITY 6.4 □ Deleting Rows

In this activity, you will delete rows from a spreadsheet. This spreadsheet shows the cost of items being sold in a retail store, the amount the items are marked up, and the selling price for each item.

```
A1: [W18] 'Online Computers Inc.                                    READY

                   A              B           C        D        E
 1  Online Computers Inc.
 2
 3  Description        Inventory No. Unit      Cost    Markup
 4
 5  Printer #5              191.00 Each       495.45   247.73
 6  Printer #8              192.00 Each       694.00   347.00
 7  Computer Mod. 350       194.00 Each       525.00   262.50
 8  Computer Mod. 460       196.00 Each       849.00   424.50
 9  Computer Mod. 640       197.00 Each       949.00   474.50
10  Computer Paper           78.00 Box         7.80     3.12
11  Diskettes--5 1/4         75.00 Box         2.22     0.89
12  Diskettes--3 1/2         95.00 Box         4.50     1.80
13
14
15
```

1. Retrieve the file ACT6-4.
2. Delete the row containing data related to Printer #5 since the Online store no longer carries Printer #5.
3. Delete the row containing data for computer Model 350 since it is not being manufactured any longer.
4. Save the file as ACT6-4.
5. Print the file.

WHAT HAPPENS TO FORMULAS AFTER COLUMNS OR ROWS HAVE BEEN DELETED?

Consider the consequences of deleting a column or row before using the Delete command. Be very careful when deleting a row or column that is part of a formula or function located elsewhere in the spreadsheet. Whenever a column or row located at the beginning or end of a range in a formula or function is deleted, the message ERR will appear in the cell assigned the formula. The ERR message means that 1-2-3 cannot complete the computation.

In the following tutorial, you will insert a new column, title it 1ST QUARTER, and enter formulas to determine the total first quarter expenses. After completion of this tutorial, you will understand that even simple column deletions should be considered carefully.

Retrieve the file QTRBGT.

Insert a new column between the March and April columns. Move the cell pointer anywhere in column E.

PRESS	/
PRESS	w (Worksheet)
PRESS	i (Insert)
PRESS	c (Column)
PRESS	↵

Move the cell pointer to E4. Enter the heading 1st Quarter in E4.

ENTER	"1st Quarter
PRESS	↵

In cell E7, enter a formula to find the sum of the January, February, and March wages.

ENTER	+b7+c7+d7
PRESS	↵

With the cell pointer at E7, copy the formula in E7 to the range E8 through E20.

PRESS	/
PRESS	c (Copy)
PRESS	↵
PRESS	↓
PRESS	. (Period key)
PRESS	↓ (12 times)
PRESS	↵

Now that the 1st Quarter expenses have been determined, remove the January column. Move the cell pointer to column B and delete the column.

PRESS \

PRESS w (Worksheet)

PRESS d (Delete)

PRESS c (Column)

Notice what has happened in the 1st Quarter column. All the cells containing formulas have the diagnostic message ERR in them as shown in Figure 6.5. The ERR message indicates that the computation cannot be completed.

```
B7: 1800                                                        READY


                    A          B          C          D          E
             4                 February   March 1st Quarter     April
             5
             6   Income
             7       Wages        1800       1800        ERR       1800
             8       Dividends       0         50        ERR
             9       Total Income  1800       1850        ERR       1800
            10                                            ERR
            11   Expenses                                 ERR
            12       Clothing       60         60        ERR         80
            13       Food          180        180        ERR        180
            14       Insurance     115        115        ERR        115
            15       Rent          450        450        ERR        450
            16       Utilities      80         80        ERR         80
            17       Misc.          90         90        ERR         90
            18       Total Expenses 975        975        ERR        995
            19                                            ERR
            20   Savings           825        875        ERR        805
            21
            22
            23
```

Figure 6.5 ☐ *ERR Messages in a Spreadsheet*

When the January expenses were deleted, the formulas in the 1st Quarter column could not be calculated. In this spreadsheet, it is evident that one should not delete the January, February, or March columns. Abandon this procedure without saving the file.

PRESS /

PRESS w (Worksheet)

PRESS e (Erase)

PRESS y (Yes)

ACTIVITY 6.5 □ Correcting Formulas after Deletions

In this activity, you will retrieve the file ACT 6-5, delete two rows, and correct formulas.

1. Retrieve the file ACT 6-5.

2. Since Martin Krause has sold his stock, he will no longer be receiving dividends this year. Therefore, delete the row for Dividends.

3. Notice that the cells showing Total Income now show ERR messages. Correct the formula in B8 for the total January income. Enter +B7 in cell B8.

4. Copy the formula in B8 to the range C8 through G8.

5. In an attempt to save more money, Krause has decided to eliminate Miscellaneous expenses from the budget. Delete the row containing Miscellaneous expenses.

6. The formulas in row 16 will show ERR messages. Change the formula in B16 to @sum(b11.b15). Copy the formula from B16 to the range C16 through G16.

7. Move the cell pointer to B18 and check the formula to determine Savings. It should be correct.

8. Save the file as ACT6-5.

9. Print the file.

C H A P T E R   6   □   T H E O R Y   E X E R C I S E S

True/False |||||||| Each of the following statements is either True or False. Indicate your choice by circling **T** for a true statement or **F** for a false statement.

1. The initial command to copy data in a spreadsheet is **/ Copy**.   1.   T   F

2. Either one cell or many cells can be copied at one time.   2.   T   F

3. Formulas should not be copied.   3.   T   F

4. Instructions to carry out the **Copy** command are displayed at the bottom of the screen.   4.   T   F

5. To copy a formula in B6 to B7, use the commands, Copy From:B6..B6 and Copy To B6..B6.   5.   T   F

6. The **Copy** command is one of the most useful commands because it saves time when entering formulas.   6.   T   F

7. To remove a column, use the **/ Worksheet Delete Column** command.   7.   T   F

8. To remove row 6, use the **/ Worksheet Delete Row 6** command.   8.   T   F

9. Before invoking the command to delete column D, you must move the cell pointer to D1.   9.   T   F

10. Only one row or one column can be deleted at a time.   10.   T   F

11. When the formula @sum(b4.d4) is entered in cell E4 and then copied to E5, the formula in E5 will change to @sum(b5.d5).   11.   T   F

12. When the formula +b5-b6 is entered in cell B7 and is copied to C7, the column letters in the formula will change.   12.   T   F

13. Labels cannot be copied.   13.   T   F

14. When the command **/ Worksheet Delete Row A4..A4** is used, only the data in row 4 will be deleted.   14.   T   F

15. When a row or column is deleted, formulas included in those rows or columns will need to be corrected.   15.   T   F

Completion ||||||||| For each item below fill in the word (or words) that completes the statement or answers the question.

1. The initial command to copy a formula or a label is _____ .

2. The initial command to delete a row is _____ .

3. So that columns and rows are not accidentally removed, it is recommended that the cell pointer be placed in the _____ or _____ to be deleted before using the **Delete** command.

4. The initial command to delete a column is _____ .

5. Before entering the command to delete Column C of a spreadsheet, you must locate the cell pointer in _____ .

6. To make a row of hyphens in the range A18 through F18, you should enter \- in A18, and copy cell _____ to the range _____ .

7. After you enter the initial Copy command, / **C**, instructions in the control panel ask you to identify the range to copy _____ and the range to copy _____ .

8. To delete columns C and D, you should locate the cell pointer in column C and enter the command / **W**orksheet **D**elete **C**olumn first. Then the Period key should be pressed to anchor the cell pointer and to allow a larger range of columns to be deleted. Finally, the _____ _____ key should be pressed followed by the Enter key.

9. When you enter the command / **W**orksheet **D**elete **R**ow A15.A18, rows numbered _____, _____, _____, and _____ will be deleted.

Answer the following questions based on the spreadsheet shown below.

```
A1: [W12] 'PROFIT FOR TURIQ OIL CO.                                    READY


        A           B         C         D         E         F         G
 1  PROFIT FOR TURIQ OIL CO.
 2  (in billions)
 3
 4                1990      1991      1992
 5  -------------------------------------
 6  Mexico City    865        49       191
 7  Houston         28        39        64
 8  Khafji          15        27        52
 9
10  Totals
11
12
13
14
```

10. To delete the heading 1990 and the 1990 data, move the cell pointer to _____ and enter the command _____ .

11. Before deleting the blank row above the totals row, move the cell pointer to row _____ first.

12. To delete the blank row above the totals row, enter the command _____ _____ .

13. To determine the total for 1990, enter the formula _____ or _____ in cell _____.

14. When copying a formula from B10 to the range C10 through D10, move the cell pointer to _____. Then enter the command / Copy and the range to copy from, _____, and the range to copy to, _____.

15. To enter a hyphenated line in row 9, first enter _____ in cell A9 and then copy that cell to the range _____ through _____.

ACTIVITY 6.6 □ Deleting Columns and Rows and Using the Copy Command

In this activity, you will enter a row of double underscores using the Copy command, delete a row, and delete a column.

```
A1: [W20] 'BUSINESS LAW CLASS                                        READY


           A              B         C         D         E        F
 1  BUSINESS LAW CLASS
 2  TEST SCORES
 3                     Test 1    Quiz 1    Test 2    Totals
 4                     Pts Poss  Pts Poss  Pts Poss
 5                        60        20        50       130
 6  NAMES
 7  Adams, Rick           45        20        48       113
 8  Jones, Mary           19        18        45        82
 9  Kassebaum, Helen      44        19        50       113
10  Lyon, Sarah           29        18        47        94
11  Smith, Phil           26        18        49        93
12  Young, Sidney         33        16        44        93
13
14  Average Scores        30        18        47        95
15
16
17
18
19
20
```

1. Retrieve the file BLAW.

2. Insert a new blank row where row 3 is located.

3. Enter double underscores in row 3 as shown.

4. Enter double underscores in row 16.

5. Since Sarah Lyon has transferred to another school, delete her name and scores from the spreadsheet.

6. Check the formulas in row 14 to see if they are still correct.

7. Since some students did not make very high scores on Test 1, the teacher has decided not to include those scores when final grades are figured. Therefore, delete the column containing the Test 1 data.

8. Correct the formulas in column D.

9. Use the **/** **R**ange **E**rase command to remove any 0s in cells in column D in which no values should appear.

10. Save the file as ACT 6-6.

11. Print the file.

CHAPTER 7

Changing Value Formats
❑ Using Absolute References and Functions

OBJECTIVES

❑ Change formats
❑ Change decimal places
❑ Use absolute and mixed references
❑ Use @AVG function
❑ Use @MAX function
❑ Use @MIN function
❑ Use @COUNT function
❑ Use @PMT function

WHY ARE SPECIAL FORMATS FOR VALUES IMPORTANT AND HOW ARE THEY DETERMINED?

A special format can make values easier to understand and analyze in a spreadsheet. Large numbers are usually easier to read if they contain commas. For example, the value 3,496,255.65 is easier to read than 3496255.65. The number of decimal places to be used depends on the degree of rounding that is considered acceptable by the users of a spreadsheet. However, when values do not require them, decimal places should not be used. Values such as 350.00, 495.00, and 224.00 are easier to read and compare if they are shown on the spreadsheet as 350, 495, and 224.

No specific rules determine whether to use percents in decimal format or with a percent sign (%) after them. Individuals or department policies may recommend one format over the other. Some individuals may prefer that a value such as two percent be shown as .02 in a spreadsheet, while others may prefer 2%.

HOW ARE FORMATS CHANGED?

The Format command changes the appearance or format of values on a spreadsheet. Values can be formatted in two different ways as mentioned in a previous chapter.

An entire spreadsheet can be formatted a certain way by using the global formatting command, **/ Worksheet Global Format.** This command changes the format of every column on a spreadsheet at once. Whereas, individual cells or a range of cells can be formatted by using the range format command, **/ Range Format.**

The following tutorials will give you more practice formatting individual cells, ranges, and the entire spreadsheet. You will use two formats used frequently in business: comma and percent.

Comma Format

Retrieve the file BLUESTEM.

This file lists the total monthly sales for each department in a retail hardware store. Your first task is to format the cells in column B in **,** (comma) format with 0 decimal places. Move the cell pointer to B7.

PRESS   /
PRESS   r (Range)
PRESS   f (Format)
PRESS   , (comma format)   .
ENTER   0
ENTER   ↵
PRESS   . (Period)
PRESS   ↓ (7 times)
PRESS   ↵

Now column B should be in **,** (comma) format with 0 decimal places.

Percent Format

Column C in the BLUESTEM file will be used to display the percent of total sales for each department. First, we will format the column. Later, we will add the formulas.

Using the file BLUESTEM, your next task is to change column C to **P**ercent format with 1 decimal place. Move the cell pointer to C7.

PRESS   /
PRESS   r (Range)

PRESS f (Format)

PRESS p (Percent format)

ENTER 1

PRESS ↵

PRESS . (Period)

PRESS ↓ (7 times)

Save the file under the name BLUESTEM.

WHAT ARE RELATIVE REFERENCES?

Relative references were used in previous formulas that you created. An example of a **relative reference** is B3. When a formula with relative references, like +B3+C3, is copied across a row or down a column, Lotus 1-2-3 automatically adjusts the cell references in the formula when it is copied to its new locations.

WHAT ARE ABSOLUTE REFERENCES AND WHEN ARE THEY USED?

An **absolute reference** is a cell address that does not change when a formula is copied from one location to another on a spreadsheet. Absolute cell references are used to keep the original column letter and/or row number constant when it is copied. Use absolute cell references only in formulas that will be copied.

To create an absolute reference, enter a $ before the column letter and row number in the cell address, i.e., $A$15. When the formula $A$15*5 is copied either down a column or across a row, neither the column letter, A, nor the row number, 15, will change. It is not necessary to precede a formula that begins with a $ with a + because the $ indicates that the entry is a formula. However, the + preceding the absolute reference does not cause any malfunction.

WHAT ARE MIXED REFERENCES?

At times you may want part of a cell address to remain constant and part of it to change in the copied formula. This is called a mixed reference. When you want a mixed cell address, precede the column letter or row number in the cell address with a dollar sign ($), i.e., $A15 or A$15. When the formula $A15*5 is copied down a column, the column letter, A, will not change, but the row number, 15, will.

When the formula A$15*5 is copied across a row, the column letter, A, will change but the row number, 15, will not change.

You may better understand the necessity for using absolute references by comparing the results of using relative and absolute references. First, you will enter a formula using relative references, and then you will correct the formula by using absolute references.

Retrieve the file BLUESTEM, if it is not on the screen.

Your job is to determine the percent of contribution each department is making toward total sales. You will need to divide each department's monthly sales by the store's total sales for the month.

Move the cell pointer to C7. Enter the formula to determine the % of Total Sales for the Clothing Department (clothing department sales/total sales).

ENTER   +b7/b14
PRESS   ↵

Copy the formula in C7 to the range C8.C13.

PRESS   /
PRESS   c (Copy)

The following data will be displayed in the control panel:

```
C7: (P1) +B7/B14                                              POINT
Enter range to copy FROM: C7..C7

        A         B         C         D         E         F         G
```

Accept this range.

PRESS   ↵

The control panel will display the following:

```
C7: (P1) +B7/B14                                              POINT
Enter range to copy TO: C7

        A         B         C         D         E         F         G
```

Identify the range to be copied to.

PRESS   ↓
PRESS   . (Period)
PRESS   ↓ (5 times)
PRESS   ↵

The spreadsheet will be displayed on your screen as shown in Figure 7.1.

```
C7: (P1) +B7/B14                                                    READY


                A         B         C         D         E         F         G
    1    BLUESTEM HARDWARE CO.
    2    MONTHLY SALES
    3
    4                            % of
    5    Department      Sales   Total Sales
    6
    7    Clothing        7941        8.4%
    8    Automotive     18690        ERR
    9    Tools          22575        ERR
   10    Garden          8689        ERR
   11    Implements     35000        ERR
   12    Animal Care     1285        ERR
   13    Housewares       263        ERR
   14       TOTAL       94443
   15
   16
```

Figure 7.1 ☐ *Error Messages in Spreadsheet*

Error Messages

Error (ERR) messages appear in column C because the calculation of the formula cannot be completed.

Move the cell pointer to C8 and read the data in the control panel. The control panel will indicate the formula is +B8/B15. Obviously, this formula cannot be calculated because the total sales is not located in B15. No values are located in B15. The formula cannot be completed because a value divided by zero is not defined.

Move the cell pointer to C7. Enter a formula using an absolute cell reference.

ENTER +b7/$B$14

PRESS ↵

PRESS /

PRESS c (Copy)

PRESS ↵

PRESS ↓

PRESS . (Period)

PRESS ↓ (5 times)

PRESS ↵

Move the cell pointer to C8 and notice the formula in the control panel. The first part of the formula has changed from B7 to B8, but the second reference in the formula, B14, has remained constant. Move the cell pointer down column C, and you will see that B14 remained constant when the formula was copied down column C.

All the formulas now express the formula: department's monthly sales divided by the store's total sales for the month.

The spreadsheet will appear on your screen as shown in Figure 7.2.

```
C8: (P1) +B8/$B$14                                                    READY


          A            B        C        D      E      F      G
 1   BLUESTEM HARDWARE CO.
 2   MONTHLY SALES
 3
 4                             % of
 5   Department      Sales   Total Sales
 6
 7   Clothing         7941      8.4%
 8   Automotive      18690     19.8%
 9   Tools           22575     23.9%
10   Garden           8689      9.2%
11   Implements      35000     37.1%
12   Animal Care      1285      1.4%
13   Housewares        263      0.3%
14      TOTAL        94443
15
16
```

Figure 7.2 ❑ *Spreadsheet with Absolute Reference*

Save the file as BLUESTEM.

Percent Format

When you use the Percent format, be careful to enter the value correctly. For example, 9.75% is keyed in as .0975.

Retrieve the file named INTEREST.

Begin by formatting the values in row 3 in Percent format with 2 decimal places. Move the cell pointer to B3.

P R E S S /

P R E S S r (Range)

P R E S S f (Format)

P R E S S p (Percent)

The control panel will display the following:

```
B3: (G) 0.0975                                                        EDIT
Enter number of decimal places (0..15): 2
          A        B        C        D      E      F      G      H
```

P R E S S ⏎

The contents of the control panel will be:

```
B3: (G) 0.0975                                                    POINT
Enter range to format: B3..B3

            A        B        C        D        E        F        G        H
```

PRESS   . (Period)

PRESS   → (3 times)

PRESS   ↵

Row 3 will now be formatted as shown in Figure 7.3.

```
B3: (P2) 0.0975                                                  READY


          A        B        C        D        E        F        G        H
    1  PRINCIPAL AND INTEREST RATE TABLE
    2
    3  RATES:       9.75%   10.50%   12.50%   14.00%
    4
    5  PRINCIPAL
    6      5000
    7      6000
    8      7000
    9      8000
   10      9000
   11
   12
```

Figure 7.3 □ *Percent Format*

Fixed Format

Use the file named INTEREST. You will change the format in the range B6 through E10 to Fixed format with 2 decimals. Fixed format will be used because the values are relatively small; they can be read quickly and accurately without commas. Move the cell pointer to B6.

PRESS /

PRESS r (Range)

PRESS f (Format)

PRESS f (Fixed)

PRESS ↵

Enter the range to be formatted.

PRESS   . (Period)

PRESS   ↓ (4 times)

PRESS   → (3 times)

The control panel will display the following:

```
E18:                                                                POINT
Enter range to format: B6..E18

            A       B       C       D       E       F       G       H
```

PRESS ↵

Currency Format

Format the values in column A in currency format with 0 decimals. Move the cell pointer to A6.

PRESS /

PRESS r (Range)

PRESS f (Format)

PRESS c (Currency)

PRESS 0

PRESS ↵

The control panel will display the following:

```
A6: 5000                                                            POINT
Enter range to format: A6..A6

            A       B       C       D       E       F       G       H
```

Enter the range to be formatted.

PRESS . (Period key)

PRESS ↓ (4 times)

PRESS ↵

Save the file as INTEREST.

Copy a Mixed Cell Reference

Retrieve the file INTEREST, if it is not on your screen.

Enter mixed cell references in a formula to calculate the amount of interest on a principal of $5,000 at an interest rate of 9.75%.

Move the cell pointer to B6.

ENTER $a6*b$3
PRESS   ↵

Using the Copy command, copy this formula to cells B6 through E10. Notice that it is acceptable to copy a formula to itself, i.e., from B6 to B6. Begin with the cell pointer at B6.

PRESS   /
PRESS   c (Copy)
PRESS   ↵
PRESS   . (Period key)
PRESS   → (3 times)
PRESS   ↓ (4 times)
PRESS   ↵

While moving the cell pointer down the various columns and across several rows, check the accuracy of the copied formulas by watching the control panel.

The screen will be displayed as shown in Figure 7.4.

```
A6: (C0) 5000                                                    READY


         A         B         C         D         E       F       G       H
1    PRINCIPAL AND INTEREST RATE TABLE
2
3    RATES:       9.75%    10.50%    12.50%    14.00%
4
5    PRINCIPAL
6    $5,000     487.50    525.00    625.00    700.00
7    $6,000     585.00    630.00    750.00    840.00
8    $7,000     682.50    735.00    875.00    980.00
9    $8,000     780.00    840.00   1000.00   1120.00
10   $9,000     877.50    945.00   1125.00   1260.00
11
12
13
14
15
16
17
18
19
20
```

Figure 7.4 ☐ Formatted Cells

Save the file as INTEREST.

ACTIVITY 7.1 □ *Using Absolute References, Formatting, and Column Width*

In this activity, you will calculate the sales commission earned by each of seven sales representatives and their total salaries.

1. Retrieve the file COMM.
2. Change the global column width to 12.
3. Format the range B7 through E13 in , (comma) format with 0 decimals.
4. Enter a formula in D7 that multiplies the total sales for D. Donahue by the commission rate.
5. Copy the formula in cell D7 to the range D8.D13.
6. Check the formulas in column D to see if they were copied correctly. If not, correct the original formula and recopy it.
7. Move the cell pointer to E7 in the Total Salary column. Enter a formula that adds Donahue's base salary and commission to calculate the Total Salary.
8. Copy the formula in E7 down column E.
9. Save the file as ACT7-1.
10. Print the file.

HOW ARE THE @MAX, @MIN, @AVG, AND @COUNT FUNCTIONS USED?

Shortcut formulas, also called **@functions,** can save you a lot of time and effort. The **@MAX function** is used to locate the largest value in a range. If the formula @max(b2.b49) is entered in cell B50, the largest value in the range B2 through B49 will be displayed in B50.

The **@MIN function** is used to locate the smallest value in a range. If the formula @min(b2.b49) is entered in cell B51, the smallest value in the range B2 through B49 will be displayed in B51.

To determine the average number in a range, the **@AVG function** is used. If the formula @avg(b2.b49) is entered in cell B52, the average of all the values in the range B2 through B49 will be displayed in B52.

The **@COUNT function** counts the number of cells in a range that are not blank. If the formula @count(b2.b49) is entered, 1-2-3 will count the number of cells in the range B2 through B49 that are not empty.

Retrieve the file named GAMES.

This file lists the names of computer games owned by an individual and the prices paid for them. First, you will determine the highest price paid for a computer game. Move the cell pointer to B20.

E N T E R	@max(b5.b18)
P R E S S	↵

The price of the most expensive computer game will be shown in
B20.

Now move the cell pointer to B21 and enter a shortcut formula
to determine the least expensive computer game.

E N T E R	@min(b5.b18)
P R E S S	↵

Move the cell pointer to B22 and enter a shortcut formula to determine the average price paid for the computer games.

E N T E R	@avg(b5.b18)
P R E S S	↵

Move the cell pointer to B23 and enter a shortcut formula to determine the number of computer games listed in column b.

E N T E R	@count(b5.b18)
P R E S S	↵

The final spreadsheet will appear as shown in Figure 7.5.

```
                    A              B        C        D        E        F
4
5     Safari Trail            29.50
6     Duck Hunter             15.00
7     Juan Carlos Adventures  35.00
8     Rendezvous              12.00
9     Pinball Whiz             8.50
10    Global Encounters       59.00
11    Spy Watch                9.98
12    Wild, Wild West         16.50
13    Sea Monsters            21.00
14    Vacations Fantasy       26.95
15    Wonders of the World    45.00
16    Tank Driver             16.95
17    Cats & Dogs              6.95
18    Outer Space              6.95
19
20    Highest Price           59.00
21    Lowest Price             6.95
22    Avg. Price              22.09
23    Count                   14.00
```

Figure 7.5 ☐ *Shortcut Formulas (Functions)*

Save the file as GAMES.

ACTIVITY 7.2 ☐ Using @MAX, @MIN, and @AVG Functions

In this activity, you will use @MAX, @MIN, and @AVG functions to determine the highest selling price, the lowest selling price, and the average selling price of stocks during a one-week period.

```
STOCK  ANALYSIS

Date                    Highland       LEC  Computers
─────────────────────────────────────────────────────
March  4                  55.375                18.625
March  5                  55.3                  17.625
March  6                  55.125                17.75
March  7                  54                    19.25
March  8                  54.5                  20.5
March  11                 53.75                 20.75
March  12                 53                    22
March  13                 53.5                  21.5
March  14                 53.125                21.375
March  15                 52                    21.75
March  18                 52.5                  20.125
March  19                 53                    20
March  20                 53.125                20.5
March  21                 53.75                 21.125
March  22                 54                    22.5
March  25                 53.5                  23
March  26                 53.5                  23.5
March  27                 54.125                23.75
March  28                 54.5                  22.125
March  29                 55.625                23.625
─────────────────────────────────────────────────────
Closing

1st  Week  High
1st  Week  Low
1st  Week  Avg.

2nd  Week  High
2nd  Week  Low
2nd  Week  Avg.

3rd  Week  High
3rd  Week  Low
3rd  Week  Avg.

4th  Week  High
4th  Week  Low
4th  Week  Avg.
```

1. Retrieve the file STOCK.

2. Move the cell pointer to B26. Enter the closing selling price for the Highland stock—the selling price on March 29. Enter +B24.

3. Move the cell pointer to C26. Enter the closing selling price for the LEC Computers stock.

4. Move the cell pointer to B28 and enter a formula to determine the highest selling price for Highland stock during the first week in March—March 4-8.

5. Copy this formula from B28 to C28.

6. Move the cell pointer to B29. Enter a formula to determine the lowest selling price for Highland stock during the first week in March.

7. Copy this formula from B29 to C29.

8. Move the cell pointer to B30. Enter a formula to determine the average selling price for Highland stock during the first week in March.

9. Copy this formula from B30 to C30.

10. Continue entering formulas to calculate the high, low, and average selling prices of the Highland and LEC Computers stocks for the second week, March 11-15, the third week, March 18-22, and the fourth week, March 25-29.

11. Save the file as ACT7-2.

12. Print the file.

HOW IS THE @PMT FUNCTION USED?

The **@PMT function** is used to calculate the amount of a periodic payment on a loan. By entering @pmt followed by the principal, interest, and term, you can display the amount of the periodic payment.

Principal = the amount of the loan
Interest = the periodic interest rate (monthly or annually)
Term = the number of payment periods (usually in months or years)

To determine the yearly payments on a loan of $10,000 at 12% annual interest to be paid over a period of 4 years, you would enter:

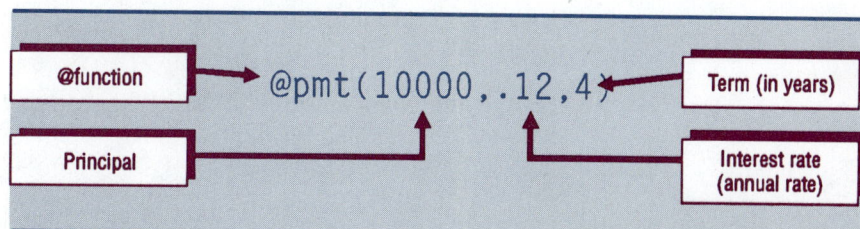

It is important to state the interest rate and the term in the same time frame. If the term is stated in months, the interest rate also must be stated in months.

To determine the monthly payments on a loan of $10,000 at 12% annual interest, compounded monthly, to be paid over a period of 36 months, you would enter the following formula:

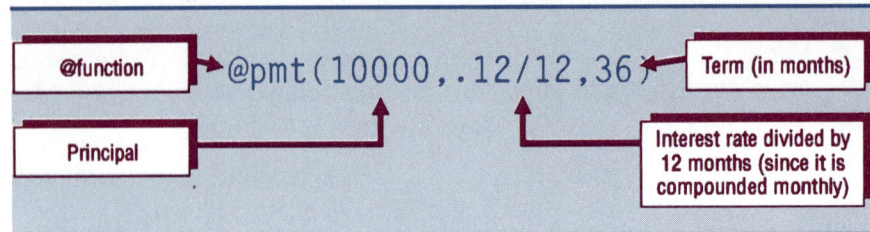

| @function | → | @pmt(10000,.12/12,36) | ← | Term (in months) |
| Principal | | | | Interest rate divided by 12 months (since it is compounded monthly) |

Each of the three parts within the parenthesis is called an **argument.** The arguments are separated with commas.

Instead of entering the values in the formula as shown previously, you can enter cell references. In the following tutorial, you will learn how to enter cell references in @PMT formulas.

Retrieve the file AUTOLOAN.

Move the cell pointer to C7.

Enter the formula to calculate the monthly payment on a $10,000 loan at 12% interest, compounded monthly, for a term of 36 months.

ENTER   @pmt(c3,c4/12,c5)

PRESS   ↵

As shown in Figure 7.6, the monthly payment on the auto loan is $332.14.

```
C7: (C2) @PMT(C3,C4/12,C5)                                          READY

          A         B         C         D         E         F         G         H
  1   AUTO LOAN PAYMENTS
  2
  3   Loan amount:         $10,000
  4   Interest rate:          12%
  5   Length of loan:       36 months
  6
  7   Monthly payment:    $332.14
  8
  9
```

Figure 7.6 ☐ Use of @PMT Formula

Change the loan amount to $12,000. Move the cell pointer to C3.

ENTER   12000

PRESS   ↵

The monthly payment will change to $398.57.

This time, change the interest rate. Move the cell pointer to C4.

ENTER .14
PRESS ↵

The monthly payment will be $410.13.
Change the term of the loan to 24 months. Move the cell pointer to C5.

ENTER 24
PRESS ↵

The monthly payment will be $576.15.
Save the file as AUTOLOAN.

ACTIVITY 7.3 □ Using the @PMT Function

In this activity, assume you are considering an auto loan for three years at an annual interest rate of 12%, compounded monthly. You have located the car you want and have negotiated a selling price of $9,799. You plan to make a $3,000 down payment on the car.

1. Retrieve the file ACT7-3.
2. Enter the selling price of the car in B3.
3. Enter the amount of the down payment.
4. Calculate the loan amount by entering a formula in C5 (Price minus Down Payment).
5. Enter the interest rate.
6. Enter the term of the loan in months.
7. Enter an @PMT formula to determine the monthly payment.
8. Print the file.
9. Since the monthly payment is higher than you expected, you have decided to buy a car that costs $4,500. You plan to make a $3,000 down payment, borrow money for the balance at 12% interest, compounded monthly, and pay for it in one year. Change the values in the spreadsheet accordingly.
10. Save the file as ACT7-3.
11. Print the file.

C H A P T E R   7   □   T H E O R Y   E X E R C I S E S

True/False IIIIIIIII   Each of the following statements is either True or False. Indicate your choice by circling **T** for a true statement or **F** for a false statement.

1. The Worksheet **G**lobal **F**ormat command is used to format an individual cell.　　1. T   F

2. The **R**ange **F**ormat command can be used to format the range B2 through G40.　　2. T   F

3. The command to format the range B2 through B15 is / **W**orksheet **R**ange **F**ormat b2.b15.　　3. T   F

4. The easiest technique to display an individual value in Currency format is to enter a $ before the value.　　4. T   F

5. The main problem with using Fixed format is that no decimal places can be displayed.　　5. T   F

6. The best principle to follow when formatting spreadsheets is to use the same format throughout the entire spreadsheet.　　6. T   F

7. When the value .15 is changed to Percent format, it will be displayed as 15%.　　7. T   F

8. An example of an absolute reference is $G$60.　　8. T   F

9. An example of a relative reference is A$16.　　9. T   F

10. Only use absolute cell references in formulas that will be copied.　　10. T   F

11. An example of a mixed reference is $B12.　　11. T   F

12. A plus (+) sign must be used before entering the formula $B$2/12.　　12. T   F

13. When a formula with relative references, like +B3+C3, is copied across a row or down a column, the cell references in the formula are adjusted automatically when the formula is copied to its new locations.　　13. T   F

14. When ERR messages appear in cells after a formula has been copied, they mean the calculation of the formula cannot be completed.　　14. T   F

15. In the cell reference $A15, only the row number will remain constant when it is copied.　　15. T   F

16. To find the average number in a range, use the @SUM function.　　16. T   F

17. To locate the number of cells in a range that are not empty, the @MAX function is used.　　17. T   F

18. To determine the smallest number in a range of cells, use the @MIN function.　　18. T   F

19. The @PMT function is used to calculate the amount of interest on a loan.   19.   T   F

20. The formula @pmt(12000,.10,5) will calculate the annual payment on a loan of $12,000 to be paid over 5 years at 10% annual interest.   20.   T   F

Completion IIIIIIII For each item below fill in the word (or words) that completes the statement or answers the question.

1. The value 7,000 is in the _____ format with _____ decimal places.

2. The value $2,500.00 is in the _____ format with _____ decimal places.

3. The value 14.375% is in the _____ format with _____ decimal places.

4. Cells can be formatted before values are entered in cells or _____ values are entered.

5. What command should be used to format an entire spreadsheet in Fixed format with 2 decimal places?

_____

6. What command should be used to format cell B22 in Currency format with 2 decimal places?

_____

7. An example of an absolute reference is _____ .

8. An example of a mixed reference is _____ .

9. An example of a relative reference is _____ .

10. Absolute references are needed in a formula only when the formula will be _____

_____ .

11. When the reference $A16 is used in a formula and is subsequently copied, the _____ will remain constant in the copied formulas.

12. What formula should be used to determine the number of cells that are not empty in the range C5 through C45?

_____

13. What formula should be used to determine the largest number in the range C5 through C45?

_____

14. What formula should be used to determine the smallest number in the range C5 through C45?

    _____

15. What formula should be used to determine the average of the values in the range C5 through C45?

    _____

16. The purpose of the @PMT function is to _____

    _____

17. The three arguments in an @PMT formula include:

    (1) _____, (2) _____, and (3) _____.

18. What formula should be used to determine the monthly payment on a $10,000 loan at 15 percent interest, compounded monthly, for a period of 36 months?

    _____

ACTIVITY 7.4 ❑ *Using @MIN and @MAX Functions*

In this activity, you will create a spreadsheet that calculates the total amount owed by customers after a 2 percent discount has been subtracted from the cost of the customers' original orders. Credit customers often receive cash discounts if they pay for their orders within 10 days after the date of the invoice. Use the following data to create the spreadsheet.

```
BURROW  BEAUTY  SUPPLY  CO.

Discount  Rate:          2%

                  Original  Amt. of    Total Amt.
Customer          Cost      Discount   of Order

A  Cut  Above     145.60
Shear  Designs     45.00
Cut  It           225.50
Sue's  Salon      380.75
George's          125.00
Mr.  &  Ms.  Shop 190.65

                  Largest   Order:
                  Smallest  Order:
```

1. Enter the labels and values shown.
2. Format the entire spreadsheet using Fixed format with 2 decimals.
3. Format the cell containing the Discount Rate in Percent format with 0 decimals.
4. Change the column widths as necessary to improve the appearance of the spreadsheet.
5. Calculate the amount of the discount for A Cut Above by multiplying the original cost of its order by the Discount Rate. Copy this formula down the Amt. of Discount column.
6. Calculate the total amount of the order for A Cut Above by subtracting the amount of the discount from the Original Cost. Copy this formula down the Total Amt. of Order column.
7. Enter a formula to calculate the largest order in the Total Amt. of Order column.
8. Enter a formula to determine the smallest order in the Total Amt. of Order column.
9. Save the file as ACT7-4.
10. Print the file.

CYCLE 2
Advanced Spreadsheet Tutorials and Exercises

CHAPTER 8

OBJECTIVES

☐ Print cell formulas
☐ Justify text
☐ Make backup copies
☐ Erase files

HOW ARE CELL FORMULAS PRINTED?

So far, the spreadsheets you have printed have shown only the values and labels in the spreadsheets. This type of printout is called an **as-displayed** printout. To correct or debug formulas in spreadsheets, it is helpful to have the formulas in a spreadsheet printed out. This is called a **cell-formulas** printout.

Cell-Formulas Printouts

To print a cell-formulas version of a spreadsheet, use the command **/ Print Printer Range Options Other Cell-Formulas Quit Align Go**. After printing the spreadsheet, you should change the type of printout back to as-displayed. This is important since most of the time you will not want cell formulas to be printed. Use the command **/ Print Printer Options Other As-Displayed Quit Quit** to change back to as-displayed printouts.

Figure 8.1 shows a cell-formulas printout. As you can see, each cell on the spreadsheet is printed on a separate line. On each line of a cell-formulas printout, the cell address is printed first, followed by any formatting symbols, and then the cell contents. The cell contents will be either a label or a formula.

Retrieve the file named BLUESTEM.

143

```
A1:   [W15]  'BLUESTEM  HARDWARE  CO.
A2:   [W15]  'MONTHLY  SALES
C4:   '% of
A5:   [W15]  'Department
B5:   'Sales
C5:   'Total  Sales
A7:   [W15]  'Clothing
B7:   (,0)   7941
C7:   (P1)   +B7/B$14
A8:   [W15]  'Automotive
B8:   (,0)   18690
C8:   (P1)   +B8/B$14
A9:   [W15]  'Tools
B9:   (,0)   22575
C9:   (P1)   +B9/B$14
A10:  [W15]  'Garden
B10:  (,0)   8689
C10:  (P1)   +B10/B$14
A11:  [W15]  'Implements
B11:  (,0)   35000
C11:  (P1)   +B11/B$14
A12:  [W15]  'Animal  Care
B12:  (,0)   1285
C12:  (P1)   +B12/B$14
A13:  [W15]  'Housewares
B13:  (,0)   263
C13:  (P1)   +B13/B$14
A14:  [W15]  'TOTAL
B14:  (,0)   @SUM(B7..B13)
```

Figure 8.1 □ *Cell-Formula Printout*

Print a cell-formulas version of the file.

PRESS /

PRESS p (Print)

PRESS p (Printer)

PRESS r (Range)

PRESS . (Period key)

PRESS ↓ (13 times)

PRESS → (3 times)

PRESS ↵

PRESS o (Options)

If you are using a 1-2-3 release earlier than Release 2.2, the second and third lines of the control panel will display as follows:

```
A1: [W15] 'BLUESTEM HARDWARE CO.                                    MENU
Header Footer Margins Borders Setup Pg-Length Other Quit
Create a header
```

If you are using Lotus 1-2-3, Release 2.2 or above, the spreadsheet file will be temporarily replaced with a settings screen as shown:

```
A1: [W15] 'BLUESTEM HARDWARE CO.                                    MENU
Header  Footer  Margins  Borders  Setup  Pg-Length  Other  Quit
Create a header
                          ───── Print Settings ─────
     Destination:   Printer

     Range:         A1..D14

     Header:
     Footer:

     Margins:
       Left 4     Right 76    Top 2    Bottom 2

     Borders:
       Columns
       Rows

     Setup string:

     Page length:  66

     Output:       As-Displayed (Formatted)
```

Now select Other from the menu.

PRESS   o (Other)

The second and third lines of the control panel will display the following:

```
A1: [W15] 'BLUESTEM HARDWARE CO.                                    MENU
As-Displayed Cell-Formulas Formatted Unformatted
Print range as displayed
```

Select *Cell-Formulas* on the menu.

PRESS   c (Cell-formulas)
PRESS   q (Quit)
PRESS   a (Align)
PRESS   g (Go)

After the cell-formulas version of the spreadsheet has been printed, change the settings back to as-displayed.

P R E S S   o (Options)
P R E S S   o (Other)

Now select *As-Displayed* on the menu.

P R E S S   a (As-displayed)
P R E S S   q (Quit)
P R E S S   q (Quit)

ACTIVITY 8.1   □   *Printing Cell-Formulas Version*

In this activity, you will print a cell-formulas version of a file.

1. Retrieve the file ACT8-1.
2. Use the appropriate print commands to print the cell formulas in this file.
3. Print the file.
4. Change the type of printout to As-Displayed.
5. Save the file as ACT8-1.
6. Erase the spreadsheet from the screen.
7. Using the printout, circle and identify in writing one example of each of the following: (a) a column width indicator and what it means, (b) a label, (c) a value, (d) a cell reference, and (e) a formula.

Text Format Displays and Printouts

The Text Format command is another technique you can use to help debug formulas in a spreadsheet. The command / **R**ange Format **T**ext will allow you to display and/or print formulas in a spreadsheet. The problem with this format is that some formulas are longer than the cell width and cannot be seen or printed in their entirety. To see entire formulas, some users increase the column widths prior to using this command.

Once a spreadsheet is displayed in text format, it can also be printed in this format. Unlike cell-formula printouts, text printouts show formulas in their original cell locations, making it easier to locate errors.

Retrieve the file BLUESTEM, if it is not already on your screen. Move the cell pointer to C7.

> *PRESS* /
>
> *PRESS* r (Range)
>
> *PRESS* f (Format)

The control panel will display the following:

```
A1: [W15] 'BLUESTEM HARDWARE CO.                                       MENU
 Fixed  Sci  Currency  ,  General  +/-  Percent  Date  Text  Hidden  Reset
 Fixed number of decimal places (x.xx)
```

Select *Text* from the menu.

> *PRESS* t (Text)

Enter the range to format.

> *PRESS* . (Period key)
>
> *PRESS* ↓ (6 times)
>
> *PRESS* ↵

The cell formulas will now be displayed on the screen as shown in Figure 8.2. As you can see, some of the cell formulas are longer than the cell width and, therefore, are not displayed in their entirety.

```
C7: (T) +B7/B$14                                                      READY

            A            B         C          D      E       F      G
 1  BLUESTEM HARDWARE CO.
 2  MONTHLY SALES
 3
 4                                % of
 5  Department       Sales   Total Sales
 6
 7  Clothing          7941  +B7/B$14
 8  Automotive       18690  +B8/B$14
 9  Tools            22575  +B9/B$14
10  Garden            8689  +B10/B$1
11  Implements       35000  +B11/B$1
12  Animal Care       1285  +B12/B$1
13  Housewares         263  +B13/B$1
14     TOTAL         94443
15
16
17
18
19
20
```

Figure 8.2 □ *Cell Formulas Displayed*

Once cell formulas are displayed, they can be printed. Print the entire spreadsheet using the range identified previously.

> *PRESS*   /
> *PRESS*   p (Print)
> *PRESS*   p (Printer)
> *PRESS*   a (Align)
> *PRESS*   g (Go)

The spreadsheet should print as it was displayed on the screen.

> *PRESS*   q (Quit)

After printing the spreadsheet, change the format back to its original format using the following instructions. Move the cell pointer to C7.

> *PRESS*   /
> *PRESS*   r (Range)
> *PRESS*   f (Format)
> *PRESS*   p (Percent)
> *ENTER*   1
> *PRESS*   ↵
> *PRESS*   . (Period key)
> *PRESS*   ↓ (6 times)
> *PRESS*   ↵

Save the spreadsheet under the name BLUESTEM. Clear the screen by using the **/ Worksheet Erase Yes** command.

ACTIVITY 8.2 ☐ *Displaying and Printing a Text Format File*

In this activity, you will first display and then print a file in Text format.

1. Retrieve the file ACT8-1 used in the previous activity.
2. Move the cell pointer to B10.
3. Change the format of the cells in row 10 to Text format.
4. Save the file as ACT8-2.
5. Print the file.
6. Erase the spreadsheet from the screen.

HOW IS A COLUMN OF TEXT JUSTIFIED AND EDITED?

The / Range Justify command is used to arrange and fit text (labels) within a width that you identify. This command can be used to create a paragraph in a spreadsheet or to fit text into a designated width for viewing or printing.

Figure 8.3 shows several rows of very long labels that may be difficult to read on the screen or to print.

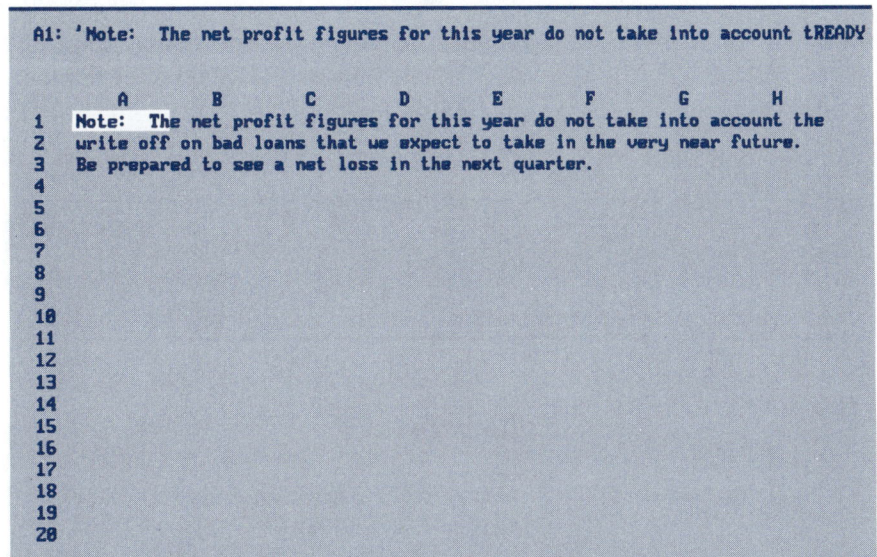

```
A1: 'Note:  The net profit figures for this year do not take into account tREADY


            A         B         C         D         E         F         G         H
1       Note:  The net profit figures for this year do not take into account the
2       write off on bad loans that we expect to take in the very near future.
3       Be prepared to see a net loss in the next quarter.
4
5
6
7
8
9
10
11
12
13
14
15
16
17
18
19
20
```

Figure 8.3 □ *Long Labels*

Figure 8.4 shows the result of justifying the same text within the range of columns A through E.

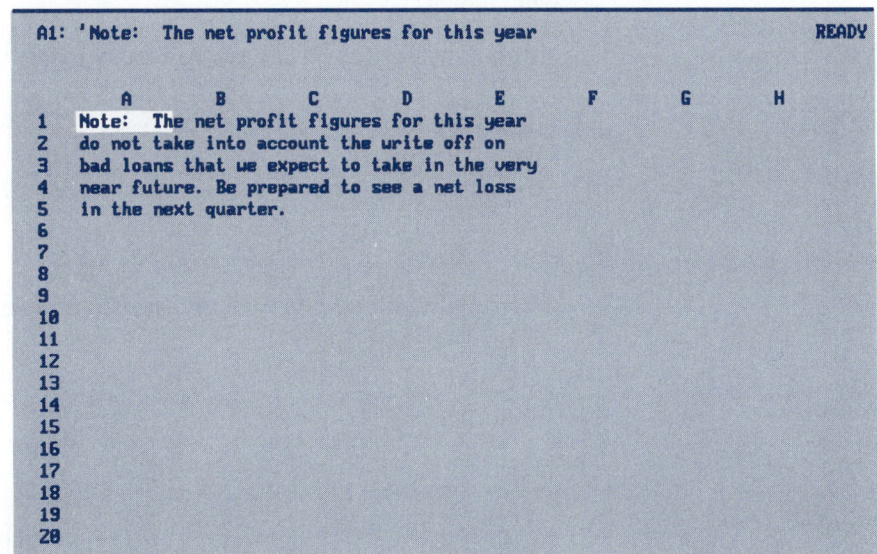

```
A1: 'Note:  The net profit figures for this year                              READY


            A         B         C         D         E         F         G         H
1       Note:  The net profit figures for this year
2       do not take into account the write off on
3       bad loans that we expect to take in the very
4       near future. Be prepared to see a net loss
5       in the next quarter.
6
7
8
9
10
11
12
13
14
15
16
17
18
19
20
```

Figure 8.4 □ *Justified Labels*

Retrieve the file ACT7-1.

Move the cell pointer to A17 and enter the text that follows. Notice that some characters will disappear from the screen as you enter the text.

ENTER Tom, As you can see, Total Sales have been very high this month. With

PRESS ↓

Enter each of the four following lines of text (including errors) in rows 18, 19, 20, and 21. Press the Down Arrow key after entering each line of text.

```
the commission added to the base salary, sales representatives are
making some of the highest paid employees in our organization. Although
I would not like to lower morale, we should consider lowering our
commission rate. What do you think?  Sandra
```

Editing Text

To correct errors in long labels, use the Edit key, F2, and the Backspace or Del key as needed.

Delete the word WITH in row 17 and replace it with AFTER. Move the cell pointer to the cell that contains this label, A17.

PRESS F2 (Edit)

PRESS ← (Backspace key 4 times)

Enter the word AFTER in the same location.

ENTER After

PRESS ↵

Move the cell pointer to A18. Insert the word IS between COMMIS-SION and ADDED.

PRESS F2 (Edit)

In the Edit mode, the Home key moves the cursor to the first character of the cell. Move the cursor to the *a* in *added* as follows:

PRESS Home

PRESS → (16 times)

ENTER is

PRESS Spacebar

PRESS ↵

Delete the word MAKING in row 19. Move the cursor to the *m* in *making*.

PRESS F2

PRESS Del (Delete key 7 times)

PRESS ↵

Save the file as LABELS.

Justifying Text

Retrieve the file LABELS, if it is not on your screen. Justify the text in the file within the range A through E.
Move the cell pointer to A17.

PRESS /

PRESS r (Range)

PRESS j (Justify)

The control panel will now display the range as shown below:

```
A17: 'Tom, As you can see, Total Sales have been very high this month.   AftPOINT
Enter Justify range: A17..A17

            A          B          C          D          E          F
```

PRESS . (Period key)

PRESS → (4 times)

PRESS ↵

Save the file as LABELS.

The text will now fit between columns A and E as shown in Figure 8.5. If justified text uses more rows than the original text, 1-2-3 moves other data in the column down. If justified text uses fewer rows than the original text, 1-2-3 moves data up in the column.

```
A22: 'rate.  What do you think?  Sandra                          READY


            A          B          C          D          E          F
  3
  4
  5  Sales Rep   Base Salary Total Sales Commission  Total Salary
  6
  7  Donahue, D.     2,500     25,800      1,290       3,790
  8  Symes, R.       2,400     22,500      1,125       3,525
  9  Sill, E.        2,500     42,699      2,135       4,635
 10  Smith, P.       2,350     34,887      1,744       4,094
 11  Holder, K.      2,800     44,000      2,200       5,000
 12  Johnson, M.     3,000     34,500      1,725       4,725
 13  Ling, A.        3,750     49,789      2,489       6,239
 14
 15  Commission Rate:             0.05
 16
 17  Tom, As you can see, Total Sales have been very high this
 18  month.  After the commission is added to the base salary,
 19  sales representatives are some of the highest paid
 20  employees in our organization.  Although I would not like
 21  to lower morale, we should consider lowering our commission
 22  rate.  What do you think?  Sandra
```

Figure 8.5 ❑ Justified Text

ACTIVITY 8.3 ❑ Justifying Text

In this activity, you will add and justify a short note at the bottom of a spreadsheet.

1. Retrieve the file ACT8-1.
2. Move the cell pointer to A12 and enter all of the following text in cell A12.

```
NOTE:    As you can see, there was a tremendous drop in profits at
our refinery in Mexico City.
```

3. Press the Down Arrow key and enter:

```
This was caused by our inability to load tankers at that port be-
cause of the oil slick caused by a tanker accident in the area.
```

4. Press the Enter key.
5. Now justify the note within the range A12 through D12.
6. Save the file as ACT8-3.
7. Print the entire file, including the text at the bottom of the spreadsheet.
8. Erase the spreadsheet from the screen.

HOW ARE BACKUP COPIES OF FILES MADE?

A **backup copy** can be made of any spreadsheet file. You can save the file by using a different filename or by saving the file to a second disk and using the same filename. If you are using Release 2.2 or above, files can be backed up with the *Backup* option under the File Save command. These backup files are given a .BAK extension automatically. Before making major changes in format or data in a spreadsheet, you may want to make routinely a backup copy of the file.

Many people who create spreadsheets develop a system for keeping backup copies of important files. It is important to make a backup copy of a file in case the original file is deleted accidentally or the disk with the original file is damaged or lost.

Natural disasters such as floods, tornadoes, and hurricanes can destroy computer equipment as well as data stored on disks. Disaster recovery procedures in businesses often require computer operators to keep backup copies of important files in remote locations. Remote locations may include branch offices, home offices for corporations, or privately owned underground storage facilities.

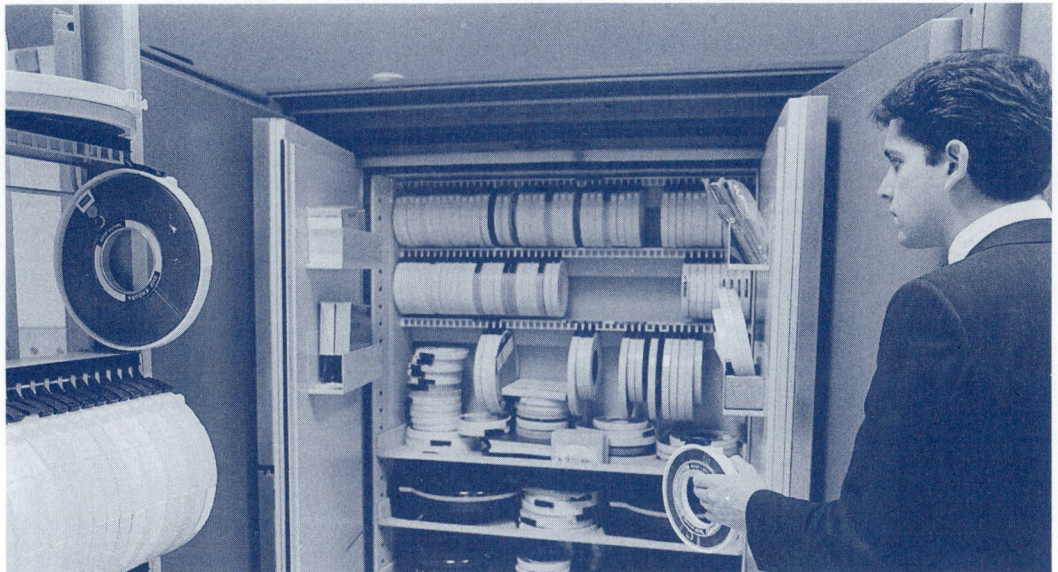

A records management storage facility may be used to protect data.

One system for making backup copies is to store the spreadsheet on two different disks. With this system, you might store the file on both a hard disk and a floppy disk, or you might store the file on two separate floppy disks. The floppy disk can be stored in a different location in the same building or off premises. When this system is used, the same filename can be used for both the original and backup files. All you need to do is retrieve the file and then save it on a different disk under the same filename.

Sometimes you may want to store a backup copy of a spreadsheet file on the same disk or in the same directory as the original file. To do this, the backup filename must not be the same as the original filename. For backup files, you may want to use BAK or BK as part of the filename. As mentioned previously, when the backup option is used with Release 2.2 or above, the extension .BAK is added automatically to the backup filename. If you are using an earlier release of 1-2-3, you may wish to use one of the systems for naming files shown in Figure 8.6.

Original Filename	Backup Filename
SALES	SALESBK
LOAN	LOANBAK
BGT	BKBGT

Figure 8.6 ☐ *Backup Filenames*

Whichever backup file system you choose, use it consistently. For example, if you begin every backup filename with BK, then you can locate all backup files in the B section of the directory.

ACTIVITY 8.4 ☐ Making a Backup File

In this activity, you will retrieve a file created previously and save it on the same disk or in the same directory as the original file. You will use a backup filename that is different from the original filename.

1. Retrieve the file GAMES.
2. Save the file under the name BKGAMES.
3. Erase the spreadsheet on the screen.
4. Retrieve the file BKGAMES.

WHEN IS THE FILE ERASE COMMAND USED?

The / File Erase command erases files on a data disk. Be very cautious when using this command. An important file can be erased accidentally. The consistent use of backup files will prevent important files from being destroyed.

Retrieve the file ACT8-3.

Before erasing ACT8-3, make a backup file and give it the filename BKACT8-3. Be sure a backup file is created before continuing with the next set of instructions.

Now erase the file ACT8-3 as follows:

P R E S S /
P R E S S f (File)
P R E S S e (Erase)

Four types of files will be displayed in the second line of the control panel as shown below:
Select Worksheet from the display.

P R E S S w (Worksheet)

The second line of the control panel will ask you to enter the name of the file you want to erase. The third line will list a directory of filenames. Erase the file ACT8-3.

E N T E R act8-3
P R E S S ⏎
P R E S S y (Yes)

Now the file ACT8-3 has been erased from the disk, but the backup file will still be there.

ACTIVITY 8.5 ☐ *Erasing Files*

In this activity, you will practice creating a backup file and erasing the original file.

1. Retrieve the file INTEREST.
2. Create a backup file for INTEREST and name it INTERBK.
3. Create a second backup file and name it BKINTER.
4. After creating the two backup files, you notice you used the wrong backup filename in instruction 2. Assume you usually use BK at the beginning of the backup filename.
5. Erase the backup spreadsheet that was named incorrectly, INTERBK.
6. Retrieve the file BKINTER.
7. Attempt to retrieve the file INTERBK. (You should not be able to retrieve this file since it has been erased.)

ACTIVITY 8.6 ☐ *Erasing Files from Chapters 1–8*

In this activity, you will erase files from the disk to make room for the files from the remaining chapters. Erase all the files in the list below that appear on your disk.

ACT2-3	ACT7-3	ECONTEST
ACT4-2	ACT7-4	EXPENSES
ACT4-4	ACT8-1	GAMES
ACT4-5	ACT8-3	INTEREST
ACT5-1	ASPEN	INVENTORY
ACT5-2	ASPENREV	JONESEXP
ACT5-3	ATTEND	LABELS
ACT6-1	AUTOLOAN	QRTBGT
ACT6-2	BKACT8-3	SALES
ACT6-3	BKGAMES	STOCK
ACT6-4	BLAW	TAXDED
ACT6-5	BLUESTEM	T-TIME
ACT6-6	COMM	WICHITA
ACT7-1	CONCESS	YOGURT
ACT7-2	DEDEXP	

CHAPTER 8 □ THEORY EXERCISES

True/False **IIIIIIIII**   Each of the following statements is either True or False. Indicate your choice by circling **T** for a true statement or **F** for a false statement.

1. A cell-formulas printout shows only labels and values.   1. T   F

2. A printout that shows cell formulas is used to correct or debug formulas.   2. T   F

3. After creating a cell-formulas printout, you should change the type of printout to an as-displayed printout.   3. T   F

4. The **/ R**ange **F**ormat **T**ext command can be used to help locate errors in labels and values in a spreadsheet.   4. T   F

5. The command to display formulas in a spreadsheet is **/ R**ange **F**ormat **T**ext.   5. T   F

6. The **/ R**ange **F**ormat **T**ext command allows you to view formulas in their entirety, no matter how wide or narrow the cell width is.   6. T   F

7. The **/ R**ange **J**ustify command arranges and fits text (labels) within a width you identify.   7. T   F

8. Text may be added to a spreadsheet to explain data in the spreadsheet.   8. T   F

9. A backup copy can be made of any spreadsheet file by saving the file using a different filename.   9. T   F

10. When you create a backup file on a disk other than the one on which the original file is stored, you must use a filename different than the original name.   10. T   F

11. An acceptable backup filename for SALES is BKSALES.   11. T   F

12. The **/ F**ile **E**rase command is used to erase a file from a data disk.   12. T   F

13. The **/ R**ange **E**rase command erases a file from memory on a data disk.   13. T   F

Completion **IIIIIIIII**   For each item below fill in the word (or words) that completes the statement or answers the question.

1. To print a cell-formulas version of a spreadsheet, use the command **/ P**rint **P**rinter **R**ange (specify the range) **O**ptions _____ Cell-Formulas.

2. After printing a spreadsheet in cell-formulas format, change the type of printout back to _____.

3. With a cell-formulas printout, each cell on the spreadsheet is printed on a

   _____ _____.

4. In each line of a cell-formulas printout, the _____ _____ is printed first, followed by any _____ symbols, and then the cell contents.

5. The problem with a Text format display is that some formulas are longer than the
   _____ _____ and cannot be seen or printed in their entirety.

6. To arrange text (labels) to fit within a specified width, the
   _____ command should be used.

7. Disaster recovery procedures in businesses often require computer operators to keep
   _____ _____ of important files in remote locations.

8. One system to make backup copies is to store the spreadsheet on two different disks
   using the same _____.

9. When making a backup copy of the file INCOME on the same disk as the original
   file, use an appropriate backup copy filename such as _____.

10. What command is used to erase a file from a disk?

    _____

ACTIVITY 8.7 □ Review Basic Spreadsheet Commands

In this activity, you will create a spreadsheet like the one that follows and revise it several times. This spreadsheet shows the revenue from television, stereo, and speaker sales for four quarters and for the year.

PRODUCT LINE REVENUE
Quarterly Summary for 1992

Televisions	Q1	Q2	Q3	Q4	1992
North America	$2,774,598	$2,271,216	$2,425,689	$3,415,407	
Europe	1,334,172	1,070,990	1,070,990	1,998,897	
International	1,969,111	1,472,400	1,473,507	2,663,202	
Total					
Stereos					
North America	$3,550,426	$2,964,777	$3,252,778	$3,610,300	
Europe	2,858,811	2,451,360	2,451,360	3,007,328	
International	3,499,340	3,313,906	3,313,906	4,017,447	
Total					
Speakers					
North America	$676,818	$917,730	$1,470,166	$1,399,826	
Europe	624,927	727,228	767,226	1,181,900	
International	840,711	1,004,775	1,053,777	1,607,520	
Total					
Worldwide Total					

Part I

1. Enter the main titles in rows 1 and 2.

2. Set the width of column A for 18 characters and the widths of columns B-F for 12 characters.

3. Enter the labels in column A. Indent the labels NORTH AMERICA, EUROPE, IN-TERNATIONAL, and TOTAL three spaces.

4. Center the labels Q1, Q2, Q3, Q4, and 1992 in appropriate cells in row 4.

5. Enter the values in columns B, C, D, and E.

6. Enter a formula in column F that calculates the Total sales of televisions in North America for all four quarters of 1992.

7. Copy this formula to appropriate cells in column F.

8. Enter a formula in cell B8 to calculate the Total sales of televisions during the first quarter, Q1. Copy that formula across row 8 to calculate the totals for the second, third, and fourth quarters, and for the Total for the year.

9. Enter formulas to calculate the total stereos sold each quarter and total speakers sold each quarter.

10. Enter a formula in cell B22 to calculate the Worldwide sales of televisions, stereos, and speakers for the first quarter.

11. Copy that formula across row 22.

12. Format the cells as shown. Format North America sales, Total sales for each product, and Worldwide Totals in currency. Format the other cells with commas.

13. Save the spreadsheet as ACT8-7.

14. Print the spreadsheet.

15. Save the spreadsheet as ACT8-7, allowing the print options to be saved also.

Part II

Continue using the same spreadsheet file.

1. Format the ranges B8-E8, B14-E14, B20-E22, and F5-F22 in Text format.

2. Print the file.

Part III

1. Retrieve the file ACT8-7 again.

2. Make a backup file of the spreadsheet and name it BKACT8-6.

3. Delete rows 10-15.

4. Correct the formulas that calculate the Worldwide Total.

5. Move the cell pointer to row 4 and insert a new row.

6. Enter a hyphenated line in row 4 from column A to column F.

7. Enter a hyphenated line in row 16 above the Worldwide Total row.

8. In A20, enter the following text and justify it between columns A-E:

```
Note:   The Worldwide revenue was relatively stable during the first
three quarters of the year, but it increased substantially during
the fourth quarter. This increase can be attributed to the
worldwide demand for televisions.
```

9. Save the file as ACT8-7 and also as BKACT8-7.

10. Print the spreadsheet.

CHAPTER 9

Freezing Titles
☐ Creating Windows

OBJECTIVES

☐ Freeze titles
☐ Create horizontal windows
☐ Create vertical windows
☐ Use synchronized scrolling
☐ Use unsynchronized scrolling

WHEN SHOULD YOU FREEZE TITLES?

In very large spreadsheets, it is difficult to see all of the pertinent data on the screen at one time. When *scrolling* (moving the cell pointer) across or down a wide or long spreadsheet, you may not remember the titles to which the values are related because the titles are no longer in view.

The **/ Worksheet Titles** command freezes horizontal titles at the top of a spreadsheet, vertical titles along the left edge, or both sets of titles. Those titles remain fixed on the screen as you scroll through the spreadsheet.

After **/ Worksheet Titles** has been entered, the control panel will display four selections: ***Both, Horizontal, Vertical,*** and ***Clear.*** Figure 9.1 shows how freezing rows 1-4 as titles lets you view data in row 23 without losing sight of the column labels. When the cell pointer is moved to row 23, rows 5-7 scroll off the screen while rows 1-4 remain.

```
B23: (C0) +B9+B15+B21                                                  READY


             A              B            C            D            E
 1   PRODUCT LINE REVENUE
 2   Quarterly Summary for 1992
 3
 4                          Q1           Q2           Q3           Q4
 8      International     1,969,111    1,472,400    1,473,507    2,663,282
 9      Total           $6,077,881   $4,814,606   $4,970,186   $8,077,506
10
11   Stereos
12      North America   $3,550,426   $2,964,777   $3,252,778   $3,610,300
13      Europe           2,858,811    2,451,360    2,451,360    3,007,328
14      International     3,499,340    3,313,906    3,313,906    4,017,447
15      Total           $9,908,577   $8,730,043   $9,018,044  $10,635,075
16
17   Speakers
18      North America     $676,818     $917,730   $1,470,166   $1,399,826
19      Europe            624,927      727,228      767,226    1,181,900
20      International     840,711    1,004,775    1,053,777    1,607,520
21      Total           $2,142,456   $2,649,733   $3,291,169   $4,189,246
22
23   Worldwide Total  │$18,128,914│ $16,194,382  $17,279,399  $22,901,827
```

Figure 9.1 ☐ *Freezing Horizontal Titles*

You can also freeze vertical titles along the left edge of a spreadsheet. Figure 9.2 shows how freezing titles in column A allows you
to examine data in column F while still seeing the row titles in column A.

```
F5:                                                                    READY


             A              C            D            E            F
 1   PRODUCT LINE REVEN
 2   Quarterly Summary
 3
 4                          Q2           Q3           Q4           1991
 5   Televisions
 6      North America   $2,271,216   $2,425,689   $3,415,407  │$10,886,910│
 7      Europe           1,070,990    1,070,990    1,998,897    5,475,049
 8      International     1,472,400    1,473,507    2,663,282    7,578,220
 9      Total           $4,814,606   $4,970,186   $8,077,506  $23,940,179
10
11   Stereos
12      North America   $2,964,777   $3,252,778   $3,610,300  $13,378,281
13      Europe           2,451,360    2,451,360    3,007,328   10,768,859
14      International     3,313,906    3,313,906    4,017,447   14,144,599
15      Total           $8,730,043   $9,018,044  $10,635,075  $38,291,739
16
17   Speakers
18      North America     $917,730   $1,470,166   $1,399,826   $4,464,540
19      Europe            727,228      767,226    1,181,900    3,301,281
20      International     1,004,775    1,053,777    1,607,520    4,506,783
```

Figure 9.2 ☐ *Freezing Vertical Titles*

At times you may want to freeze both horizontal and vertical
titles. In Figure 9.3, both horizontal and vertical titles are frozen so
that values in rows 8-23 and columns C-F can be viewed. This makes
it easier to analyze and interpret the data.

```
F23: (C0) @SUM(B23..E23)                                          READY


         A              C            D            E            F
 1  PRODUCT LINE REVEN
 2  Quarterly Summary
 3
 4                      Q2           Q3           Q4           1991
 8     International    1,472,400    1,473,587    2,663,282    7,578,220
 9     Total           $4,814,606   $4,970,186   $8,077,506  $23,940,179
10
11  Stereos
12     North America   $2,964,777   $3,252,778   $3,610,300  $13,378,281
13     Europe          2,451,360    2,451,360    3,007,328   10,768,859
14     International    3,313,906    3,313,906    4,017,447   14,144,599
15     Total           $8,730,043   $9,018,044  $10,635,075  $38,291,739
16
17  Speakers
18     North America   $917,730     $1,470,166   $1,399,826   $4,464,540
19     Europe          727,228      767,226      1,181,900    3,301,281
20     International    1,004,775    1,053,777    1,607,520    4,506,783
21     Total           $2,649,733   $3,291,169   $4,189,246  $12,272,604
22
23  Worldwide Total    $16,194,382  $17,279,399  $22,901,827  $74,504,522
```

Figure 9.3 ◻ *Both Horizontal and Vertical Titles are Frozen*

Placement of the cursor prior to using the **Titles** command is important. Position the cursor as follows:

◻ For horizontal titles, place the cell pointer one row below the rows you want to freeze.

◻ For vertical titles, place the cell pointer one column to the right of the columns you want to freeze.

◻ For both horizontal and vertical titles, place the cell pointer one row below and one column to the right of the rows and columns you want to freeze.

After the **Titles** command has been entered, it will remain in effect until you use the **/ Worksheet Titles Clear** command.

Horizontal Titles

In this tutorial, you will retrieve a file that shows first quarter profits for a company for two years—1990 and 1991. You will freeze the horizontal titles at the top of the spreadsheet and scroll to the bottom of the spreadsheet.

Retrieve the file PROFIT.

Move the cell pointer to row 5 and freeze the titles above row 5.

PRESS /

PRESS w (Worksheet)

To select titles from the second line of the control panel:

PRESS   t (Titles)

If you are using Release 2.2 or above, the control panel will display the following:

```
FZ3: (C0) @SUM(BZ3..EZ3)                                    MENU
Both  Horizontal  Vertical  Clear
Freeze all rows and columns above and to the left of the cell pointer
```

If you are using a Lotus release earlier than Release 2.2, the second and third lines of the control panel will display the following:

```
FZ3: (C0) @SUM(BZ3..EZ3)                                    MENU
Both  Horizontal  Vertical  Clear
Set both horizontal and vertical titles
```

Select **Horizontal** titles from the menu.

PRESS   h (Horizontal)

Try to move the cell pointer into the frozen titles area—into rows 1, 2, 3, or 4. Once titles are frozen, you cannot move the cursor into the titles area. No changes can be made to the titles while they are frozen.

The spreadsheet does not appear to be different, but it is. Move the cell pointer down to row 19. Then continue moving the cell pointer so that row 19 is located directly beneath the titles at the top of the screen.

Now, clear the horizontal title setting.

PRESS   /

PRESS   w (Worksheet)

PRESS   t (Titles)

PRESS   c (Clear)

Move the cell pointer to rows 1, 2, or 3, and you will find that the titles are no longer frozen.

Vertical Titles

In this next tutorial, you will freeze the vertical titles at the left edge of the spreadsheet.

Retrieve the file PROFIT, if it is not on the screen.

Move the cell pointer to column B to freeze all titles to the left of that column.

PRESS   /

PRESS   w (Worksheet)

PRESS   t (Titles)

PRESS   v (Vertical)

Scroll to the April figures and keep scrolling to the right until only the titles in column A and the April figures appear on the screen.

Try to move the cell pointer anywhere in column A. You will find that the cell pointer cannot enter title areas that are frozen.

Now, clear the vertical title setting.

PRESS   /

PRESS   w (Worksheet)

PRESS   t (Titles)

PRESS   c (Clear)

Both Horizontal and Vertical Titles

In the following tutorial, you will freeze both horizontal and vertical titles simultaneously.

Retrieve the file PROFIT, if it is not on your screen.

Move the cell pointer to B6, one row below the horizontal titles to be frozen and one column to the right of the vertical titles to be frozen.

PRESS   /

PRESS   w (Worksheet)

PRESS   t (Titles)

PRESS   b (Both)

Scroll down to the bottom of the spreadsheet and then to the right side of the spreadsheet. Change the Legal Fees for June to 700 and notice the change in the profit for June.

Again, you will find the cell pointer will not move into the titles areas.

Clear the title setting.

PRESS   /

PRESS   w (Worksheet)

PRESS   t (Titles)

PRESS   c (Clear)

ACTIVITY 9.1 □ Using the Titles Command

In this activity, you will retrieve a very wide spreadsheet showing a personal budget for a high school student for the months June through May.

1. Retrieve the file ACT9-1.
2. Scroll to the right side of the spreadsheet to view the TOTALS column. Notice that when you scroll to the right side, you can view the values, but you no longer know which values relate to which labels.
3. Scroll to the bottom of the spreadsheet to view the row showing savings for College Education. As you can see, the months of the year no longer appear at the top of the screen, making it difficult to change, analyze, or interpret the data.
4. Move the cell pointer to the appropriate location to freeze the titles in rows 1-4.
5. Freeze the horizontal titles located above the cell pointer.
6. Change the estimated gasoline expense for September through May to 26.
7. Clear the horizontal titles setting.
8. Move the cell pointer to the appropriate location to freeze the titles along the left side of the spreadsheet.
9. Scroll to the February column and change the amount of the Misc. expense to 25.
10. Clear the vertical titles setting.
11. Move the cell pointer to the appropriate location and set both horizontal and vertical titles in rows 1-4 and column A.
12. Move the cell pointer to N34 to view the total amount saved for college during the year.
13. Clear the titles setting.
14. Print the spreadsheet.
15. Erase the spreadsheet from the screen so that your revisions are not saved.

WHY SHOULD WINDOWS BE CREATED?

The / Worksheet Window command divides the screen into two windows. It lets you split the screen horizontally or vertically into two windows, enabling you to see simultaneously cells that are far apart on the spreadsheet. Each window displays a different part of the same spreadsheet, allowing you to make changes in one section and to see the results of those changes in another section. Each window can be of equal size, or one can be large and one small.

The Windows command allows you to work in both windows and to make editing changes. Whereas, the Titles command does not allow changes to be made in the titles area. Determine the appropriate command to use by analyzing the types of editing that need to be done.

Vertical Windows

The / Worksheet Window Vertical command allows you to create two windows. The screen is split vertically at the column the cell pointer is in. Figure 9.4 shows a spreadsheet split vertically. This makes it easy to view the labels in one window and the total revenue for 1992 in the second window. By using two windows, you note the revenue shown in columns B-E can be hidden from sight.

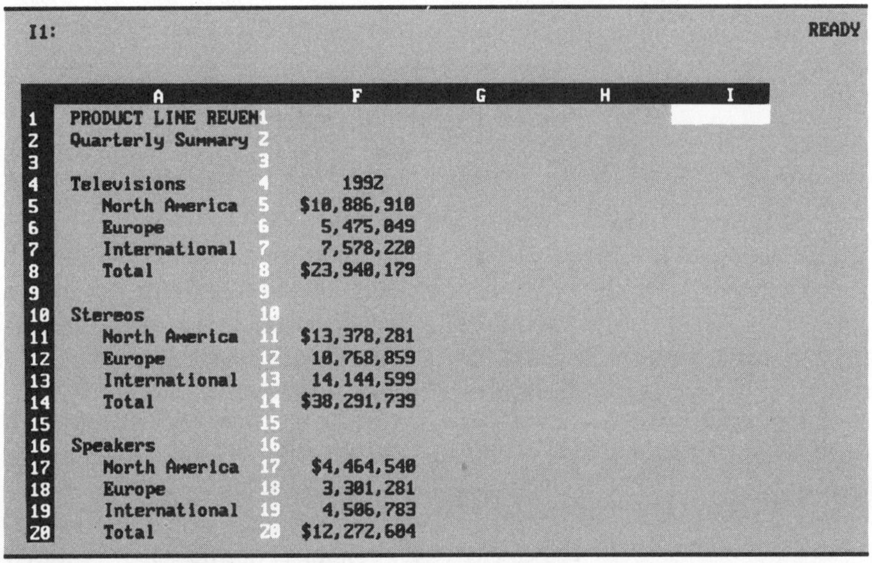

Figure 9.4 ◻ *Vertical Windows*

Retrieve the file PROFIT.

Move the cell pointer to the column in which you will split the screen, column E.

PRESS /

PRESS w (Worksheet)

PRESS w (Window)

PRESS v (Vertical)

Notice the difference between the placement of the cell pointer when setting titles and windows. The Windows command takes affect in the column or row where the cell pointer is positioned. The cell pointer is then located in the left or top screen.

Now the screen is split into two windows.

PRESS F6 (Window key)

The cell pointer should be in the right window.

PRESS → (3 times)

The January-March and April-June figures should be visible on the screen. By splitting the screen, windowing allows you to compare the figures for the first quarter of the year to those for the second quarter easily.

Now practice using the F6 key to move the cell pointer from one window to another.

PRESS F6 (Window key)

The cell pointer should be in the left window in the cell that it had been positioned in previously.

PRESS F6 (Window key)

Practice moving the cell pointer up, down, left, and right in each window to see how the spreadsheet scrolls in each individual window. Notice that the same column(s) can appear in both windows simultaneously.

Clearing Windows

The **/ Worksheet Window Clear** command restores the full screen spreadsheet. Prior to changing from vertical windows to horizontal windows or vice versa, you must clear the window setting.

With the WINDOWS file on the screen:

PRESS /
PRESS w (Worksheet)
PRESS w (Window)
PRESS c (Clear)

Horizontal Windows

The **/ Worksheet Window Horizontal** command allows you to split the screen horizontally at the row the cell pointer is in. As shown in Figure 9.5, the top window shows the revenue from Televisions. In the bottom window, the same spreadsheet has been scrolled to show only the Worldwide Total, thus allowing comparisons of revenue from television sales to worldwide sales of all products. Notice that rows 9-21 do not appear on the screen.

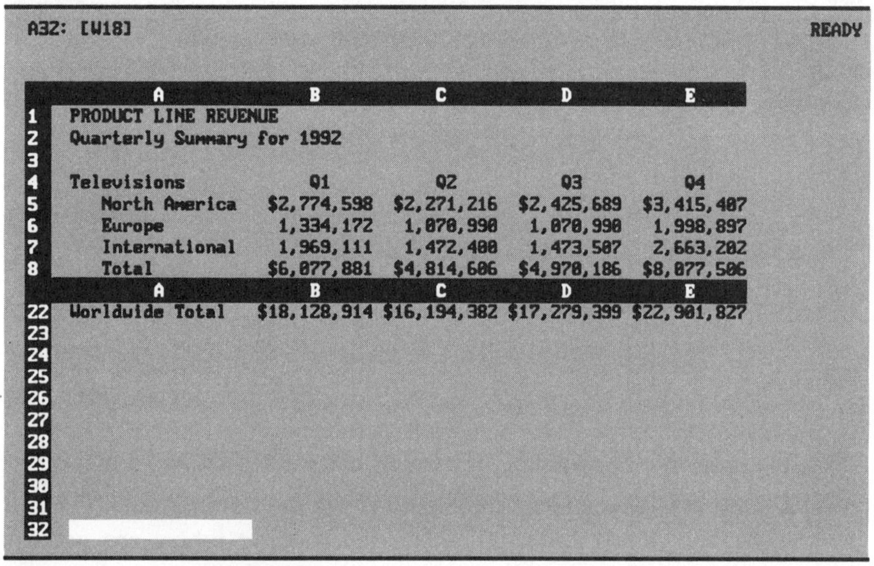

```
A32: [W18]                                                      READY

           A          B          C          D          E
 1  PRODUCT LINE REVENUE
 2  Quarterly Summary for 1992
 3
 4  Televisions         Q1         Q2         Q3         Q4
 5    North America  $2,774,598 $2,271,216 $2,425,689 $3,415,407
 6    Europe          1,334,172  1,070,990  1,070,990  1,998,897
 7    International    1,969,111  1,472,400  1,473,507  2,663,202
 8    Total          $6,077,881 $4,814,606 $4,970,186 $8,077,506
           A          B          C          D          E
22  Worldwide Total $18,128,914 $16,194,382 $17,279,399 $22,901,827
23
24
25
26
27
28
29
30
31
32
```

Figure 9.5 ☐ *Horizontal Windows*

Retrieve the file PROFIT, if it is not on the screen. Move the cell pointer to row 7.

PRESS /

PRESS w (Worksheet)

PRESS w (Window)

PRESS h (Horizontal)

Move the cell pointer to the bottom window.

PRESS F6 (Window key)

PRESS ↓ (until cell pointer is in row 30)

The screen will now display Income figures in the top window and Total Expenses and Profit in the bottom window. As you can see on your screen, the Window command can be used to hide some rows or columns from view, making it possible to analyze and interpret data more easily. Rows 7-17, containing a listing of individual expenses, have been hidden from view. This makes it easy to analyze increases or decreases in Income, Total Expenses, and Profit in January, February, and March.

Now clear the horizontal windows.

PRESS /

PRESS w (Worksheet)

PRESS w (Window)

PRESS c (Clear)

ACTIVITY 9.2 □ Using Vertical and Horizontal Windows

In this activity, you will use vertical and horizontal windows and make editing changes in the spreadsheet.

1. Retrieve the file used in the previous activity, ACT9-1.
2. Split the screen vertically at column B.
3. Move the cell pointer to the right window.
4. Since the class ring will be paid for in April, change the class ring payment in May to 0.
5. Increase the allowance in December to 35.
6. Change the Miscellaneous expense for September to 60. Notice how difficult it is to locate the appropriate cell when the column labels are not displayed.
7. Use the command to clear the windows.
8. Split the screen horizontally at row 10.
9. With the cell pointer in the top window, press the Home key.
10. Move the cell pointer to the bottom window.
11. Change the Miscellaneous expense for October to 50.
12. Save the file as ACT9-2.
13. Print the file.

Unsynchronized Windows

The command / Worksheet Window Unsync allows windows to scroll independently of each other in all directions. Neither columns nor rows remain the same in both windows when scrolling data in one window.

Unsynchronized Horizontal Windows In this tutorial, you will create unsynchronized horizontal windows.

Retrieve the file PROFIT, if it is not already on the screen. Move the cell pointer to row 7.

PRESS /

PRESS w (Worksheet)

PRESS w (Window)

PRESS h (Horizontal)

Now create unsynchronized windows.

PRESS /

PRESS w (Worksheet)

PRESS w (Window)

PRESS u (Unsync)

PRESS F6

Press the Right and Down Arrow keys until columns F-L and rows 4-16 appear in the bottom window.

The top window displays data from columns A-F, while the bottom window displays data in columns F-L, as shown in Figure 9-6. The income for January, February, and March of 1990 can be compared with the income for January, February, and March of 1991 quite easily since they are both visible on the same screen.

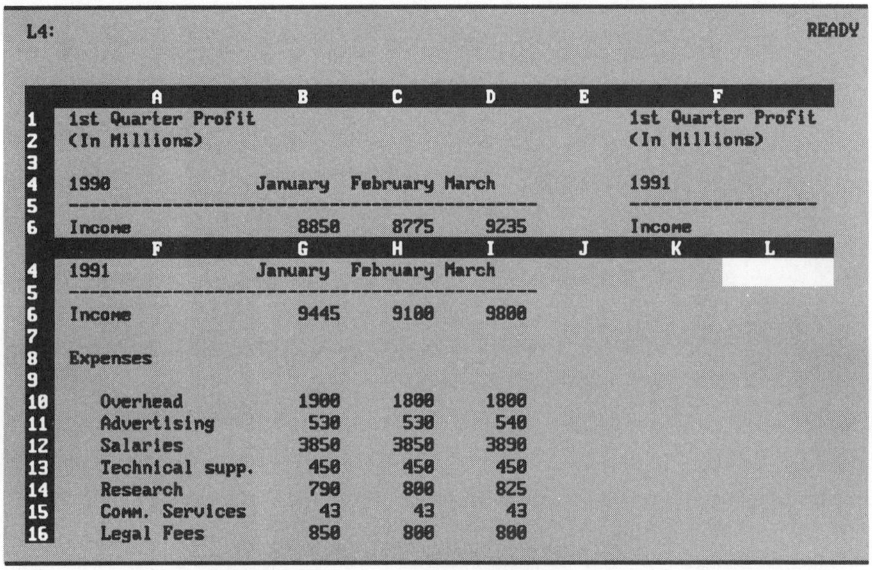

Figure 9.6 □ *Unsynchronized Horizontal Windows*

Practice on your own scrolling through the data in the top window so that the Profit for January-March 1990 appears. Then scroll through the data in the bottom window so that the January-March Profits appear directly beneath the 1990 figures.

After you are finished practicing scrolling, use the following instructions to clear the windows.

PRESS /

PRESS w (Worksheet)

PRESS w (Window)

PRESS c (Clear)

Unsynchronized Vertical Windows The command / Worksheet Window Unsync is also used to create unsynchronized vertical windows.

Retrieve the file PROFIT, if it is not on your screen. Move the cell pointer to column C and create vertical unsynchronized windows.

P R E S S /

P R E S S w (Worksheet)

P R E S S w (Window)

P R E S S v (Vertical)

P R E S S /

P R E S S w (Worksheet)

P R E S S w (Window)

P R E S S u (Unsync)

Move the cell pointer down to row 30 in the left window. Notice that the row numbers in the left window are different than those in the right window.

P R E S S Home

To move the cell pointer to the right window:

P R E S S F6

Move the cell pointer to I6. Notice that the column letters in the right window are different than those in the left window. Unsynchronized scrolling allows windows to scroll independently in all directions.

Practice moving the cell pointer up, down, left, and right in each window.

Clear the windows and display one full screen.

P R E S S /

P R E S S w (Worksheet)

P R E S S w (Window)

P R E S S c (Clear)

Erase the spreadsheet from the screen without saving it.

ACTIVITY 9.3 ◻ *Using Unsynchronized Scrolling*

In this activity, you will use unsynchronized scrolling.

1. Retrieve the file ACT9-3.
2. Scroll down until row 21 is displayed on the screen. Then split the screen horizontally at row 20.
3. Set up unsynchronized scrolling.
4. Be sure that rows 2-19 and columns A-C are displayed in the top window.
5. Move the cell pointer to the bottom window.
6. Move the cell pointer to row 21 and press the Right Arrow key 3 times so that columns B-G are displayed. The Amount of Change column, column D, should be visible in the bottom window. Notice that the columns displayed in the top window are not the same as those displayed in the bottom window.
7. Move the cell pointer to the top window.
8. Change the amount of General Merchandise in 1991 to 3,255.30 and watch the value change in the Total Amount of Change cell, D21, shown in the bottom window.
9. Change the Miscellaneous amount for 1991 to 30.52.
10. Clear the windows.
11. Save the spreadsheet as ACT9-3.
12. Print the spreadsheet.

Synchronized Windows

Another window option allows synchronized scrolling. When you use the command / Worksheet Window Sync, the two windows scroll in unison. When you use horizontal windows, Sync keeps the same columns on the screen in both windows as you scroll through columns in one window. When you use vertical windows, Sync keeps the same rows on the screen in both windows as you scroll through rows in one window. Synchronized scrolling is the initial default setting.

Synchronized Horizontal Windows Figure 9.7 shows horizontal windows with synchronized scrolling. Notice that the same columns are in both windows in this example, but different rows appear in the two windows.

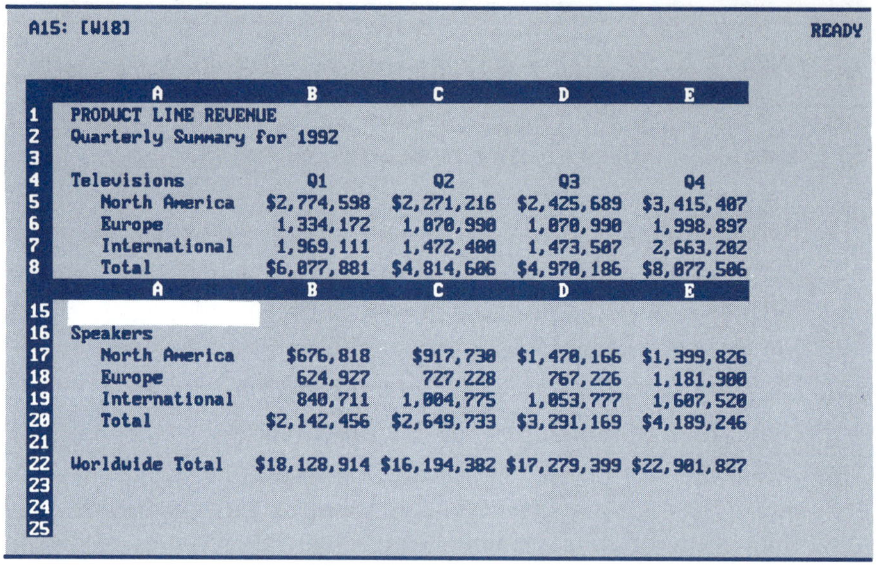

```
A15: [W18]                                                              READY

            A              B            C            D            E
 1  PRODUCT LINE REVENUE
 2  Quarterly Summary for 1992
 3
 4  Televisions          Q1           Q2           Q3           Q4
 5    North America   $2,774,598   $2,271,216   $2,425,689   $3,415,407
 6    Europe           1,334,172    1,070,990    1,070,990    1,998,897
 7    International     1,969,111    1,472,400    1,473,507    2,663,202
 8    Total           $6,077,881   $4,814,606   $4,970,186   $8,077,506
            A              B            C            D            E
15
16  Speakers
17    North America     $676,818     $917,730   $1,470,166   $1,399,826
18    Europe             624,927      727,228      767,226    1,181,900
19    International      840,711    1,004,775    1,053,777    1,607,520
20    Total           $2,142,456   $2,649,733   $3,291,169   $4,189,246
21
22  Worldwide Total  $18,128,914  $16,194,382  $17,279,399  $22,901,827
23
24
25
```

Figure 9.7 □ *Synchronized Horizontal Windows*

Create synchronized horizontal windows using the following instructions:

Retrieve the file PROFIT, if it is not on the screen.

Move the cell pointer to row 7.

PRESS /

PRESS w (Worksheet)

PRESS w (Window)

PRESS h (Horizontal)

PRESS /

PRESS w (Worksheet)

PRESS w (Window)

PRESS s (Sync)

Move the cell pointer to the bottom window.

PRESS F6

PRESS → (10 times)

As you can see, the column letters remain the same in both windows. Now move the cell pointer to the top window.

PRESS F6

PRESS ← (10 times)

Again, the column letters remain the same in both windows.

PRESS ↓ (7 times)

The row numbers will change in the top window but not in the bottom window. With synchronized horizontal windows, only the column letters remain the same in both windows.

Now clear the windows.

PRESS /

PRESS w (Worksheet)

PRESS w (Window)

PRESS c (Clear)

Synchronized Vertical Windows When vertical windows are used, the synchronized scrolling command keeps the row numbers the same in both windows as shown in Figure 9.8. However, the columns can be different in each window. The left window shows the 1990 data, and the right window shows the 1991 data.

H1:							READY
	A	**B**	**C**	**D**		**G**	**H**	**I**
1	1st Quarter Profit				1			
2	(In Millions)				2			
3					3			
4	1990	January	February	March	4	January	February	March
5	---------------				5	---------------		
6	Income	8850	8775	9235	6	9445	9100	9800
7					7			
8	Expenses				8			
9					9			
10	Overhead	1800	1700	1700	10	1900	1800	1800
11	Advertising	530	530	540	11	530	530	540
12	Salaries	3778	3800	3800	12	3850	3850	3890
13	Technical supp.	434	434	434	13	450	450	450
14	Research	790	800	825	14	790	800	825
15	Comm. Services	45	45	45	15	43	43	43
16	Legal Fees	720	720	720	16	850	800	800
17					17			
18	Total Expenses	8097	8029	8064	18	8413	8273	8348
19	---------------				19	---------------		
20	Profit	753	746	1171	20	1032	827	1452

Figure 9.8 □ *Synchronized Vertical Windows*

Retrieve the file PROFIT, if it is not on your screen. Move the cell pointer to column B and create vertical windows.

PRESS /

PRESS w (Worksheet)

PRESS w (Window)

PRESS v (Vertical)

Now enter the command for synchronized scrolling.

PRESS   \

PRESS   w (Worksheet)

PRESS   w (Window)

PRESS   s (Sync)

PRESS   Home

PRESS   F6

Scroll to the right until the 1991 figures for January, February and March appear on the screen as shown in Figure 9.9. As you can see, the column letters are different in each window.

```
K1:                                                              READY

          A                 G       H       I       J     K     L
  1  1st Quarter Profit 1
  2  (In Millions)      2
  3                     3
  4  1990               4   January  February March
  5  ----------------   5   -----------------------------
  6  Income             6     9445     9100    9800
  7                     7
  8  Expenses           8
  9                     9
 10     Overhead       10     1900     1800    1800
 11     Advertising    11      530      530     540
 12     Salaries       12     3850     3850    3890
 13     Technical supp.13      450      450     450
 14     Research       14      790      800     825
 15     Comm. Services 15       43       43      43
 16     Legal Fees     16      850      800     800
 17                    17
 18  Total Expenses    18     8413     8273    8348
 19  ----------------  19   -----------------------------
 20  Profit            20     1032      827    1452
```

Figure 9.9 □ *Synchronized Vertical Windows*

Scroll down the spreadsheet to row 25. The row numbers in both windows have remained the same. With synchronized vertical windows, only column letters can be different in each window.

PRESS   /

PRESS   w (Worksheet)

PRESS   w (Window)

PRESS   c (Clear)

ACTIVITY 9.4 ◻ *Using Synchronized Windows*

In this activity, you will use synchronized scrolling with vertical and horizontal windows.

1. Retrieve the file ACT9-1, which was used in a previous activity.
2. Split the screen vertically at column B.
3. Set up synchronized scrolling.
4. Move the cell pointer to the right window.
5. Scroll to the right until only the TOTALS column, column N, appears in this window.
6. Move the cell pointer to row 34. Notice that the row numbers in the left window are the same as those in the right window.
7. Clear the windows. Move the cell pointer to A1.
8. Set a horizontal window at row 10.
9. Set up synchronized scrolling.
10. Move the cell pointer to the bottom window.
11. Position the cell pointer in G34. Look at the column headings in both windows. With synchronized scrolling, they are the same in both windows.
12. Move the cell pointer to the top window.
13. PRESS the Home key. Both windows will have column A at the left edge of the screen.
14. Erase the worksheet from the screen.

C H A P T E R   9   □   T H E O R Y   E X E R C I S E S

True/False ‖‖‖‖‖‖‖   Each of the following statements is either True or False. Indicate your choice by circling **T** for a true statement or **F** for a false statement.

1. The / Worksheet Titles Horizontal command freezes horizontal titles at the top of a spreadsheet, vertical titles along the left edge, or both sets of titles.

        1. T   F

2. Even though titles have been frozen, the cell pointer can enter those title areas and changes can be made.

        2. T   F

3. Titles that have been frozen remain fixed on the screen as you scroll through a spreadsheet.

        3. T   F

4. Either horizontal or vertical titles can be frozen, but not both.

        4. T   F

5. The command to clear titles is **/ w t c**.

        5. T   F

6. To freeze horizontal titles, place the cell pointer one row below the rows you want to freeze.

        6. T   F

7. To freeze vertical titles, place the cell pointer on the column you want to freeze.

        7. T   F

8. To freeze both horizontal and vertical titles, place the cell pointer one row below and one column to the right of the rows and columns you want to freeze.

        8. T   F

9. Windowing lets you split the screen horizontally or vertically into two windows, enabling you to see simultaneously cells that are far apart on the spreadsheet.

        9. T   F

10. The / Window Vertical command allows you to create two windows with the screen split vertically at the column the cell pointer is in.

      10. T   F

11. The Window key is the F6 key.

      11. T   F

12. The / Worksheet Window Clear command restores the full screen spreadsheet.

      12. T   F

13. To move the cell pointer from one window to another, use the F8 key.

      13. T   F

14. The / Worksheet Window Horizontal command allows you to split the screen horizontally at the row the cell pointer is in.

      14. T   F

15. When the command / Worksheet Window Sync is used, the two windows scroll independently of each other.

      15. T   F

16. The command / Worksheet Window Unsync allows windows to scroll independently of each other in all directions.

      16. T   F

Completion IIIIIIIII For each item below fill in the word (or words) that completes the statement or answers the question.

1. To freeze horizontal titles at the top of a spreadsheet, use the command

   _____.

2. To freeze horizontal titles in rows 1-3, place the cell pointer in row _____ prior to entering the **Titles** command.

3. To freeze vertical titles at the left edge of a spreadsheet, use the command

   _____.

4. To freeze vertical titles in column A, place the cell pointer in column _____ prior to entering the **Titles** command.

5. After the **Titles** command has been entered, it will remain in effect until you use the **/ Worksheet Titles** _____ command.

6. To freeze both horizontal and vertical titles, use the command

   _____.

7. Where should the cell pointer be placed to freeze at the same time horizontal titles in rows 1-3 and vertical titles in column A?

   _____

8. The **/ Worksheet Window** command splits the screen horizontally or _____ into _____ windows.

9. Where should the cell pointer be placed to split the screen vertically at column C?

   _____

10. After using windows, what command restores the full screen spreadsheet?

    _____

11. The command to create a horizontal window is _____.

12. The command to create a vertical window is _____.

13. What command should be used to make two windows scroll in unison?

    _____

14. What type of scrolling is being used when one window displays columns A-D and rows 1-6 and the other window displays columns F-I and rows 3-11?

    _____

ACTIVITY 9.5 ❐ *Reviewing Titles and Window Commands*

In this activity, you are asked to retrieve any of the previous files you have worked with.

1. Practice setting horizontal titles, vertical titles, and then both titles simultaneously.
2. Clear the titles.
3. Set horizontal windows.
4. Use unsynchronized scrolling and then synchronized scrolling.
5. Clear the horizontal windows and set vertical windows.
6. Scroll through the data using unsynchronized scrolling and then synchronized scrolling.
7. Erase the spreadsheet from the screen when you are through practicing these activities. No printout is required for this activity.

OBJECTIVES

❑ Answer what-if questions
❑ Design spreadsheets for what-if decision making
❑ Use manual recalculation
❑ Use automatic recalculation
❑ Use protect and unprotect commands

WHAT IS WHAT-IF DECISION MAKING?

What-if decision making is a powerful feature of Lotus 1-2-3. It is easy to ask "What if the cost of producing a product increases by $.25? What will be the effect on our selling price?" By changing one value in a spreadsheet, you can quickly calculate the answer. Doing the same calculations manually is a tedious task that could take you 10-20 minutes to do. Because values and formulas can be changed so easily in spreadsheets, we can ask these what-if questions and make personal and business decisions based on the answers.

As you can see in Figure 10.1, the spreadsheet shows the number of hours worked each day of the week and the hourly wages Jesse received. Since Jesse works at two different jobs, the hourly wages are different for each job.

In this next tutorial, you will calculate Jesse's wages for each day of the week, his total wages, and then answer some what-if questions.

Retrieve the file JESSE.

On your own, enter the formulas needed to calculate Jesse's daily wages and total wages.

Did Jesse earn enough money in one week to buy a computer game that costs $75.00?

Obviously, the answer is no. If Jesse works two more hours on Sunday and two more hours on Friday, will he earn enough for the computer game?

```
A1: 'EARNINGS FROM JESSE'S PART-TIME JOB                              READY

          A           B           C           D           E           F
1    EARNINGS FROM JESSE'S PART-TIME JOB
2
3
4                   No. of      Hourly      Daily
5                   Hours       Wage        Wage
6
7    Sunday           4          4.58
8    Monday           3          3.85
9    Tuesday          8          3.85
10   Wednesday        3          3.85
11   Thursday         8          3.85
12   Friday           3          3.85
13   Saturday         4          4.58
14                                        -----------
15             TOTAL WEEKLY EARNINGS
16
```

Figure 10.1 ◻ *Weekly Earnings Spreadsheet*

Use the following instructions to find the answer. Move the cell pointer to B7.

ENTER   6
PRESS   ↵

Move the cell pointer to B12.

ENTER   5
PRESS   ↵

Now Jesse has earned enough money to buy a $75 computer game.

If Jesse works the same number of hours each week for four weeks, how much money will he earn in a month?

Use the following instructions to answer the question. Move the cell pointer to B17.

ENTER   TOTAL MONTHLY EARNINGS
PRESS   ↵

Move the cell pointer to D17.

ENTER   +D15*4
PRESS   ↵

The answer to the question is $349.40.

Save the file as JESSE. You have just completed an example of how values, labels, and formulas can be changed or how new ones can be entered to answer what-if questions.

ACTIVITY 10.1 ☐ *Using What-If Calculations*

In this activity, you will calculate the total cost of producing a bottle of soft drink and its selling price.

1. Retrieve the file ACT10-1.
2. Enter a formula in E6 to determine the total cost per bottle (Cost of Ounce * No. of Ounces + Cost of Bottle + Labor).
3. Copy the formula from E6 down column E.
4. This soft drink wholesale company wants to make a profit of $.09 per bottle, no matter how many ounces the bottle contains. Enter this amount in the column labeled Profit.
5. Enter a formula in column G to calculate the Selling Price (Total Cost + Profit).
6. Determine what the selling price is for a 32-ounce bottle costing $.09 for labor, $.01 per ounce of syrup, and $.10 for the bottle.
7. Print the spreadsheet.
8. Determine the effect on selling price of an increase in the cost of syrup to $.02 per ounce.
9. Save the file as ACT10-1.
10. Print the spreadsheet.

DESIGN PRINCIPLES

As mentioned in Chapter 3, it is helpful to place variable information used in separate cells to make what-if decisions. Placing a description next to the variable can be helpful to you and others who may analyze the data in a spreadsheet.

There are several reasons for not placing variable information within formulas. For one thing, the variable may be difficult to locate. When the variable is located, a formula has to be edited and, in many cases, the new formula must be copied to a range of cells. This becomes a time-consuming task.

Figure 10.2 shows an example of a variable, 20 percent, entered in a separate cell with the description of the variable, % of Down Payment, next to it. This makes it easy to recalculate the amount of down payment merely by changing one value, the percent of down payment.

In this next tutorial, you will calculate next year's school budget by entering a variable amount and description at the bottom of the spreadsheet.

```
C1: (F2) 0.2                                                          READY


           A          B           C           D           E           F
    1   % of Down Payment                  0.20
    2
    3
    4      Cost of              Amt. of Down
    5       House                 Payment
    6      $50,000                $10,000
    7       80,000                 16,000
    8      100,000                 20,000
    9
   10
```

Figure 10.2 ☐ *A Variable in a Spreadsheet*

The spreadsheet you will be working with shows the school expenses budgeted for this year. Since the school district may allow only a 1 or 2 percent increase in the budget for next year, calculate the budgeted expenses for each possibility using the following instructions:

Retrieve the file SCHOOL.

Move the cell pointer to A2.

ENTER % of Increase

PRESS ↵

Move the cell pointer to C2.

ENTER .01

PRESS ↵

Now calculate the amount budgeted for Utilities for next year.

Move the cell pointer to E6.

ENTER +d6+d6*c2

PRESS ↵

Copy this formula to the appropriate cells in column E.

Save the spreadsheet as **SCHOOLA** and print it.

Move the cell pointer to C2 and change the percent of increase.

ENTER .02

PRESS ↵

Save the spreadsheet as SCHOOLB and print the spreadsheet.

In some cases, what-if decision making involves personal manipulation of the data, not merely changing one value and calculating the answer. In this next tutorial, you are asked to use your own judgment in a what-if decision making situation. This time, the school district asks that you cut the budget for next year to 5,000,000. However, you cannot decrease salaries or utilities.

Retrieve the file SCHOOLB.

Use the arrow keys to move the cell pointer to E29.

ENTER   @sum(e6.e27)
PRESS   ↵

Move the cell pointer to row 19 and set up windows.

PRESS   /
PRESS   w (Worksheet)
PRESS   w (Window)
PRESS   h (Horizontal)

Move the cell pointer as follows:

PRESS   F6 (Window key)

Scroll the data in the bottom window so that only the TOTALS row appears in the bottom window.

PRESS   F6

In the top window, move the cell pointer to column E.

On your own, enter the same values in column E as in column D for the items that cannot be decreased. In the rest of column E, enter values that are reasonable decreases based on your own judgment. While the expenses decrease, keep watching the total in the bottom window until it is 5,000,000.

Use the following instructions to clear the windows:

PRESS   /
PRESS   w (Worksheet)
PRESS   w (Window)
PRESS   c (Clear)

Save the spreadsheet as SCHOOLC and print the spreadsheet.

ACTIVITY 10.2 ☐ *Making What-If Decisions*

In this activity, you will change values in a personal budget and analyze the results of those changes.

1. Retrieve the file ACT10-2.
2. Change the values in this file to answer the following questions:
   a. What if the income from the fast-food restaurant was reduced by $20 a month? What would be the total income for the whole year? What would be the amount of savings for college education by the end of May?
   b. In addition, what if the Entertainment expense were decreased to $10 for the months September through May? Then how much would be saved for college education by the end of May?
   c. What if $1,300 was needed to attend college? Decrease variable expenses so that the savings for college at the end of the year is $1,300. Do not increase income.
3. Save the file as ACT10-2.
4. Print the spreadsheet.

WHAT IS RECALCULATION?

Recalculation refers to the way 1-2-3 calculates the spreadsheet. **Automatic recalculation** means that all formulas in a spreadsheet are recalculated each time a value used in one of those formulas is changed. **Manual recalculation** means that the spreadsheet is only recalculated when you tell it to do so.

To use manual recalculation, enter the command / Worksheet Global Recalculation Manual. Once the spreadsheet is in the manual recalculation mode, press the F9 key, the Recalc key, when you want the spreadsheet to be recalculated.

When values are changed in very large spreadsheets containing many formulas, automatic recalculation of the spreadsheet can take a long time. To save time, use the manual recalculation mode, enter all changes, and then recalculate formulas.

When you save a spreadsheet, the current recalculation mode being used will be saved with it. Therefore, if you have been using manual recalculation but want the file to be saved in the automatic recalculation mode, enter the / Worksheet Global Recalculation Automatic command before saving the file.

In this tutorial, you will retrieve a file, change to manual recalculation mode, edit the file, use the Recalc key, and change back to automatic recalculation.

Retrieve the file JESSE.

To change to manual recalculation:

PRESS /
PRESS w (Worksheet)
PRESS g (Global)
PRESS r (Recalculation)
PRESS m (Manual)

Move the cell pointer to B8.

ENTER 4
PRESS ↵

Move the cell pointer to B11.

ENTER 2
PRESS ↵
PRESS F9 (Recalc key)

Move the cell pointer to C7.

ENTER 4.55
PRESS ↵
PRESS F9

To change back to automatic recalc:

PRESS /
PRESS w (Worksheet)
PRESS g (Global)
PRESS r (Recalculation)
PRESS a (Automatic)

Move the cell pointer to C13.

ENTER 4.55
PRESS ↵

Save the file as JESSE.

ACTIVITY 10.3 ☐ Using Manual Recalculation

In this activity, you will use the manual recalculation mode and the Recalc key. Then you will change to automatic recalculation mode. The spreadsheet shows income (cash inflow) and expenses (cash outflow) for a university medical center.

1. Retrieve the file MEDICAL.
2. Enter the command for manual recalculation.
3. Decrease the student fees for January to 6,500.
4. Decrease the state appropriations for each month to 5,000.
5. Decrease the student aid for February to 3,500.
6. Press the Recalc key.
7. Decrease the cash outflow for organized research to 2,670 in February and to 2,000 in December.
8. Increase the student fees to 6,500 in August, to 5,700 in September, and to 5,000 in October.
9. Press the Recalc key.
10. Change to automatic recalculation.
11. Save the file as ACT10-3.
12. Print the file.

WHAT IS CELL PROTECTION?

Data in unprotected cells can be changed; data in **protected cells** cannot be changed. If you try to change the data in protected cells, the computer will beep and the error message *Protected cell* will be displayed at the bottom of the screen.

When a spreadsheet is created, the cells are unprotected. After checking the data, you may wish to protect some cells so they are not accidentally changed. Labels, values, or formulas that will not change should be protected. Before letting someone else use a spreadsheet you created, protect important labels, values, and/or formulas in it.

First, you must protect the entire worksheet by using the command / Worksheet Global Protection Enable. Once all the cells are protected, use the / Range Unprotect command to unprotect cells that you want to allow to change. To determine whether a cell is protected or unprotected, move the cell pointer to that cell. If the status line displays the letter *U*, it is an unprotected cell. If it displays *PR*, it is a protected cell. On color monitors, unprotected cells appear in green and are easily seen.

If you accidentally unprotect a cell, you can protect it again by using the command the **/ R**ange **P**rotect. However, this command only works when global protection has been enabled.

To make editing changes to numerous protected cells in a spreadsheet, disable global protection by using the command **/ W**orksheet **G**lobal **P**rotection **D**isable. After making the changes, turn on global protection, and the cells will be protected exactly as they were before you disabled protection.

In the following tutorial, you will enable global protection and then unprotect a range of cells.

Retrieve the file JESSE.

E N T E R   **/**

E N T E R   w (Worksheet)

E N T E R   g (Global)

E N T E R   p (Protection)

E N T E R   e (Enable)

Unprotect the shaded cells shown in Figure 10.3 according to the following instructions:

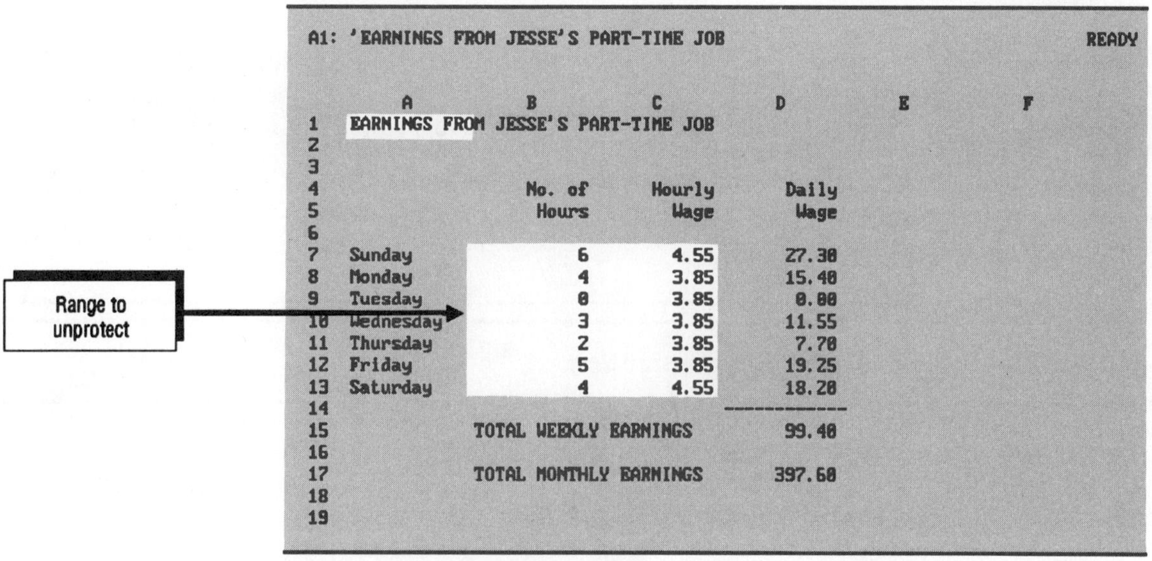

```
A1: 'EARNINGS FROM JESSE'S PART-TIME JOB                              READY

           A              B            C           D          E          F
  1   EARNINGS FROM JESSE'S PART-TIME JOB
  2
  3
  4                     No. of      Hourly      Daily
  5                     Hours        Wage        Wage
  6
  7   Sunday              6           4.55       27.30
  8   Monday              4           3.85       15.40
  9   Tuesday             0           3.85        0.00
 10   Wednesday           3           3.85       11.55
 11   Thursday            2           3.85        7.70
 12   Friday              5           3.85       19.25
 13   Saturday            4           4.55       18.20
 14                                             -------------
 15          TOTAL WEEKLY EARNINGS              99.40
 16
 17          TOTAL MONTHLY EARNINGS            397.60
 18
 19
```

Range to unprotect

Figure 10.3 □ *Unprotected Cells*

E N T E R   **/**

E N T E R   r (Range)

E N T E R   u (Unprotect)

E N T E R   b7.c13

P R E S S   ⏎

Move the cell pointer to D7. Notice that the status line indicates that it is a protected cell by displaying *PR* in front of the formula.

Move the cell pointer to C8. Notice that the status line displays a *U*, indicating that it is an unprotected cell.

Move the cell pointer to A1.

ENTER   MONTHLY EARNINGS

PRESS ↵

The computer beeped at you when you pressed the Enter key. Why? Because A1 is a protected cell. No changes can be made to protected cells when the worksheet protection is enabled.

To allow the cell pointer to move:

PRESS   Esc (Escape key or the Enter key to return to READY mode)

Now move the cell pointer to B7.

ENTER 5

PRESS ↵

Unlike data in protected cells, data in unprotected cells can be changed.

Save the file as JESSE. No printout is needed.

ACTIVITY 10.4 □ *Using Cell Protection*

In this activity, you will use protect and unprotect commands.

1. Retrieve the file MEDICAL.
2. Enter the global protection command.
3. Unprotect the range B18 through M21.
4. Change the amount allocated for organized research in February to 1,000.
5. Disable global protection.
6. Change the monthly state appropriations to 6,000 for each month.
7. Enable global protection.
8. Save the file as ACT10-4.
9. Print the file.

C H A P T E R   1 0 □ *T H E O R Y   E X E R C I S E S*

True/False **IIIIIIII** Each of the following statements is either True or False. Indicate your choice by circling **T** for a true statement or **F** for a false statement.

1. Since values and formulas can be changed in spreadsheets, what-if questions can be answered quickly.   1. T   F

2. A spreadsheet cannot be used to answer the question "What will be the effect on our company's profit if all employees receive a 7 percent pay increase?"   2. T   F

3. Variable information should be placed within formulas to make what-if decision making easier.   3. T   F

4. To make it easy to locate variables and understand their meaning, labels describing the variable should be entered in a cell adjacent to the variable itself.   4. T   F

5. In manual recalculation mode, you must press the F9 key to recalculate formulas.   5. T   F

6. The **/ Range Recalculation Manual** command must be entered when you want to use manual recalculation.   6. T   F

7. When a spreadsheet is saved, the current recalculation mode being used will be saved with the file.   7. T   F

8. To change from manual recalculation mode to automatic recalculation, enter **/ Worksheet Global Recalculation Automatic.**   8. T   F

9. Data in unprotected cells cannot be changed.   9. T   F

10. To prevent values or formulas from being changed accidentally, use the command **/ Worksheet Global Protection Enable.**   10. T   F

11. Only labels, values, or formulas that will not change in a spreadsheet should be protected.   11. T   F

12. After all cells are protected in a spreadsheet, the **/ Range Unprotect** command can be used to unprotect cells that you want to change.   12. T   F

13. If a status line displays D8: PR +B7*20, it means that cell D8 is unprotected.   13. T   F

14. The **/ Range Protect** command is used if you accidentally unprotect cells that need to be protected.   14. T   F

15. The **/ Range Protect** command only works when global protection has been enabled.   15. T   F

16. To turn global protection off, use the command **/ Worksheet Global Protection Disable.**   16. T   F

Completion IIIIIIII For each item below, fill in the word (or words) that completes the statement or answers the question.

1. Using 1-2-3 to answer the question "What will be the selling price of a television if we sell it at 25 percent off the ticketed price?" is an example of 1-2-3's ability to do _____ analyses.

2. Where should you place variable information that will be used to make what-if decisions? _____

3. To enter the manual recalculation mode, enter the command

   _____.

4. Once in manual recalculation mode, use the _____ key to recalculate formulas in a spreadsheet.

5. When a spreadsheet is saved, the current recalculation mode (will/will not) _____ be saved with it.

6. To change from the manual recalculation mode to automatic recalculation, enter the command _____.

7. Protected cells (can/cannot) _____ be changed.

8. When one tries to change data in a protected cell, the computer will _____.

9. To protect an entire spreadsheet, use the command **/ Worksheet Global Protection**

   _____.

10. Once all cells are protected in a spreadsheet, the **/** _____ _____ command can be used to unprotect cells that need to be changed.

11. If the status line displays N20: PR +B6/N19, cell N20 is a (an) _____ cell.

12. If the status line displays N20: U +B6/N19, cell N20 is a (an) _____ cell.

13. The **/ Range Protect** command only works when global protection has been _____.

14. To make numerous changes in protected cells in a spreadsheet, use the command **/ Worksheet Global Protection** _____ to unprotect the entire spreadsheet.

ACTIVITY 10.5 ☐ *Reviewing Manual Recalculation and Cell Protection*

In this activity, you will practice using the manual and automatic recalculation commands, the Recalc key, global cell protection, and cell unprotect commands.

1. Retrieve the file ACT10-5.
2. Enter the command for manual recalculation.
3. Change the amount of sales in the automotive department to 19,230.
4. Change the amount of sales in housewares to 325.
5. Press the Recalc key to recalculate the formulas.
6. Change to automatic recalculation mode.
7. Enable global cell protection.
8. Unprotect the values in B7 through B13.
9. Disable global cell protection.
10. Change the title in A2 to MONTHLY SALES REPORT.
11. Enable global cell protection.
12. Save the spreadsheet as ACT10-5.
13. Print the spreadsheet.

CHAPTER 11

OBJECTIVES

- ☐ Use a predesigned template
- ☐ Plan a template design
- ☐ Create a template
- ☐ Use a template

WHAT IS A TEMPLATE?

A **template** is a spreadsheet model that includes titles, column labels, row labels, and formulas for a particular type of application that is used frequently such as a weekly sales report or a monthly balance sheet. A template also includes the column widths and numeric format. Sometimes a template will include values that will not change each time the template is used. A template is stored on disk and filled in with new figures each time it is used. The new data is then saved under a different filename.

The left side of Figure 11.1 shows a monthly sales template with labels and formulas as it would appear on the screen. Notice that wherever a formula has been entered on the template, either an *ERR* message is displayed or a *0* is displayed. They will be replaced by values when data are entered on the spreadsheet. ERR appears when a formula calls for division by zero (which is an error). A zero (0) appears when a formula, lacking data, results in zero. The right side of Figure 11.1 shows the template as it would appear in Text format.

WHEN IS A TEMPLATE USED?

Templates are created for any spreadsheet that is used over and over again. Many spreadsheet tasks are quite repetitive. They require the same spreadsheet format, labels, and formulas each month, quarter, or year. For example, financial statements that are created every month or even once a year should be created as template files. A template not only saves creation time, but it also makes the com-

```
A1: [W15] 'BLUESTEM HARDWARE CO.              A1: [W15] 'BLUESTEM HARDWARE CO.


          A         B        C        D    E            A         B        C        D    E
1   BLUESTEM HARDWARE CO.                        1   BLUESTEM HARDWARE CO.
2   MONTHLY SALES                                2   MONTHLY SALES
3                                                3
4                       % of                     4                       % of
5   Department    Sales   Total Sales            5   Department    Sales   Total Sales
6                                                6
7   Clothing              ERR                     7   Clothing              +B7/B$14
8   Automotive            ERR                     8   Automotive            +B8/B$14
9   Tools                 ERR                     9   Tools                 +B9/B$14
10  Garden                ERR                    10   Garden                +B10/B$1
11  Implements            ERR                    11   Implements            +B11/B$1
12  Animal Care           ERR                    12   Animal Care           +B12/B$1
13  Housewares            ERR                    13   Housewares            +B13/B$1
14      TOTAL        0                           14      TOTAL     @SUM(B7.
15                                               15
16                                               16
17                                               17
18                                               18
19                                               19
20                                               20
```

Figure 11.1 ☐ *Monthly Sales Template*

parison and analysis of data from month to month or year to year much easier. For example, if the home office of a retail clothing store chain wants to compare sales in each of its three stores, the comparison is much easier when the sales data is presented in the same format.

Templates should be created whenever similar data is gathered from several departments or branches within an organization. When this occurs, the same templates should be used by all the departments or branches. For example, if the home office of a pizza chain requires that each of its 25 stores turn in weekly sales reports, the weekly sales report should be created as a template, and all 25 stores should use the same template.

Employees who use the same type of spreadsheets may collaborate on the development of a template so that it meets the needs of everyone. In some businesses, however, one or two people specialize in the creation of spreadsheet templates to be used by others in the organization.

A template can save a user hours of time and effort. People working in the accounting, banking, engineering, and other specialized fields, can purchase entire disks containing template files. That way, they do not have to create their own templates. Although these templates may not fit each businesses' needs perfectly, the templates can be modified in a matter of minutes to meet the requirements of a particular business.

HOW IS A TEMPLATE USED?

A template is used as a skeleton or shell to create other spreadsheets. To use a template, you retrieve the template file and enter the appropriate values. After you enter the values, you save the file under a new name so that two files exist—the template file and the newly created spreadsheet file. For instance: "The monthly balance sheet template is stored on the disk as BALSHEET. When the January figures are entered, the revised balance sheet would be saved as JANBAL. As a result, the basic template, BALSHEET, can be reused each month."

Some problems can arise when several people use the same template. Lengthy, complex formulas can be accidentally erased or edited, or entire columns or rows can be accidentally deleted. To prevent these problems, protection commands are used to keep users from entering or modifying certain cells on a template. The other cells are left unprotected so the user can enter appropriate values.

As you may recall from the previous chapter, first the / Worksheet Global Protection Enable command is used to protect the entire worksheet. Then the / Range Unprotect command is used to unprotect cells in which values will be entered later—ones that do not contain labels or formulas.

In the following tutorial, you will use a template to calculate the statistics for a basketball game. The protection command has been used to prevent you from entering the cells containing labels and formulas. If you accidentally attempt to enter data in a protected cell, press ESC to return to the READY mode and move the cell pointer to an unprotected cell.

Retrieve the file T-BASKET.

Move the cell pointer to B7.

ENTER April 18

PRESS ↵

In column B, enter the values shown in Figure 11.2.

Enter the values in columns C-H that are shown in Figure 11.2. Save the spreadsheet as BSKTAP18.

BASKETBALL STATISTICS ANALYSIS
3 PT. FIELD GOAL MADE = 3 POINTS EACH
2 PT. FIELD GOAL MADE = 2 POINTS EACH
FREE THROWS MADE = 1 POINT EACH

DATE: *April 18*

PLAYER'S NAME	3 PT. FIELD GOALS MADE	3 PT. FIELD GOALS ATTEMPTED	2 PT. FIELD GOALS MADE	2 PT. FIELD GOAL ATTEMPTS	FREE THROWS MADE	FREE THROW ATTEMPTS
Barbee, Greg	0	1	2	8	2	2
Gonzalez, Danny	1	2	3	7	2	4
Gadison, Jesse	1	4	3	11	5	8
Holiday, Roger	0	2	2	4	0	2
Johnson, Phil	1	1	1	3	1	4
Peterson, Dan	2	5	3	12	2	2
Robinson, Billy	3	4	4	14	4	7
Uphoff, Andy	2	5	4	9	7	8

Figure 11.2 ❑ *Filling in a Template*

ACTIVITY 11.1 ☐ *Using a Template*

In this activity, you will retrieve and use a template designed to figure wages for part-time employees at a fast-food restaurant.

1. Retrieve the file named T-BURGER.
2. Move the cell pointer to B4 and enter March 3-9.
3. Enter the following hours worked by Bates: Sunday, 0; Monday, 3; Tuesday, 2; Wednesday, 2; Thursday, 0; Friday, 3; and Saturday, 4.
4. Enter the following hours worked by Hanschu: Sunday, 4; Monday, 3; Tuesday, 3; Wednesday, 3; Thursday, 2; Friday, 3; and Saturday, 0.
5. Enter the following hours worked by Linton: Sunday, 4; Monday, 3; Tuesday, 2; Wednesday, 3; Thursday, 3; Friday, 3; and Saturday, 0.
6. Enter the following hours worked by Yi: Sunday, 2; Monday, 0; Tuesday, 3; Wednesday, 2; Thursday, 3; Friday, 3; and Saturday, 2.
7. Save the file as WGMCH3-9.
8. Print the file.

HOW DO YOU DESIGN A TEMPLATE?

Many of the principles of spreadsheet design are also useful when designing templates. Most templates are read from the upper left-hand corner down to the lower right-hand corner. This means that the titles and main headings usually begin in the upper left portion of the template. Titles placed in the upper left-hand corner are easily visible when the file is retrieved.

Titles and labels should be clear and understandable. Very short abbreviations make it difficult for you and others to use and/or analyze the spreadsheets at a later date. Figure 11.3 shows both a good and a bad example of label usage.

One general principle used in planning template layout is to display as much of the spreadsheet on the screen as possible. For small templates, this is easy to achieve. It means having a design that is longer than it is wide. Figure 11.4 shows two examples of the same template—one that is horizontally oriented and cannot be displayed in its entirety on the screen and the other vertically oriented to show the entire template. For large templates, it may not be possible to display all of the template on the screen at once no matter which orientation is used.

```
                    Unit Costs                                    Unit Cost
                    ──────                                        ──────
Unit Prod.                         Unit Production

                    =========                                     =========
Var. Costs:                        Variable Costs:
  Dir. Mat.                          Direct Materials
  Dir. Lab.                          Direct Labor
                    ──────                                        ──────
  Total Var. Costs    $0.00           Total Variable Costs  $0.00

Fixed Costs:                       Fixed Costs:
  Depr.                              Depreciation
  Maint.                             Maintenance
  Sal.                               Salaries
  Util.                              Utilities
                    ──────                                        ──────
  Total Fixed Costs   $0.00           Total Fixed Costs     $0.00
Total Prod. Costs     $0.00        Total Production Costs   $0.00
```

Figure 11.3 ☐ *Examples of Proper and Improper Use of Labels*

```
VIDEO CONNECTION
MONTHLY SALES

          January February March    April May    June    July    August   September October  November December Totals
Omaha                                                                                                             0
Dallas                                                                                                            0
Seattle                                                                                                           0
```

```
VIDEO CONNECTION
MONTHLY SALES

                    Omaha        Dallas       Seattle
January
February
March
April
May
June
July
August
September
October
November
December
                    ──────────────────────────────────
Totals                0            0            0
```

Figure 11.4 ☐ *Horizontal and Vertical Template Orientation*

References

Another rule to follow is to place all formulas that refer to other cell references below or following those cell references. Formulas at the end of a row or bottom of a column will recalculate faster than if they precede the data used in the calculation.

A formula should not refer to its own cell reference. In other words, formulas should not depend on themselves for the answer. This situation occurs only when a closed loop of cell references, called a **circular reference,** is used. When this occurs, a *CIRC* message appears at the bottom of the screen. Try to eliminate all such circular references in templates and spreadsheets.

Figure 11.5 shows circular references. As you can see, the formula in A1 includes a reference to A3; and the formula in A3 includes a reference to A1, thereby creating a circular reference. Even after values have been entered, the CIRC message still appears at the bottom of the screen.

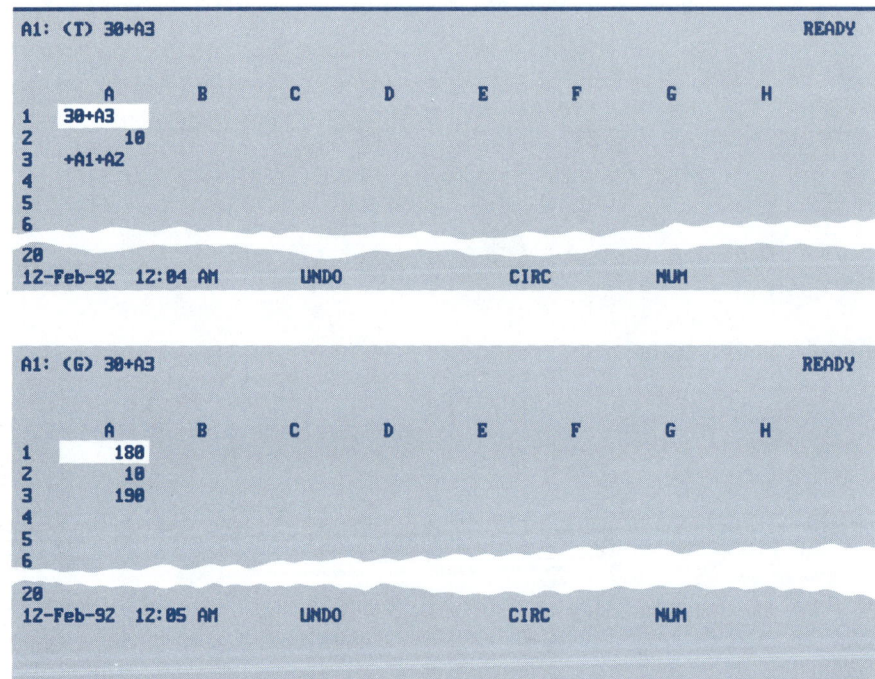

Figure 11.5 ☐ *Circular References*

Variables

As stated in an earlier chapter, clearly identify and place any variables that may change in separate cells rather than within formulas. When placed in separate cells, variables are easy to identify and change if necessary.

In the template shown in Figure 11.6, the variable is a 3 percent increase in salary. The variable is hidden within the formula, and the formula can only be seen in the control panel when the cell pointer is in C5, C6, or C7. This is not an appropriate technique to use because the printout will not show the percent of salary increase. Also, each formula will have to be edited to change the percent of increase.

```
C5: (,0) [W17] +B5+B5×0.03                                          READY


         A              B                 C            D        E
1  PROJECTED SALARY INCREASES
2  COMPUTER AGE STORES
3
4              Present Salary   Projected Salary
5  Adams, A.             24,000            24,720
6  Dunlap, R.            21,000            21,630
7  Hawkins, M.           26,000            26,780
8
9
10
11
```

Figure 11.6 ◻ *Inappropriate Use of Variables in Templates*

An appropriate use of variables is shown in Figure 11.7. The variable is presented at the top of the template, is labeled, and will appear on a printout. The formula includes the cell address of the variable, B4, rather than the value of the variable. To change the variable, you need to change only the value in B4.

```
C7: (,0) [W17] +B7+B7×$B$4                                         READY


         A              B                 C            D        E
1  PROJECTED SALARY INCREASES
2  COMPUTER AGE STORES
3
4  % of Increase          0.03
5
6              Present Salary   Projected Salary
7  Adams, A.             24,000            24,720
8  Dunlap, R.            21,000            21,630
9  Hawkins, M.           26,000            26,780
10
11
```

Figure 11.7 ◻ *Appropriate Use of Variables in Templates*

Creation of the Template

There are seven steps for creating the template:

1. Create the template title, column headings, and row labels.
2. Enter subtotal and total lines.
3. Enter any values that will not change.
4. Enter the formulas.
5. Set the numeric format for the entire template.
6. Set the column width.
7. Save the template.

After its creation, a template should be tested. Values should be entered, and the results should be compared to those derived using manual calculations. If a template is designed to replace calculations previously done manually, the accuracy of the template can easily be checked against the previous data.

In the following tutorial, you will be asked to create a template that will calculate the increase or decrease in utilities from last month to this month. Rod Landry, the owner of Rod's Antique Car Shop, believes that utility bills have increased substantially. In fact, he plans to keep track of how much the bills have increased from month to month. Last month the electricity bill was $165.98; the gas bill, $295.47; and the phone bill, $65.20. This month the electricity bill was $195.40; the gas bill, $311.60; and the phone bill, $59.50.

Begin creating a template by entering the titles in the upper left corner of the template.

Move the cell pointer to A1.

ENTER	ROD'S ANTIQUE CAR SHOP
PRESS	↓
ENTER	UTILITY BILL COMPARISON
PRESS	↵

Enter the following labels in column A. Move the cell pointer A5.

ENTER	Electric
PRESS	↓
ENTER	Gas
PRESS	↓
ENTER	Phone
PRESS	↓ (2 times)
ENTER	Totals
PRESS	↵

Move the cell pointer to B4.

ENTER	"Last Month
PRESS	→
ENTER	"This Month
PRESS	→
ENTER	"Inc or Dec
PRESS	↵

Move the cell pointer to B8.

ENTER \-

PRESS ↵

ENTER /

ENTER c (copy)

PRESS ↵

ENTER . (period)

PRESS → (2 times)

PRESS ↵

Move the cell pointer to B9.

ENTER @sum(b5.b7)

PRESS ↵

PRESS /

ENTER c (copy)

PRESS ↵

ENTER . (period)

PRESS → (2 times)

PRESS ↵

Move the cell pointer to D5.

ENTER +c5−b5

PRESS ↵

ENTER /

ENTER c (Copy)

PRESS ↵

ENTER . (Period)

PRESS ↓ (2 times)

PRESS ↵

Change the global column width.

ENTER /

PRESS w (Worksheet)

ENTER g (Global)

ENTER c (Column-width)

ENTER 12

PRESS ↵

Change the format.

```
ENTER   /
ENTER   w (Worksheet)
ENTER   g (Global)
ENTER   f (Format)
ENTER   f (Fixed)
ENTER   2
PRESS   ↵
```

Now save the template.

```
ENTER   /
ENTER   f (File)
PRESS   s (Save)
ENTER   t-util
PRESS   ↵
```

To see if the template works, enter the following values. In cell B5:

```
ENTER   165.98
PRESS   →
ENTER   195.40
PRESS   ↵
```

In cell B6:

```
ENTER   295.47
PRESS   →
ENTER   311.60
PRESS   ↵
```

In cell B7:

```
ENTER   65.20
PRESS   →
ENTER   59.50
PRESS   ↵
```

Save the file using the name UTILMAY.

ACTIVITY 11.2 ◻ *Creating a Template*

In this activity, you will create a template that will be used to determine the amount of profit Rod Landry makes on each antique car he sells. Although his profits have been good over the last year, he has never kept track of his profits based on sales each month. Use the following information to create a template.

Rod Landry usually sells no more than five cars a month. He keeps a record of the amount he paid when he purchased each antique car, the total cost of repairs, and the selling price for each car. He wants a record of the year of the automobile, the make (Chevrolet, Ford, Volkswagon, Buick, Oldsmobile, etc.), the model (Impala, Corvair, Trans Am, Camaro, etc.), the type (2-door, 4-door, or convertible), the purchase price, cost of repairs, selling price, and profit. The profit will be based on the selling price minus the sum of the purchase price and the cost of repairs.

Allow a place on the template for the current month and year. Use some type of line to separate the labels from the values. Set column widths to accommodate the usual makes, models, and types of cars purchased. Use the comma format with zero decimals. Use the protection command to protect all labels and formulas in the template.
Save the file as T-PROFIT. Print the file.

CHAPTER 11 □ THEORY EXERCISES

True/False ‖‖‖‖‖‖ Each of the following statements is either True or False. Indicate your choice by circling **T** for a true statement or **F** for a false statement.

1. A template is a spreadsheet model that includes titles, column labels, row labels, and formulas for a particular type of application that is used frequently.

        1. T   F

2. A template uses default settings for column widths and formats so they can be changed when data is entered.

        2. T   F

3. Templates only include values that will not change each time the template is used.

        3. T   F

4. The process of using a template includes retrieving the template file, entering values, and saving it under the template filename.

        4. T   F

5. Templates are created for spreadsheet tasks that are used over and over again.

        5. T   F

6. Monthly financial statements should be created as templates.

        6. T   F

7. Templates should always be designed by one person to assure having a design that is easy for everyone to understand.

        7. T   F

8. Predesigned template disks can be purchased that contain spreadsheet files for specialized fields such as accounting or banking.

        8. T   F

9. To prevent users of templates from accidentally erasing formulas, the protection command can be used.

        9. T   F

10. Very short abbreviations within templates are recommended so that more information can be seen on the screen at one time.

        10. T   F

11. One general principle for template layout is to display as much of the spreadsheet on the screen as possible.

        11. T   F

12. All formulas that refer to other cell references should be placed below or following those cell references.

        12. T   F

13. A formula should not refer to its own cell reference.

        13. T   F

14. Variables should be identified clearly and placed in separate cells rather than within formulas.

        14. T   F

15. Template designs do not need to be tested because any errors will be located the first time it is used.

        15. T   F

Completion   IIIIIIII For each item below fill in the word (or words) that completes the statement or answers the question.

1. A spreadsheet model that includes titles, column labels, row labels, and formulas for a particular type of application is called a _____.

2. _____ statements that are created on a periodic basis should be created as template files.

3. Any spreadsheet that is used every month should be created as a

   _____.

4. Employees who use the same type of spreadsheets may _____ on the development of a template so that it meets the needs of everyone using it.

5. The purpose of a template is to save a spreadsheet _____ time and effort.

6. A template is used as a skeleton or _____ to create other spreadsheets.

7. The _____ command is used to keep users from entering or modifying certain cells on a template.

8. Titles and main headings usually begin in the upper _____ portion of the template.

9. Very short abbreviations (should/should not) _____ be used in templates.

10. A template should be designed so that most, if not all, of the spreadsheet can be

    _____ on the screen at one time.

11. Formulas at the end of a row or bottom of a column will _____ faster than if they precede the data used in the calculation.

12. If the formula +b3*b4-b5 is entered in B5, the message _____ will appear on the screen.

13. All circular references in templates should be _____.

14. Templates usually include titles, labels, and _____.

15. After a template has been created and saved, it should be _____.

16. List two types of spreadsheet applications that should be created as templates.

    a._____

    b._____

ACTIVITY 11.3   □   *Testing a Template*

In this activity you will test the template created in ACTIVITY 11-2.

1. Retrieve the file T-PROFIT.

2. Enter the following data based on May 199– (use the current year) automobile sales for Rod's Antique Car Shop.

   a. 1962 Chevrolet Corvette convertible; purchased for $3,500; spent $4,000 on repairs; sold it for $12,500

   b. 1959 Chevrolet Impala, 2-door; bought it for $500; put $4,575 worth of repairs in it; sold it for $8,000

   c. 1965 Ford Mustang; 2-door; paid $650 for it; spent $5,000 for repairs; and sold it for $10,500

   d. 1969 Chevrolet Camaro; 2 door; paid $300 for it; spent $3,500; sold it for $5,000

   e. 1977 Volkswagon Beetle convertible; purchased for $500; spent $2,200 for repairs; sold it for $3,800

3. Correct the format, column widths, and/or formulas if necessary.

4. Save the file as MAYPROF.

5. Print the file.

6. If you made any changes in the format, column widths, or formulas, delete the data entered in Step 2 in order to create a revised template.

7. Use the worksheet protection command to protect all labels and formulas from being entered. Unprotect the cells in which values would be entered.

8. Move the cell pointer to the first cell in which a value would be entered at a later time by a user of the template.

9. Save the template file as T-PROFIT.

10. Print the file only if you made corrections to it.

ACTIVITY 11.4   □   *Creating, Testing, and Using a Balance Sheet Template.*

In this activity, you will create a balance sheet template for a retail store. Then you will test it and use it to create a balance sheet.

At the end of each month, the accountant for Sea & Ski Center, a retail store, prepares a balance sheet. A balance sheet shows the assets, liabilities, and capital for the store. Assets include cash on hand, account receivables—money owed to the store by customers, and merchandise inventory—the merchandise in the store. Liabilities are debts that the store owes such as unpaid bills for ski equipment. Capital is calculated by subtracting total liabilities from total assets.

```
SEA & SKI CENTER
BALANCE SHEET
September 30, 1992
─────────────────────────

ASSETS
  Cash                          $4,312.00
  Accounts Receivable           $6,947.00
  Merchandise Inventory        $20,163.00
    Total Assets               $31,422.00
LIABILITIES
  Accounts Payable              $5,125.00
    Total Liabilities           $5,125.00

CAPITAL                        $26,297.00
```

Based on the format for the September Balance Sheet that is shown, create a template that can be used at the end of each month.

1. Use appropriate column widths and formats.

2. Enter only the labels and values that will stay the same each month. Enter any formulas that are needed.

3. Use worksheet protect and unprotect commands.

4. Save the template as TM-BAL.

5. Test the template using the figures for the September template.

6. Make any corrections necessary. Then delete the values entered in Step 5.

7. Move the cell pointer to the first cell that data will be entered.

8. Save the file as TM-BAL.

9. Create a balance sheet for October 31, 1992 using the template. Enter the following figures: Cash, $4,650.00; Accounts Receivable, $6,515.50; Merchandise Inventory, $18,250.25; and Accounts Payable $4,950.30.

10. Save the file as BALOCT.

CHAPTER 12

OBJECTIVES

- ❏ Create a macro
- ❏ Name a macro
- ❏ Document a macro
- ❏ Use a macro

WHAT IS A MACRO?

Creating spreadsheets often involves entering the same long sequences of commands, formulas, and labels over and over again. To eliminate entering repetitive keystrokes, you can create macros. A **macro** is a series of keystrokes that has been stored for later use. A two-keystroke command will invoke a set of macro instructions stored previously.

Macros can be created to save or print a spreadsheet, enter labels, or calculate formulas or an entire spreadsheet. Macros are designed to save time and effort. They should be used whenever you use the same keystrokes repeatedly or when keystrokes are difficult to remember.

HOW IS A MACRO CREATED?

The process of creating a macro involves four steps: (1) plan the macro, (2) create the macro, (3) name the macro, and (4) document the macro. In this section, each of these four steps will be described.

Plan the Macro

The process of planning a macro involves practicing manually the procedure the macro is to perform. While going through the process manually, write in the proper order every keystroke involved in the procedure. For example, the process for saving a spreadsheet involves the keystrokes shown in Figure 12.1.

Keystroke	Purpose
/	Access Command mode
f	Select File command
s	Select Save command

Figure 12.1 ❑ *Planning a Macro to Save a Spreadsheet*

After recording manually the sequence of keystrokes, you should translate the keystrokes into **macro language** (instructions). For command keystrokes, macro language uses the first character of the command; i.e., **f** for **F**ile, **s** for **S**ave, **p** for **P**rint, etc. Cursor and other function keys are entered within braces, { }, using special abbreviated names. These braces are sometimes called curly brackets. The macro language uses the tilde symbol, (~), to represent the Enter key. Examples of these types of macro keystrokes and their purposes follow.

COMMAND   KEY SEQUENCES

/fs~r   / File Save [Enter] Replace
/ppagq   / Print Printer Align Go Quit (to print a
                                 file with a print range identified
                                 previously)

LABELS

WEEKLY SUMMARY   To enter the label WEEKLY SUMMARY
ABC Corp.   To enter the label ABC Corp.

POINTER OR CURSOR KEYS

{Up}   {Down}   {Left}   {Right}

{Pgup}   {Pgdn}   {Tab}   {Home}

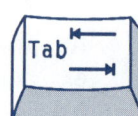

FUNCTION AND EDITING KEYS

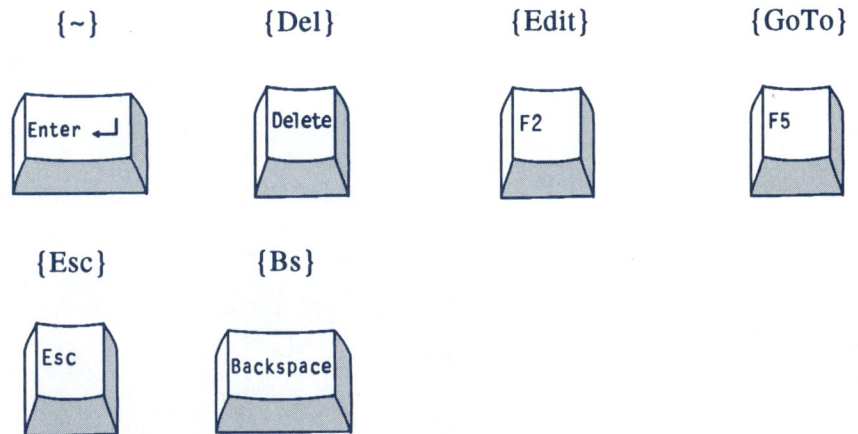

{~}   {Del}   {Edit}   {GoTo}

Enter ↵   Delete   F2   F5

{Esc}   {Bs}

Esc   Backspace

Consult your software instruction manual for a complete list of macro instructions.

Create the Macro

Macros should be located either below the data section or below and to the right of the data section of a spreadsheet. Locations are shown in Figure 12.2.

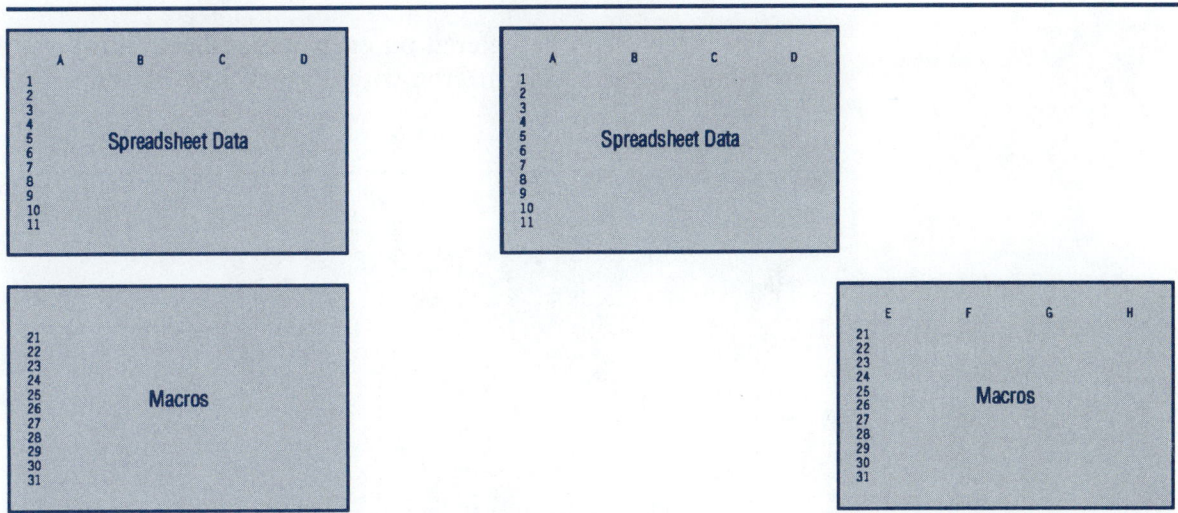

Figure 12.2 □ *Macro Locations*

The following rules should be followed when entering macros:

1. Any macro that does not begin with a label must be preceded with a label prefix—an apostrophe, ('); a quotation mark, ("); or a caret mark, (^). For example, the **File Save** command should be entered as **'/fs**. If you begin a macro with a /, 1-2-3 will change to the command mode immediately. All macros must be entered as labels.

2. A macro can be entered either in a horizontal row across a worksheet or in sections in a column as shown in Figure 12.3. An entire set of macro instructions can be stored in one cell, as long as it does not exceed the maximum amount of cell memory for your software. (The limit is 240-512 characters, depending on the version of software you are using). The macro works down the column, cell by cell, until it reaches a blank cell. The blank cell causes the macro to stop.

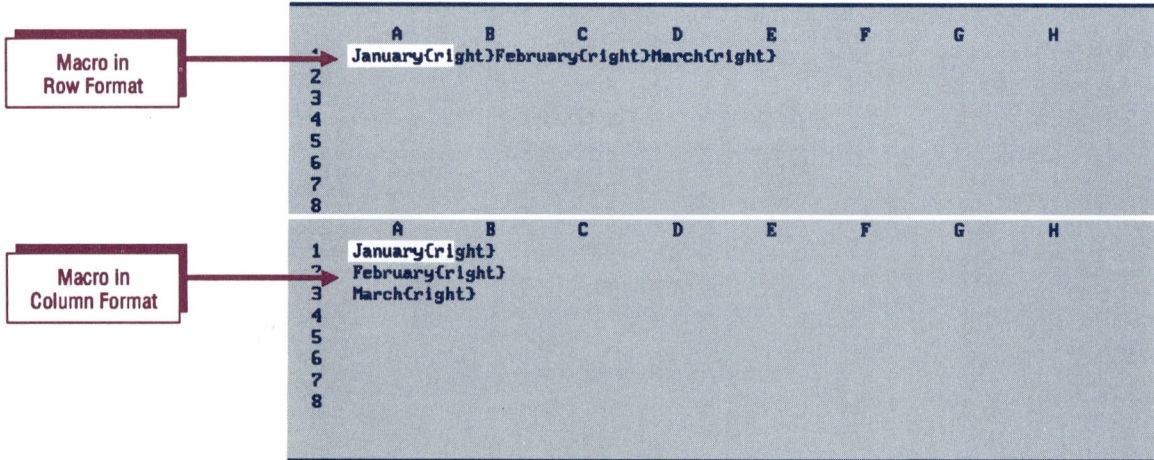

Figure 12.3 ▢ Macros in a Row Format and a Column Format

3. Many macros can be entered on each spreadsheet. However, you must separate the macros with a blank row as shown in Figure 12.4.

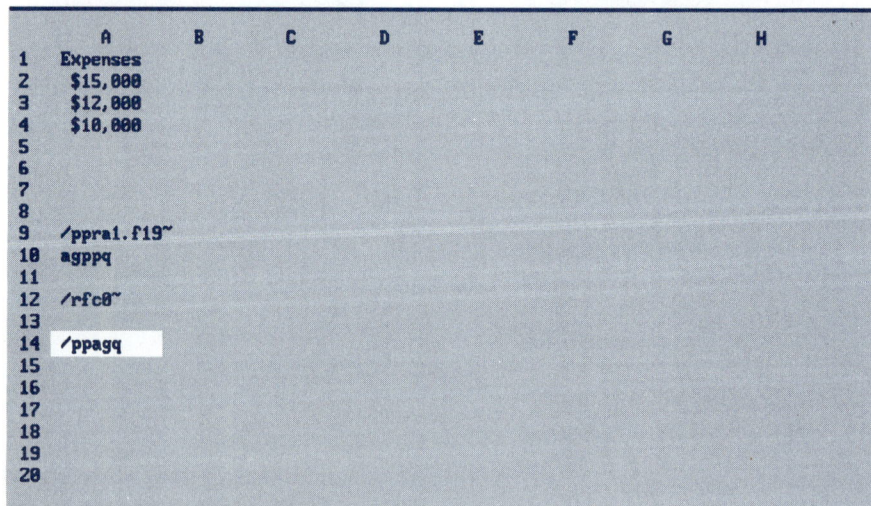

Figure 12.4 ▢ Macros Separated by Blank Rows

By following these rules, you can create macros that run properly and are placed in the same location consistently.

Name the Macro

Before you can use a macro, you must give it a name. A **macro name** consists of two characters. The first is the backslash, (\), and the second is a single letter, (a, b, c,. . . x, y, z). Use a character that relates to the macro task such as \s to save a file, \c to set currency format, or \o to enter the label Operating Expenses.

Plan all the macros you want to use and select appropriate names before you create them. This prevents giving two different macros the same name. For example, if a spreadsheet needs macros both to save a file and to sum a column of values, two different names should be given to these macros. One can be named \s, but the other should be given a different name.

To name a macro, use the **/ R**ange Name Create command. After entering this command, you will see the second line of the control panel displaying the following:

```
A45: '/ppagq                                              EDIT
Enter name:

      A      B      C      D      E      F      G      H
```

You will enter the name of the macro on the second line of the control panel. Remember: The macro name must begin with a backward slash, (\), and have only one letter following the slash. After entering the name, press the Enter key. Then, the second line of the screen will ask you to enter the range where the macro is to be located. In the following example, the name \p has been entered and the range identified as A45..A45.

```
A45: '/ppagq                                            POINT
Enter name: \p                    Enter range: A45..A45

      A      B      C      D      E      F      G      H
```

To save time and effort, move the cell pointer to the beginning cell in which the macro is located before using the **Range Name** command. Another timesaver is to identify the range by the first cell. There is no need to highlight the entire macro because the macro operates from the beginning cell until the next blank cell. For example, in Figure 12.4, only cell A9 would need to be highlighted when using the **Range Name** command.

Document the Macro

Documenting a macro means entering the macro name and a brief explanation of the purpose of the macro on the spreadsheet. Place the macro name consistently to the left or right of each macro. Enter an explanation of its use consistently to the left or right of the macro. Two systems for documenting macros are shown in Figure 12.5.

	A	B	C	D	E	F
25	Macro		Macro Name	Explanation		
26	=========	=========	=========	=========	=========	=========
27						
28	/fs~r		\s	Saves spreadsheet		
29						
30	/ppagq		\p	Prints spreadsheet		
31						
32						

	A	B	C	D	E	F
22	Name	Macro			Explanation	
23	=========	=========	=========	=========	=========	=========
24	\s	/reB5.D10~			Erase a range of cells--	
25					B5 through D10	
26						
27	\g	{goto}B5~			Move to cell B5	
28						
29						
30						

Figure 12.5 ☐ *Documenting a Macro*

HOW IS A MACRO INVOKED?

After creating and documenting a macro, invoke or execute it. To invoke a macro, hold down the Alt key and press the letter of the macro name. As shown in Figure 12.6, the macro /ppagq has been entered in a cell and named \p. To invoke this macro, you must hold down the Alt key and press the letter p. When you invoke this macro, Lotus 1-2-3 will automatically print the spreadsheet.

Macro to print spreadsheet

Hold down the **Alt** key and enter the letter **p** to invoke the macro

	A	B	C	D	E	F
25	Macro		Macro Name	Explanation		
26	=========	=========	=========	=========	=========	=========
27						
28	/ppagq		\p	Prints spreadsheet		
29						
30						
31						
32						
33						
34						
35						
36						
37						
38						
39						

Figure 12.6 ☐ *Invoking a Macro*

Remember when invoking a macro, you do not enter the backslash, (\). Enter only the letter of the macro name.

It is always important to save the cell pointer at a logical point, which is usually A1. However, before invoking a macro that enters labels or calculates formulas, move the cursor to the cell in which the first label is to be entered or to the cell in which the formula is to be used. As shown in Figure 12.7, to display in A16 the macro created in B25, you would move the cursor to A16 and then invoke the macro.

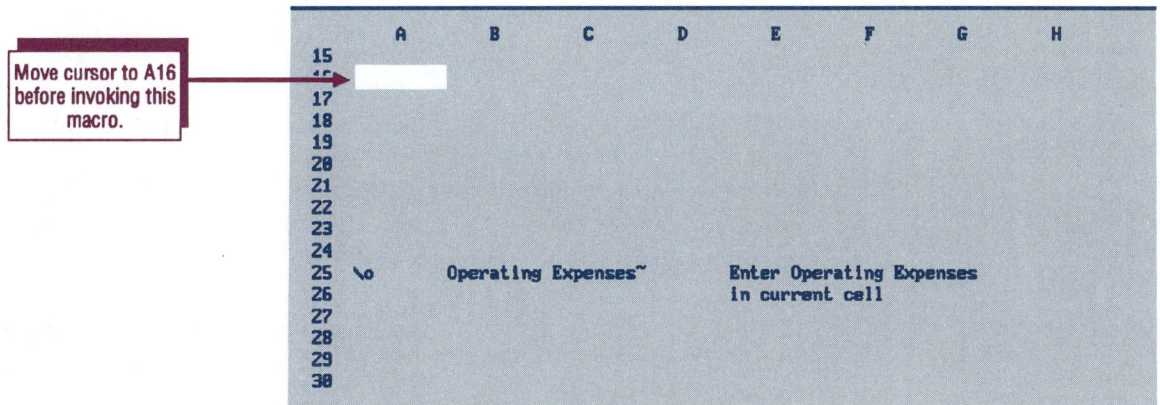

Figure 12.7 ◻ *Invoking a Label Macro*

After documenting and testing a macro by invoking it, the spreadsheet should be saved so the documentation is saved along with the macro itself.

CORRECTING A MACRO

If the macro stops, look at the error message on the screen or at the control panel to determine at what point the macro had trouble executing the commands. To exit the incomplete macro, press the Ctrl and Break keys simultaneously or the Esc key until you have exited from the macro commands.

Look at the macro to determine the error. The following errors are frequently made:

1. A tilde was omitted.
2. Parentheses, ( ), or brackets, [ ], were entered instead of braces, { }.
3. Macro steps were not preceded with an apostrophe.
4. The backslash, (\), was used instead of the forward slash, (/), at the beginning of the command.
5. The forward slash,(/), was used in the **R**ange **N**ame **C**reate command instead of the backslash, (\). If the backslash is not present, the macro will not execute at all.

Once the error has been located, use the F2 key to edit the macro. Once finished with editing, save the file containing the macro.

CREATING MACROS

In the tutorials and activities that follow, you will apply your skills to create command macros, label macros, and formula macros.

Creating Command Macros

In the following tutorial, you will plan, create, name, and invoke a macro to print a spreadsheet that has had a print range identified previously.

Retrieve the file named SALARY.

Plan for the creation of a macro that will print the spreadsheet. Since the print range has already been identified, do not include the **R**ange command in the procedure.

Begin by performing the procedure to print the spreadsheet and exit from the print commands. While performing this procedure, write each keystroke that you enter.

1. _____

2. _____

3. _____

4. _____

5. _____

6. _____

The keystrokes you wrote down should be the same as the ones that you will enter in the following tutorial instructions.

Move the cell pointer to A25, the cell that will contain the macro.

ENTER '/ppagq

PRESS ↵

You can correct any errors made while entering the macro by reentering the macro or by using the Edit key, F2, to delete or insert characters. Move the cell pointer to A25. To name the macro:

ENTER /

ENTER r (Range)

ENTER n (Name)

ENTER c (Create)

The control panel will display the following:

```
A25: '/ppagq                                              EDIT
Enter name:

          A       B       C       D       E       F       G       H
```

ENTER	\p
PRESS	↵

The control panel will display the following:

```
A25: '/ppagq                                                         POINT
Enter name: \p                              Enter range: A25..A25

        A        B        C        D        E        F        G        H
```

Since you moved the cell pointer to A25 before entering the **Range Name** command, the correct macro location, A25..A25, appears in the control panel. To accept this range:

PRESS	↵

Now, move the cell pointer to B25 and document the macro by entering the macro name and its purpose as follows:

ENTER	'\p
PRESS	↵

Move the cell pointer to C25 and enter the following explanation.

ENTER	To print the spreadsheet
PRESS	↵

To invoke the macro, make sure your printer is turned on and:

PRESS AND HOLD	Alt (Alt key)
PRESS	p

Watch the control panel as the macro keystrokes are automatically entered. The print range was not part of the macro since it had been identified previously and stored with the file.

To save the macro and the macro documentation under the same filename:

ENTER	/
ENTER	f (File)
ENTER	s (Save)
PRESS	↵
ENTER	r (Replace)

In the tutorial instructions that follow, you will create a second macro on the same spreadsheet. This macro will be used to save the file. If the SALARY file is not on your screen, retrieve that file before proceeding.

Move the cell pointer to A27, two rows below the other macro.

ENTER   '/fs~r
PRESS   ↵

With the cell pointer in A27:

ENTER   /
ENTER   r (Range)
ENTER   n (Name)
ENTER   c (Create)

The control panel will display the following:

```
A27: '/fs~r                                                              NAMES
Enter name:
\P
          A        B        C        D        E        F        G        H
```

Notice that the third line of the control panel displays the names of macros created previously.

ENTER   \s
PRESS   ↵

The control panel will display the following:

```
A27: '/fs~r                                                              POINT
Enter name: \s                          Enter range: A27..A27
          A        B        C        D        E        F        G        H
```

To accept that range:

PRESS   ↵

To document the macro, move the cell pointer to B27 and:

ENTER   '\s
PRESS   ↵

To enter an explanation of the macro, move the cell pointer to C27 and:

ENTER   To save the spreadsheet

PRESS   ↵

To separate the spreadsheet data from the macros, move the cell pointer to A24 and enter the following:

ENTER   MACRO

PRESS   →

ENTER   MACRO NAME

PRESS   →

ENTER   EXPLANATION

PRESS   ↵

To save the changes in the spreadsheet by invoking the \s macro:

*PRESS
AND
HOLD*   Alt (Alt key)

PRESS   s

Watch the control panel as the **File Save** commands are automatically executed.

Correcting Macros

If the macro does not work when you invoke it, you need to find the error(s) and correct it (them). Notice that when the macro stops working, the error message will show where the macro stopped functioning. This will indicate the first error in the macro. Another simple way to locate errors in short macros is to go through the procedure manually and press each keystroke that was entered in the macro.

ACTIVITY 12.1 □ *Creating, Naming, and Invoking Command Macros*

1. Retrieve the file ACT12-1.
2. Below the spreadsheet data, create a macro that saves the file under the same file-name.
3. Name the macro \s.
4. Use adjacent cells to document the macro. Include the macro name and an explanation of its purpose.
5. Change the % of Increase in the spreadsheet to 6 percent by entering .06.
6. Invoke the macro.
7. Create a macro to print the range A1.D13. Enter /ppra1.c13~agq as the macro.
8. Name the macro \p.
9. Document the macro.
10. Invoke the macro to print the spreadsheet.
11. Invoke the macro to save the file.

Label Macros

In the next tutorial, you will create, name, and execute a macro that displays labels across a row. The labels will be days of the week. Each day of the week, except Saturday, will be followed by the name of the macro instruction that represents the Right Arrow key. Saturday will be followed with the tilde symbol.

Retrieve the file named RECCTR.

Move the cell pointer to M30, the cell that will contain the macro. Remember, pressing the Tab key moves the cell pointer one screen to the right.

E N T E R	Sunday{right}Monday{right}Tuesday{right}Wednesday{right} Thursday{right}Friday{right}Saturday~
P R E S S	↵

Keep the cell pointer in M30. To name the macro:

E N T E R	/
E N T E R	r (Range)
E N T E R	n (Name)
E N T E R	c (Create)
E N T E R	\d
P R E S S	↵

To accept the range M30:

PRESS   ↵

To document the macro, move the cell pointer to J30.

ENTER   '\d
PRESS   ↵

Move the cell pointer to K30.

ENTER   Days of the Week
PRESS   ↵

Move the cell pointer to B6. To invoke the macro:

PRESS
AND
HOLD   Alt (Alt key)
PRESS   d

Move the cell pointer to B20. To invoke the macro:

PRESS
AND
HOLD   Alt (Alt key)
PRESS   d

The following instructions will show you how to create a macro that displays the various activities available at the Good Times Recreation Center.

Retrieve the file RECCTR if it is not on your screen.

In cell M33, enter the following:

ENTER   Swimming{down}Fun Run{down}Acrobatics{down}
Basketball{down}Volleyball~
PRESS   ↵

To name the macro:

ENTER   /
ENTER   r (Range)
ENTER   n (Name)

ENTER   c (Create)
ENTER   \a
PRESS   ⏎

To accept the range M33:

PRESS   ⏎

To document the macro, move the cell pointer to J33.

ENTER   '\a
PRESS   ⏎

Move the cell pointer to K33.

ENTER   List of Activities
PRESS   ⏎

Move the cell pointer to A7. To invoke the macro:

PRESS
AND
HOLD   Alt (Alt key)
PRESS   a

If the macro is not correct, edit and invoke it again.
   Now move the cell pointer to A21. To invoke the macro:

PRESS
AND
HOLD   Alt (Alt key)
PRESS   a

At this point, the spreadsheet template, RECCTR, can be stored until
the number of participants involved in each activity has been ob-
tained.

ENTER   /
ENTER   f (File)
ENTER   s (Save)
PRESS   ⏎
ENTER   r (Replace)

After creating macros, remember to test them by invoking them. If they execute successfully, save the file so it contains the macros and the spreadsheet data.

Macros Using Labels, Formulas, and Formats

In this tutorial, you will create a macro to enter the years 1989, 1990, and 1991 in the locations shown in Figure 12.8. You will also create a macro to calculate the totals and format them in Currency format with two decimal places.

```
A1: [W15] 'Centre High School Store                                          READY


           A              B              C              D              E
 1  Centre High School Store
 2  Sales for 1989-1991
 3
 4                        1989           1990           1991
 5  Food
 6      Candy bars        245.75         285.00         300.50
 7      Soft drinks       560.00         625.50         640.00
 8      Potato chips      125.25         110.00         105.00
 9  Totals
10
11
12  Supplies
13      Pencils           45.00          48.00          44.00
14      Notebooks         35.50          47.50          52.00
15      Paper             60.50          75.00          83.50
16  Totals
17
18
19  Clothing
20      T-shirts          475.00         525.00         395.00
```

Figure 12.8 □ Creating Several Macros for One Spreadsheet

Retrieve the file CENTRE.

Move the cell pointer to D28. To create the macro to display and center the years within each cell:

ENTER ^1989{right}^1990{right}^1991~

PRESS ↵

Keep the cell pointer in D28. To name the macro \y:

ENTER /

ENTER r (Range)

ENTER n (Name)

ENTER c (Create)

ENTER \y

PRESS ↵

To accept the range D28:

PRESS ⏎

To document the macro, move the cell pointer to A28.

ENTER '\y
PRESS →
ENTER Years
PRESS ⏎

Now, create a macro to calculate totals for each of the three types of merchandise sold in the store and format the totals in Currency with two decimal places. Begin by moving the cell pointer to D30.

ENTER '@sum({up}{up}{up}.{down}{down})~/rfc2~~
PRESS ⏎

To name the macro \s:

ENTER /
ENTER r (Range)
ENTER n (Name)
ENTER c (Create)
ENTER \s
PRESS ⏎

To accept the range D30:

PRESS ⏎

Move the cell pointer to A30. To document the macro:

ENTER '\s
PRESS →
ENTER Formula and Format
PRESS ⏎

Move the cell pointer to B4. To invoke the macro to display the years:

PRESS	
AND	
HOLD	Alt (Alt key)
PRESS	y

Move the cell pointer to B11. To invoke the macro:

PRESS	
AND	
HOLD	Alt (Alt key)
PRESS	y

Move the cell pointer to B18. To invoke the macro:

PRESS	
AND	
HOLD	Alt (Alt key)
PRESS	y

Move the cell pointer to B9. To invoke the @SUM and Currency format macro:

PRESS	
AND	
HOLD	Alt (Alt key)
PRESS	s

Move the cell pointer to C9. To invoke the macro:

PRESS	
AND	
HOLD	Alt (Alt key)
PRESS	s

Move the cell pointer to D9. To invoke the macro:

PRESS	
AND	
HOLD	Alt (Alt key)
PRESS	s

On your own, move the cell pointer to the other appropriate locations on the spreadsheet and invoke the same macro to calculate the totals.

To save the file:

ENTER /

ENTER f (File)

ENTER s (Save)

PRESS ↵

ENTER r (Replace)

Before erasing the spreadsheet from the screen, save the file that contains the macros.

ACTIVITY 12.2 □ Creating Label and Formula Macros

In this activity you will create macros that will enter the months of the year across a row of a spreadsheet and enter a formula to calculate the sum of a column.

1. Retrieve the file THEME.
2. Move the cell pointer to Q13. Enter:

   January{right}February{right}March{right}April{right}May{right}
   June{right}July{right}August{right}September{right}October{right}
   November{right}December~

3. Name the macro \m.
4. Document the macro by entering the name in O13 and a description in P13.
5. Move the cell pointer to Q15. Enter:

   '@sum({up}{up}{up}{up}.{down}{down}{down})~{right}

6. Name the macro \s.
7. Document the macro by entering the name in O15 and a description in P15.
8. Move the cell pointer to B5 and invoke the macro designed to display the months of the year.
9. Move the cell pointer to B10. Invoke the macro to calculate the total for the column. If the macro does not work, you need to find the error(s) in it. Notice that when the macro stops working, the error message will show where the macro stopped functioning. Correct the macro and invoke it again.
10. Continue invoking the \s macro to calculate all the other totals in row 10.
11. Save the file as THEME.
12. First, print the spreadsheet data range. Then, print the range that includes the macros and their descriptions.

CHAPTER 12 □ THEORY EXERCISES

True/False ‖‖‖‖‖‖‖ Each of the following statements is either True or False. Indicate your choice by circling **T** for a true statement or **F** for a false statement.

1. Macros are created to eliminate entering repetitive keystrokes.   1. T   F

2. A macro is a series of keystrokes that has been stored for later use.   2. T   F

3. A macro is more likely to be correct if the procedure it is to perform is practiced manually and every keystroke is written.   3. T   F

4. A macro to save a file should be entered as /wfs~r.   4. T   F

5. The Up cursor key is entered as (Up) in a macro.   5. T   F

6. The Enter key is indicated by a tilde symbol in a macro.   6. T   F

7. Macros should be placed above the data section in a spreadsheet so they can be seen.   7. T   F

8. Any macro that does not begin with a label must be preceded with an apostrophe, a quotation mark, or a caret.   8. T   F

9. An entire set of macro instructions can be stored in one cell, as long as it does not exceed the maximum amount of cell memory for the software.   9. T   F

10. When you enter several macros on a spreadsheet, separate the macros with a blank row between them.   10. T   F

11. A macro name consists of one character.   11. T   F

12. To name a macro, use the command **/ Range Name Create**.   12. T   F

13. Documenting a macro means entering the macro name and a brief explanation of its purpose.   13. T   F

14. To invoke a macro, hold down the Ctrl key and press the letter of the macro name.   14. T   F

15. Before invoking a macro that enters labels in cells, move the cell pointer to the cell in which the first label is to be entered.   15. T   F

16. An acceptable name for a macro listing the months of the year is \mth.   16. T   F

Completion ||||||||| For each item below fill in the word (or words) that completes the statement or answers the question.

1. As a macro, the \ **F**ile **S**ave **R**eplace command would be entered as

   _____.

2. Macros are used to eliminate entering _____ keystrokes.

3. One rule for planning a macro is to perform the procedure _____ and write each keystroke involved.

4. Macros should be positioned _____ the data section or below and to the right of the data section of a spreadsheet.

5. The _____ symbol is used in macro language to represent the Enter key.

6. When entering the macro /ppagq, an apostrophe, a _____ mark, or a _____ mark must precede it.

7. A macro can be entered in a single cell or in a _____.

8. When two macros are entered on a spreadsheet, they must be separated by a

   _____ _____.

9. To enter and center the labels 1990, 1991, and 1992 in adjacent cells in a row, you should enter the macro as _____.

10. To name a macro, use the _____ command.

11. To document a macro named \o, you should enter the macro name as _____.

12. To invoke a macro named \t, hold down the _____ key and press _____.

13. To invoke a macro containing labels, move the cell pointer to the cell in which the first _____ is to be entered.

ACTIVITY 12.3 ▢ *Creating and Invoking Macros*

In this activity, you will plan and create a spreadsheet like the one shown. You will create macros to display the labels January, February, March, and Totals, and the labels, Sun Valley, Keystone, and Vail, and to calculate the total attendance for each ski resort for the first three months of 1990 and 1991. You will also create a macro to print the data in the spreadsheet.

	A	B	C	D	E	F	G
1	HIGH COUNTRY SKI SLOPES						
2	Attendance Figures (in thousands)						
3							
4	1990						
5		January	February	March	Totals		
6	Sun Valley	42	77	64	183		
7	Keystone	55	52	64	171		
8	Vail	64	58	69	191		
9							
10							
11							
12	HIGH COUNTRY SKI SLOPES						
13	Attendance Figures (in thousands)						
14							
15	1991						
16		January	February	March	Totals		
17	Sun Valley	43	75	63	181		
18	Keystone	57	53	67	177		
19	Vail	65	68	72	205		
20							

Part I Planning the Macros

1. Plan a macro that will right align the labels January, February, March, and Totals in consecutive cells in a row. Write the keystrokes that need to be included in this macro.

   _____

2. Select an appropriate name for the macro described in Step 1. _____

3. Plan a macro that will enter the resort names in consecutive cells down a column.

   _____

   _____

4. Select an appropriate name for the macro described in Step 3. _____

5. Plan a macro that will use a @SUM formula to calculate the total attendance for January-March for each ski slope. Plan this macro by going through the procedure manually and writing down each character and/or keystroke entered.

_____

_____

_____

6. Select an appropriate name for the macro described in Step 5. _____

7. Plan a macro that will print the data but not the macros in the spreadsheet. In the macro, enter the appropriate range to be printed. Use capital letters for the letters in the cell addresses. Also include the command to exit from the print menu. Plan this macro by going through the print procedure manually and writing each character and/or keystroke entered.

_____

_____

8. Select an appropriate name for the macro described in Step 7. _____

Part II Creating the Macros

1. In I24, create a macro to right align the labels January, February, March, and Totals in consecutive cells in a row.
2. Name and document the macro.
3. In I26, create a macro to enter the resort names in consecutive cells down a column.
4. Name and document the macro.
5. In I28, create a macro containing a @SUM formula that will calculate the total attendance for January-March for each ski slope.
6. Name and document the macro.
7. In I30, create a macro to print the spreadsheet.
8. Name and document the macro.

Part III Creating the Spreadsheet

1. Begin creating the spreadsheet by entering the titles shown in A1, A2, A12, and A13.
2. Enter 1990 in A4 and 1991 in A15.
3. In B5, invoke the macro to enter January, February, March, and Totals.

4. In A6, invoke the macro to enter the resort names.

5. Enter the values shown.

6. In E6, E7, and E8, invoke the macro to calculate the column totals.

7. Continue using the macros to create the rest of the spreadsheet that shows the 1991 figures. Enter the values manually.

8. Save the file as ACT12-3.

9. Invoke the macro to print the spreadsheet data.

10. Print only the macros and the documentation for them.

CYCLE 3
Graphics Tutorials and Exercises

CHAPTER 13

Creating Graphs and Bar Charts

OBJECTIVES

- ☐ Select a graph type
- ☐ Create a bar chart
- ☐ Select the X axis labels
- ☐ Select data ranges
- ☐ View a graph
- ☐ Enter titles and legends
- ☐ Name a graph
- ☐ Save a graph
- ☐ Print a graph

WHAT IS A GRAPH?

A **graph** shows numeric information in picture form. The most common graphs are bar charts, line graphs, pie charts, and xy graphs. Each of these graphs may have several variations. Bar charts, for example, may be single, multiple, or stacked.

WHY ARE GRAPHS IMPORTANT?

Graphs have a visual impact that long columns and rows of numbers in a spreadsheet do not always have. While written reports may contain very complete and complex information that cannot be replaced by graphs, that information can be effectively supplemented with graphs.

Graphs are important because they enable people to understand information quickly and easily. They can be used effectively to compare and analyze numeric data. Graphs express data in a form that is eye-catching, interesting, and often more understandable than text.

WHAT ARE THE MAIN ELEMENTS OF GRAPHS?

All graphs, except pie charts, have at least two main elements—the vertical or Y-axis and the horizontal or X-axis as shown in Figure 13.1. Other elements that may be included are first titles or main headings, second titles or secondary headings, X-axis titles, Y-axis titles, legends, and labels.

ABC CORPORATION
Gross Sales

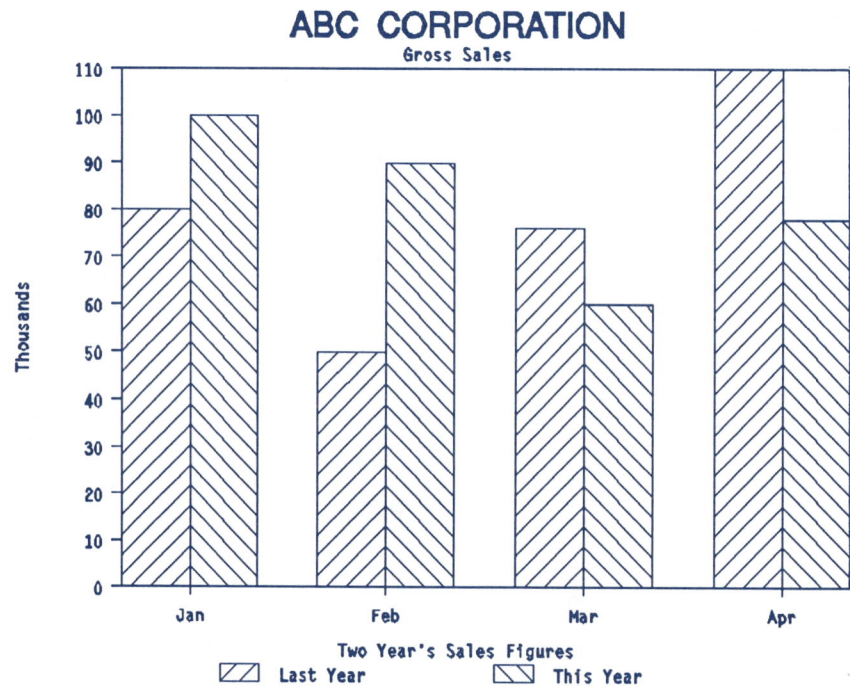

Figure 13.1 ☐ *Elements of Graphs*

A **first** title is an overall description of the graph. A **second** title is a brief description or explanation of the data in the graph. The first title in Figure 13.1 is *ABC CORPORATION* and the second title is *Gross Sales*.

X-axis and Y-axis titles can also be included on a graph. *Two Year's Sales Figures* is the X-axis title in Figure 13.1 and *Thousands* is the Y-axis title. The Y-axis title *Thousands* indicates that all of the numbers are expressed as thousands.

X-axis labels identify the points or bars in a graph or the pieces in a pie chart. They can be either name or value labels. In Figure 13.1, months of the year are used as X-axis labels. By default, 1-2-3 creates graphs with the X-axis appearing across the bottom of the graph.

Crosshatching is the pattern of diagonal lines shown in a bar or piece of a pie chart to distinguish one bar or pie piece from another. Crosshatching is done automatically by the software.

Legends include information to describe what each line or type of crosshatching represents. In Figure 13.1, the legends show the type of crosshatching used for the two different sets of data.

Each set of numeric values used in a graph is called a **data series.** These series are identified as series A, B, C, D, E, or F. Only six series of values can be entered on a 1-2-3 graph. Figure 13.2 shows the two data series, *A* and *B*, used to create the bar chart shown in Figure 13.1.

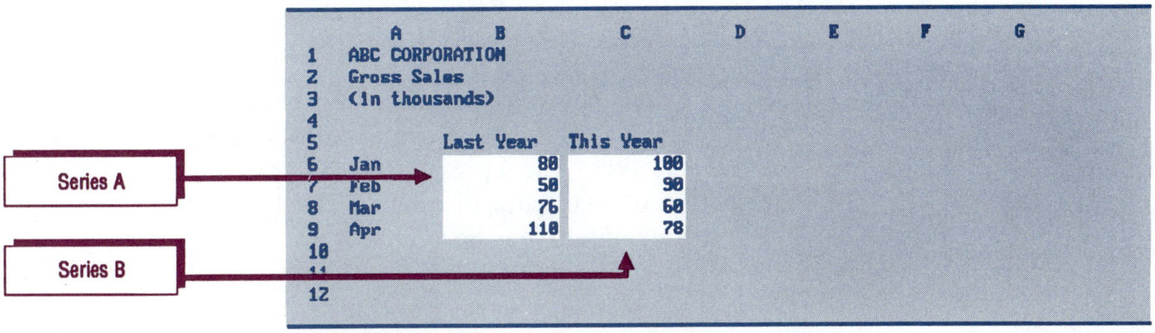

Figure 13.2 □ *Data Series Used to Create Bar Chart*

GRAPH TYPES AND USES

You should select the type of graph based on the type of data to be depicted. The following paragraphs provide a brief description of each type of graph that can be created with 1-2-3.

1. A **bar chart** uses rectangles or bars to represent a set of numbers. A simple bar chart uses only one series of numbers. It can have no more than six sets of values depicted. The most common type of bar chart, the vertical bar chart, has bars beginning on the horizontal or X-axis and has labels under each bar.

   Bar charts are used to show information over a period of time, such as changes in inventory or in sales over several years. Generally, bar charts should not be used to represent percentages or parts of a whole.

2. **Multiple bar charts** show the same information as simple bar charts but use several series or sets of data.

3. A **stacked bar chart** shows the cumulative effect of several sets of data. Each bar is divided into two or more parts and represents more than one numeric value.

4. A **line graph** represents a set of numeric values as vertical distances connected by a line. Each numeric value is represented by a dot or a symbol on the line. Line graphs are often used to depict changes in data over a period of time.

5. A **multiple line graph** represents several sets of data on the same chart. Each line is of a different type—single, double,

broken, or dotted. Multiple line graphs are used to track measurements for several sets of data.

6. A **pie chart** is used to compare values that represent parts of a whole. The whole amount is illustrated as a circle with each slice representing one of the values. Only one data set can be represented by a pie chart.

7. An **xy graph** shows the relationship between two sets of data by displaying numeric values on both the vertical and horizontal axes. The xy graph allows the user to plot the intersection of two pairs of values. The intersections are represented by symbols on the graph.

CREATE A BAR CHART

In this tutorial, you will create a bar chart showing attendance figures at a ski resort. You will use data from a spreadsheet created in a previous chapter.

Retrieve the file ACT12-3.

To create a bar chart:

PRESS /

PRESS g (Graph)

If you are using Version 2.1, the second and third lines of the control panel will display:

```
A1:                                                              MENU
Type  X  A  B  C  D  E  F  Reset  View  Save  Options  Name  Quit
Set graph type
```

If you are using a newer version of 1-2-3, the second and third lines of the control panel will display:

```
A1:                                                              MENU
Type  X  A  B  C  D  E  F  Reset  View  Save  Options  Name  Group  Quit
Line  Bar  XY  Stack-Bar  Pie
```

To select the type of graph you will create:

PRESS t (Type)

The second and third lines of the control panel will display the following:

```
A1:                                                          MENU
Line  Bar  XY  Stack-Bar  Pie
Line graph
```

To select a bar graph:

PRESS   b (bar)

The second and third lines of the control panel will display the following:

```
A1:                                                          MENU
Type  X  A  B  C  D  E  F  Reset  View  Save  Options  Name  Group  Quit
Line  Bar  XY  Stack-Bar  Pie
```

To select the labels that will be displayed on the X-axis:

PRESS   x

The second line of the control panel will display the following:

```
A1:                                                          POINT
Enter x-axis range: A1
```

The range displayed in the control panel will be the present location of the cell pointer. Therefore, a cell address other than A1 may appear if you have moved the cell pointer.

    To select the X-axis range, including January, February, and March, move the cell pointer to B5 and:

PRESS   . (Period)
PRESS   → (2 times)
PRESS   ↵

Do not include the label Totals in the X-axis range.

Select X-Axis Data Ranges

    Since only one series of data will be graphed, only the first data range, range A, will be selected. To indicate the data you want to display,

PRESS   a

The second line of the control panel will display the following:

```
A1:                                                                    POINT
Enter first data range: A1
```

The range shown in the control panel is the present location of the cell pointer.

Move the cell pointer to B6.

PRESS . (Period)

PRESS → (2 times)

PRESS ↵

View a Graph

At any point while creating a graph, you can view it. To view the graph:

PRESS v (View)

To return to the graphing menu:

PRESS Esc (Esc key or Enter key to return to the graphing menu)

Create Titles

As you may have noticed, the graph did not include any titles to describe the data. To add titles:

PRESS o (Options)

The second and third lines of the control panel will display the following:

```
A1:                                                                    MENU
Legend  Format  Titles  Grid  Scale  Color  B&W  Data-Labels  Quit
Create legends for data ranges
```

To select titles from this menu:

PRESS t (Titles)

The second and third lines of the control panel will display the following:

```
A1:                                                            MENU
First  Second  X-Axis  Y-Axis
Assign first line of graph title
```

PRESS   f (First)

The control panel will prompt you to enter a title.

ENTER   High Country Ski Slopes
PRESS   ↵

To enter a second title:

PRESS   t (Titles)
PRESS   s (Second)
ENTER   Attendance Figures
PRESS   ↵
PRESS   q (Quit)

To view the graph that you created:

PRESS   v (View)

To return to the graph menu:

PRESS   Esc

Create X-axis Titles

To add the title Sun Valley on the horizontal axis:

PRESS   o (Options)
PRESS   t (Titles)
PRESS   x (X-axis)
ENTER   Sun Valley
PRESS   ↵

Create Y-Axis Titles

To add the title In Thousands on the vertical axis:

PRESS   t (Titles)

PRESS   y (Y-axis)

ENTER   (in thousands)

PRESS   ↵

PRESS   q (Quit)

To view the graph:

PRESS   v (View)

To escape from the graphing menus:

PRESS   Esc (3 times)

Name a Graph

It is very important to name a graph so that 1-2-3 can remember the graph settings. Naming a graph stores the graph settings with the current spreadsheet file. After naming a graph, you can develop a new graph from the same spreadsheet and still have the specifications for the first graph stored to view and modify at a later time.

With the graph menu on the screen, name the graph using the following instructions:

PRESS   /

PRESS   g (Graph)

PRESS   n (Name)

PRESS   c (Create)

ENTER   bar1

PRESS   ↵

If you want to retrieve a named graph into the current file and display it on the screen at a later time, you would use the **/ Graph Name Use** command.

Save a Graph for Printing

The **/ Graph Save** command saves a picture of the graph on disk so that it can be printed. Use the same filename used to name the graph. The filename extension will end with .PIC to indicate that it is a pictorial file, not a spreadsheet file.

To save the graph on disk for printing at a later time:

PRESS s (Save)

ENTER bar1

PRESS ↵

PRESS Esc (2 times)

The selections used to make the graph should also be stored with the spreadsheet file ACT12-3. If you save a spreadsheet with **/ File Save**, 1-2-3 stores the graph settings, too. At a later time, you can redraw the graph by retrieving the file and pressing the F10 (Graph) key. To save the graph settings made previously:

PRESS /

PRESS f (File)

PRESS s (Save)

PRESS ↵

PRESS r (Replace)

View a List of Graph Files

To view a list of graph files that have been stored:

PRESS /

PRESS f (File)

PRESS l (List)

PRESS g (Graph)

A list of the graph files with .PIC extensions should appear. At this point, only the BAR1 file should be listed. To escape from this list:

PRESS Esc (5 times)

Use the Graph Key to View a Graph

To view the graph you have been working with, use the Graph key.

PRESS F10

To return to the spreadsheet that the graph is associated with:

PRESS Esc

Reset Graph Commands

The **/ Graph Reset Graph** command cancels all graph settings currently in effect. However, it does not affect settings stored under a graph name nor does it delete a saved graph.

To reset graph commands:

PRESS   /

PRESS   g (Graph)

PRESS   r (Reset)

PRESS   g (Graph)

PRESS   q (Quit)

This command is useful when creating a second or third graph using the same spreadsheet data.

ACTIVITY 13.1 ☐ *Creating a Simple Bar Chart*

In this activity you will create a simple bar chart using a spreadsheet created in the previous chapter. You will chart the changes in sales of candy bars from 1989 through 1991.

1. Retrieve the file CENTRE.
2. Choose the type of graph you will create—a bar chart.
3. Select the X-axis labels—1989, 1990, and 1991. They are located in B4 through D4.
4. Select the series A data range, representing candy bar sales in 1989, 1990, and 1991—B6 through D6.
5. Enter a first-line title—Centre High School Store.
6. Enter a second-line title—Sales for 1989-1991.
7. Enter an X-axis title—Candy Bars.
8. Enter a Y-axis title—(in dollars).
9. View the graph. If needed, make any corrections by reentering titles or data ranges.
10. Name the graph CANDY.
11. Save the graph under the same name, CANDY.
12. Save and replace the spreadsheet file under the same name, CENTRE.

CREATE A MULTIPLE BAR CHART

In this tutorial you will create a multiple bar chart using three series of data.

Retrieve the file KRAUSE. To create a multiple bar chart:

PRESS /
PRESS g (Graph)
PRESS t (Type)
PRESS b (Bar)

To select the labels that will be displayed on the X-axis:

PRESS x

To select the X-axis range, move the cell pointer to B4 and:

PRESS . (Period)
PRESS → (3 times)
PRESS ↵

To indicate the first data series you want to display:

PRESS a

Move the cell pointer to B6.

PRESS . (Period)
PRESS → (3 times)
PRESS ↵

To indicate the second data series you want to display:

PRESS b

Move the cell pointer to B7.

PRESS . (Period)
PRESS → (3 times)
PRESS ↵

To indicate the third data series you want to display:

PRESS c

Move the cell pointer to B8.

PRESS . (Period)
PRESS → (3 times)
PRESS ↵

To add titles to the graph:

PRESS o (Options)
PRESS t (Titles)
PRESS f (First)
ENTER Krause Manufacturing
PRESS ↵

To enter a second title:

PRESS t (Titles)
PRESS s (Second)
ENTER Quarterly Sales for Three Product Lines
PRESS ↵

To add a title on the vertical axis:

PRESS t (Titles)
PRESS y (Y-axis)
ENTER Net Sales
PRESS ↵

To create legends for the A range data:

PRESS l (Legend)
PRESS a (Range A)

The second line of the control panel will display the following:

```
A1: [W18] 'Krause Manufacturing                                    EDIT
Enter legend for first data range:
```

ENTER   Automotive

PRESS   ↵

To create a legend for the B range data:

PRESS   l (Legend)

PRESS   b (Range B)

ENTER   Electrical

PRESS   ↵

To create a legend for the C range data:

PRESS   l (Legend)

PRESS   c (Range C)

ENTER   Engineering

PRESS   ↵

PRESS   q (Quit)

To view the graph:

PRESS   v (View)

To return to the graphing menu:

PRESS   Esc

To name the graph:

PRESS   n (Name)

PRESS   c (Create)

ENTER   bar2

PRESS   ↵

To save the graph for printing at a later time:

PRESS   s (Save)

PRESS   bar2

PRESS   ↵

PRESS   Esc (2 times)

The selections used to make the graph should also be stored with the spreadsheet file KRAUSE. To save these selections:

PRESS /

PRESS f (File)

PRESS s (Save)

PRESS ↵

PRESS r (Replace)

To view a list of graph files that have been stored:

PRESS /

PRESS f (File)

PRESS l (List)

PRESS g (Graph)

Verify that BAR2.PIC appears on the list. If it does not, repeat the Graph Save sequence and list the graph files again.

PRESS Esc (5 times)

Later in this chapter you will print the file BAR2.PIC.

ACTIVITY 13.2 ☐ *Creating a Multiple Bar Chart*

In this activity, you will create a multiple bar chart using the spreadsheet created in the previous chapter. In this activity, you will chart the changes in sales of pencils, notebooks, and paper over a three-year period.

1. Retrieve the file CENTRE.
2. Before creating this graph, enter the command **/ Graph Reset Graph** in order to remove the previous graph settings.
3. Choose the type of graph you will create—a bar chart.
4. Select the X-axis labels located in B11 through D11.
5. Select the first data range—range A located in B13 through D13. This range shows the pencil sales for 1989-1991.
6. Select the second data range—range B located in B14 through D14. This range shows the notebook sales for 1989-1991.
7. Select the third data range—range C located in B15 through D15. This range shows the paper sales for 1989-1991.

8. Enter a first line title—Supplies Sold.

9. Enter a second line title—1989-1991.

10. Enter a legend for the series A data—Pencils.

11. Enter a legend for the series B data—Notebooks.

12. Enter a legend for the series C data—Paper.

13. Enter a Y-axis title—(in dollars).

14. Name the graph SUPPLIES.

15. Save the graph under the same name SUPPLIES.

16. Save the file as CENTRE.

PRINT A GRAPH

In this tutorial, you will learn how to print a graph. Several steps are necessary to print a graph. You must select *PrintGraph* from the 1-2-3 main menu, choose the name of the graph to be printed, and send the graph image to the printer.

To access the Printgraph Menu:

PRESS /

PRESS q (Quit)

PRESS y (Yes)

The Lotus Access System menu will appear on the screen as shown in Figure 13.3.

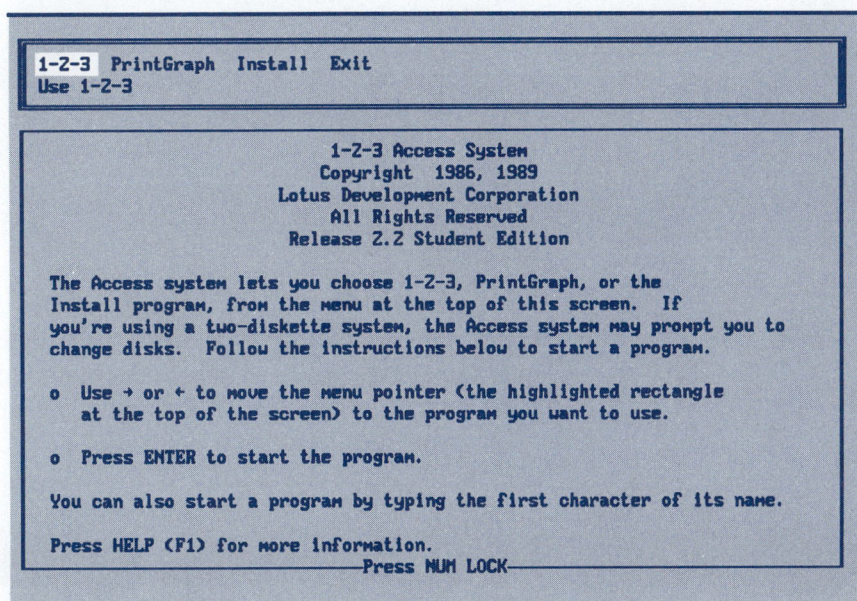

```
1-2-3  PrintGraph  Install  Exit
Use 1-2-3

            1-2-3 Access System
            Copyright  1986, 1989
          Lotus Development Corporation
             All Rights Reserved
          Release 2.2 Student Edition

  The Access system lets you choose 1-2-3, PrintGraph, or the
  Install program, from the menu at the top of this screen.  If
  you're using a two-diskette system, the Access system may prompt you to
  change disks.  Follow the instructions below to start a program.

  o  Use → or ← to move the menu pointer (the highlighted rectangle
     at the top of the screen) to the program you want to use.

  o  Press ENTER to start the program.

  You can also start a program by typing the first character of its name.

  Press HELP (F1) for more information.
                 ─Press NUM LOCK─
```

Figure 13.3 ☐ Lotus Access System Menu

P R E S S   p (Printgraph)

If you are using a release of 1-2-3 that requires the System Disk to be in Drive A, a prompt will appear on the screen to remove the Lotus 1-2-3 System disk and to insert the Lotus 1-2-3 PrintGraph Disk in Drive A. When you press the Enter key, the Printgraph program will load.

If you are using 1-2-3 on a hard disk system, the Printgraph screen will be displayed as shown in Figure 13.4. The third line of the screen displays the Printgraph Menu. Below the menu, the default settings for graphs are displayed.

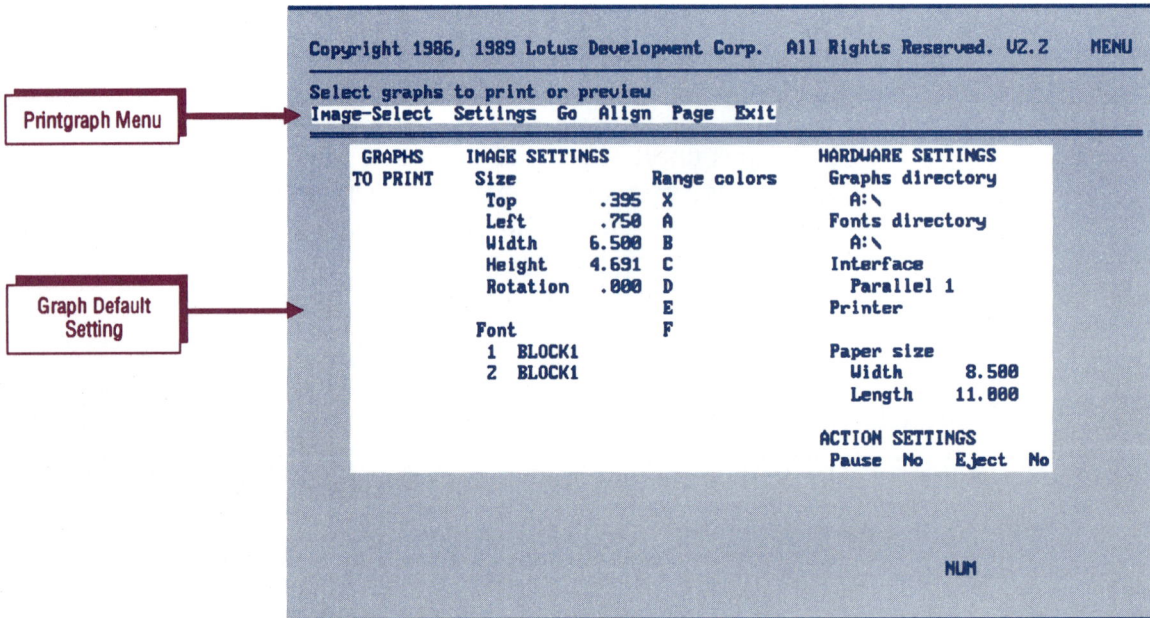

```
Copyright 1986, 1989 Lotus Development Corp.  All Rights Reserved. V2.2    MENU

Select graphs to print or preview
Image-Select  Settings  Go  Align  Page  Exit

     GRAPHS     IMAGE SETTINGS                    HARDWARE SETTINGS
     TO PRINT   Size              Range colors    Graphs directory
                Top       .395    X                 A:\
                Left      .750    A               Fonts directory
                Width    6.500    B                 A:\
                Height   4.691    C               Interface
                Rotation  .000    D                 Parallel 1
                                  E               Printer
                Font              F
                1  BLOCK1                         Paper size
                2  BLOCK1                           Width      8.500
                                                    Length    11.000

                                                 ACTION SETTINGS
                                                 Pause  No    Eject  No



                                                                        NUM
```

Printgraph Menu

Graph Default Setting

Figure 13.4 ❏ *Printgraph Screen*

To print a graph:

P R E S S   i (Image-select)

The screen that appears will list the names of all the graphs created. Whenever several graph filenames are listed, use the cursor arrow keys, the Home key, and the End keys to move the highlighting bar to the appropriate graph filename before pressing the Spacebar.

To print the first graph you created, use the arrow keys to highlight the name BAR1 if it is not already highlighted.

P R E S S   Spacebar

Pressing the Spacebar causes a pound sign, (#), to appear in front of the graph name and marks it to be printed. If you have incorrectly marked a name, the # sign can be removed by pressing the Spacebar a second time. Several graphs can be selected for printing by marking each of the graph names with the # sign.

With the # sign in front of the BAR1 name:

PRESS F10 (Graph key)

The graph will appear on the screen as it will be printed. After viewing the graph:

PRESS Esc (2 times)

To print the graph:

PRESS a (Align)
PRESS g (Go)

To exit the Printgraph Menu and return to the spreadsheet:

PRESS e (Exit)
PRESS y (Yes)
PRESS 1 (1-2-3)

If you are using a release of 1-2-3 that requires the System Disk to be in Drive A, a prompt will appear on the screen to remove the PrintGraph Disk and to insert the System Disk in Drive A. Only then can you continue to create spreadsheets or graphs.

ACTIVITY 13.3 ❑ *Printing Graphs*

In this activity, you will print the graphs created in ACTIVITIES 13-1 and 13-2. You will print the two graphs named CANDY and SUPPLIES.

1. Load 1-2-3 and access the Printgraph Menu.
2. Select the graphs to be printed—CANDY.PIC and SUPPLIES.PIC.
3. Print both graphs.

C H A P T E R   1 3 □ T H E O R Y   E X E R C I S E S

True/False ||||||||| Each of the following statements is either True or False. Indicate your choice by circling **T** for a true statement or **F** for a false statement.

1. The X-axis is the horizontal axis at the bottom of a graph based on 1-2-3 default settings.   1. T   F

2. The main heading on a graph is called the first title.   2. T   F

3. A second title is a brief description of the data in the graph that appears at the bottom of the graph.   3. T   F

4. X-axis titles are the same as X-axis labels.   4. T   F

5. Y-axis titles appear next to the vertical axis at the left side of the graph.   5. T   F

6. Crosshatching is the pattern of diagonal lines shown in a bar or piece of a pie chart to distinguish one bar or pie piece from another.   6. T   F

7. Legends are used to describe what each line or type of cross-hatching represents.   7. T   F

8. Each data series is identified as either series 1, 2, 3, 4, 5, or 6.   8. T   F

9. A bar chart can have six sets of values depicted.   9. T   F

10. A pie chart is used to depict changes in data over a period of time.   10. T   F

11. A line graph is used to compare values that represent parts of a whole.   11. T   F

12. The Graph key is the F10 key.   12. T   F

13. The initial command to create titles is **/ Graph Options Titles**.   13. T   F

14. The command to view a graph is **/ Graph View**.   14. T   F

15. To view and work with a named graph, use the command **/ Graph Name Use**.   15. T   F

16. To save a picture of a graph on disk so that it can be printed, use the command **/ Graph Name Create**.   16. T   F

17. The command **/ File Save** stores the spreadsheet and the graph settings too.   17. T   F

18. To print a graph, you must access the Printgraph Menu and then select the **Image-Select** command.   18. T   F

19. To mark a filename for printing, press the Spacebar.   19. T   F

20. Several file names can be marked at the same time with a # sign to indicate all of those files will be printed.   20. T   F

Completion IIIIIIIII For each item below fill in the word (or words) that completes the statement or answers the question.

1. The vertical axis is called the _____.

2. The horizontal axis is called the _____.

3. An overall description of a graph that is displayed at the top of the graph is called a _____ title.

4. The pattern of diagonal lines shown in a bar or piece of a pie chart to distinguish one bar or pie piece from another is called _____.

5. A label used to describe what a type of crosshatching represents is called a _____.

6. The command to select the type of graph to be created is / Graph _____.

7. The command to view a current graph is / Graph _____.

8. The command to create an X-axis title is

_____.

9. The key used to view a graph is the _____ key.

10. The same graph name should be used when naming and _____ a graph.

11. To save graph settings with the spreadsheet file, use the command

_____.

12. The file extension added to a graph filename is _____.

13. To mark a filename for printing, press the _____.

14. To remove the # sign from a filename marked for printing, press the

_____.

ACTIVITY 13.4　□　*Creating, Saving, and Printing a Bar Chart*

In this activity, you will retrieve the file ACT13-4 and create a multiple bar chart on your own using the data in the spreadsheet.

1. Retrieve the file ACT13-4.
2. Create a bar chart. Select appropriate first and second titles and a Y-axis title. Include X-axis labels and legends for the three series of data shown in the spreadsheet.
3. Name and save the graph under the name COLLEGE.
4. Save the file ACT13-4.
5. Print the graph.

CHAPTER 14

Creating Stacked-Bar Charts and Line Graphs

OBJECTIVES

- ☐ Create stacked bar charts
- ☐ Create single line graphs
- ☐ Create multiple line graphs
- ☐ Change the scale
- ☐ Use grids
- ☐ Use data labels

WHAT IS A STACKED BAR CHART?

A **stacked bar chart** shows the cumulative effect of several sets of data. Each bar is divided into two or more related parts. The data depicted in each bar represents more than one numeric value. Different types of crosshatching are used to represent the various sections within each bar. Since crosshatching is used, legends are needed to explain what each section of a bar represents.

The stacked bar chart shown in Figure 14.1 shows the sales of sporting goods over four seasons. This type of graph is useful to compare sales for two seasons. However, a stacked bar chart is not as useful if you want to compare baseball sales in the spring and fall. If you wanted to make such a comparison, a multiple bar chart or line graph would be more useful.

Before using a stacked bar chart, consider the type of data being depicted and the types of comparisons you wish to make. Each item within a stacked bar must be related to the other items in the bar.

WHAT IS A LINE GRAPH?

A **line graph** is used to show trends or cycles over a period of time. A line graph shows a set of numeric values as vertical distances connected by a line. This type of graph is extremely effective in illustrating trends or making comparisons over a period of time such as for costs, budgets, sales, and distribution information.

SPORTING GOODS SALES
SEASONAL TRENDS

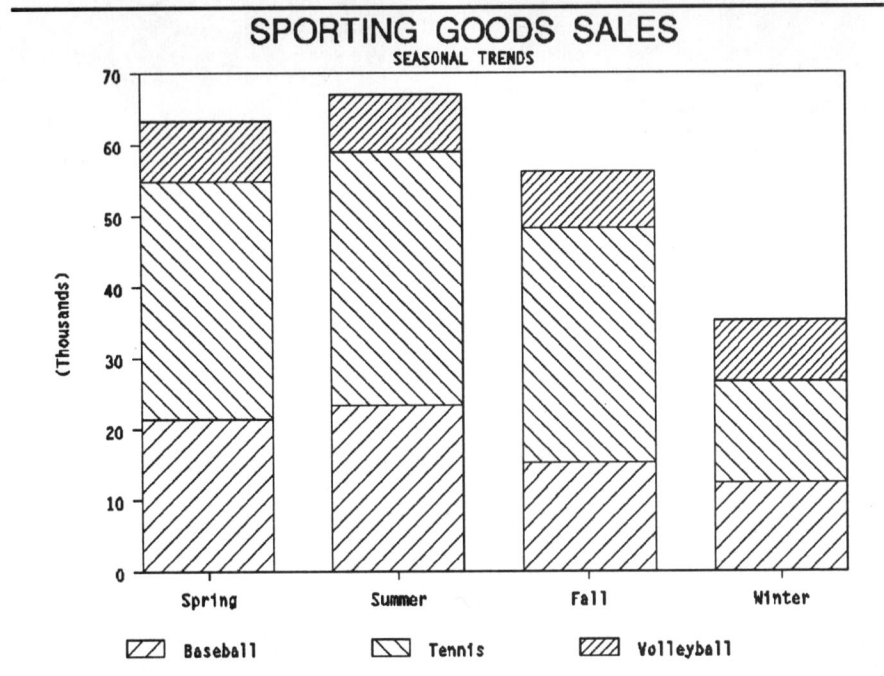

Figure 14.1 □ *Stacked Bar Chart*

Line graphs are often used in the financial pages of newspapers to show the changes in stock prices over a period of time. The line graph in Figure 14.2 shows changes in the Dow Jones averages over a period of three months.

DOW JONES INDEX
Index of 30 Industrial Stocks

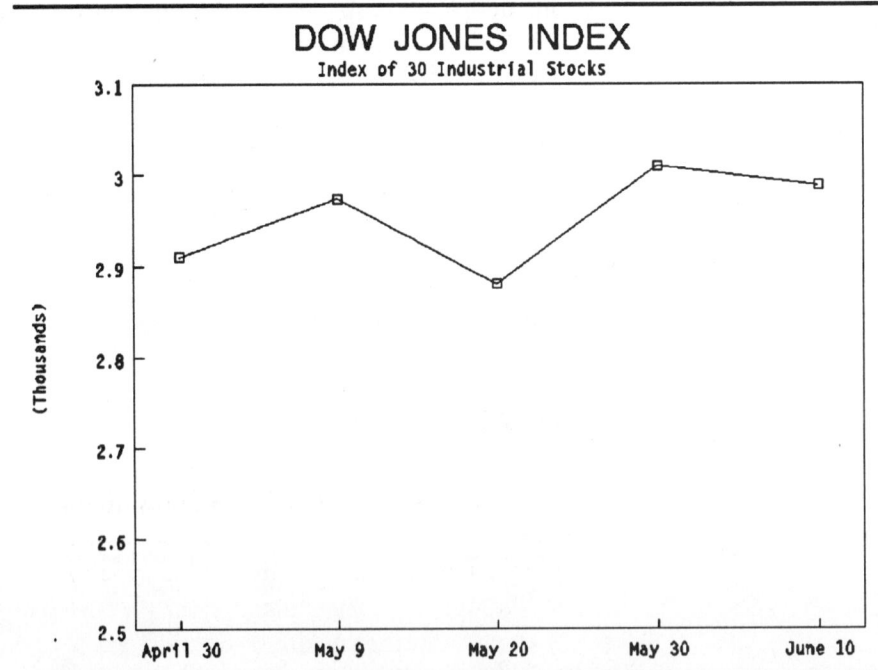

Figure 14.2 □ *Line Graph*

A **multiple line graph** shows several sets of data on the same chart. Each line represents a different set of data. The symbols used on each line vary. Legends are used to explain what each type of point represents. Multiple line graphs, like single line graphs, are used to track data over a period of time. Figure 14.3 shows the seasonal trends in sales of sporting goods.

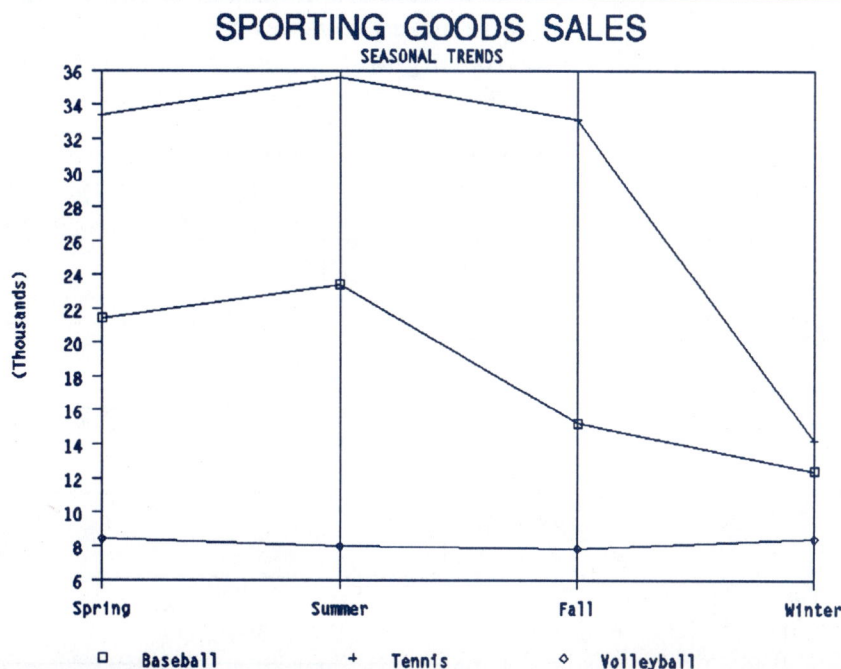

Figure 14.3   ◻   *Multiple Line Graph*

WHAT IS SCALING?

The term **scale** refers to the numbers that appear on the y-axis of all graph types and both the X- and Y-axis for xy graphs. In all previous activities, 1-2-3 automatically inserted the numbers on the Y-axis scale. For some situations, however, you may wish to set your own low and high values on the scale. Manual scaling allows you to set the range of numbers to be printed on the Y-axis (vertical) for all graph types and on both the X- and Y-axis for xy graphs. The lower limit can be set below 0 to allow negative values to be depicted on a graph.

In Figure 14.2 the lower scale number on the Y-axis has been set manually at 2,550, and the upper scale has been set at 3,050. 1-2-3 automatically used the values 2.5 through 3.1 and added the Y-axis title (Thousands).

To set the lower number on the scale to 2,550, use the command **/ Graph Options Scale Y-Scale Manual Lower 2550**. To set the upper number on the scale to 3,050, use the command **/ Graph Options Scale Y-Scale Manual Upper 3050**. Any time you want to return to automatic scaling on the Y-axis, use the command / Graph Options Y-scale Scale Automatic.

WHAT ARE GRID LINES?

Grid lines are horizontal or vertical lines across a graph that are used to make the values represented by bars or lines clearer. To add horizontal grid lines, use the command / Graph Options Grid Horizontal. The line graph in Figure 14.4 includes a horizontal grid.

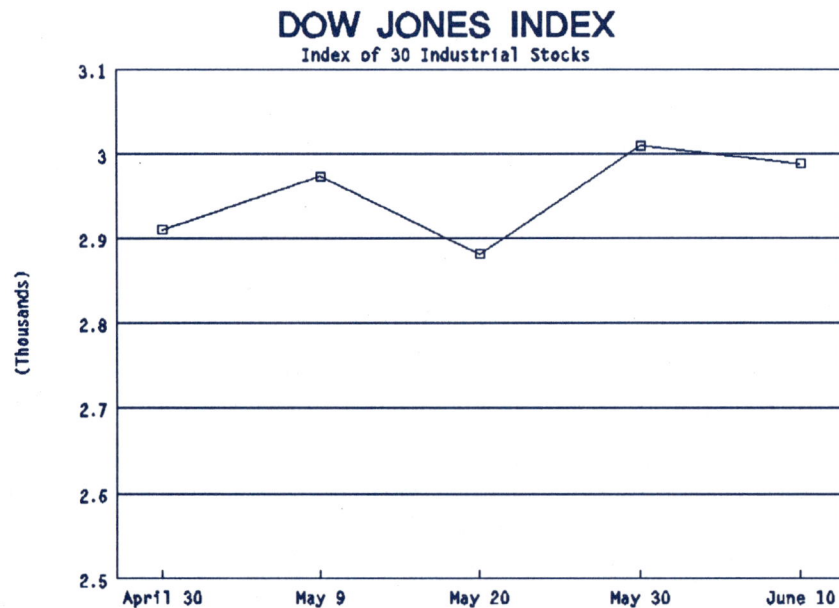

Figure 14.4 ☐ *Horizontal Grid*

Horizontal grid lines can help you determine more precisely the value represented by a point on a line graph or by a bar on a bar chart. In some cases, grid lines distract from the graph itself and should not be used.

To add vertical grid lines, use the command / Graph Options Grid Vertical. The line graph shown in Figure 14.5 includes a vertical grid.

Like horizontal grid lines, vertical grid lines can help you interpret data in a graph. Generally, vertical grid lines are confusing in bar charts. They are more useful in line graphs that contain numerous labels on the X-axis. Vertical grids should be used only when they enhance the graph.

Both horizontal and vertical grid lines can be added to a graph using the command / Graph Options Grid Both. Be careful when using both horizontal and vertical grid lines. They may clutter the graph and make it more difficult to understand the data being graphed. If you wish to experiment using grid lines and then want to remove them, use the command / Graph Options Grid Clear.

DOW JONES INDEX
Index of 30 Industrial Stocks

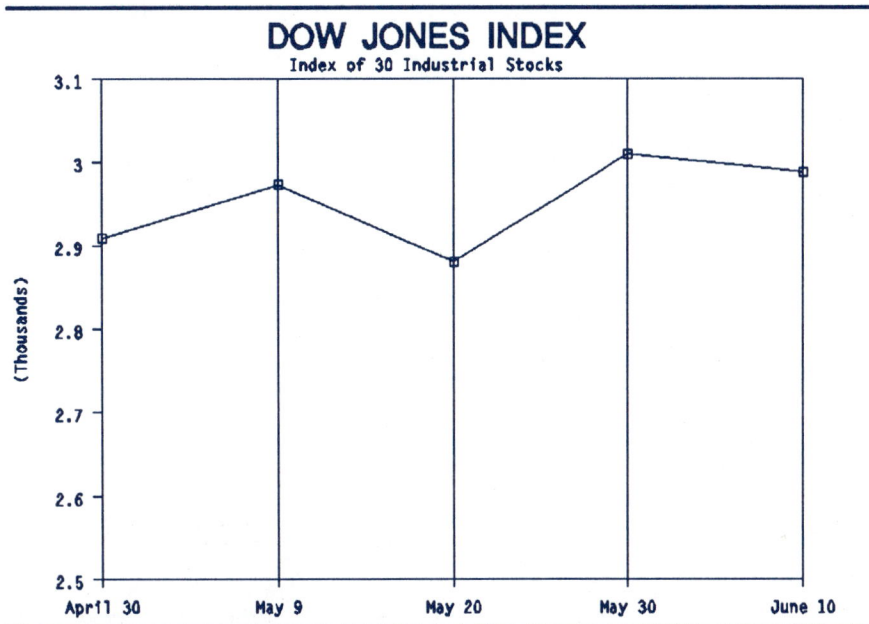

Figure 14.5 ☐ Vertical Grid

WHAT ARE DATA LABELS?

Data labels are used to help clarify the values of the data points on a graph. The initial command to add data labels is **/ Graph Options Data-Labels.** After you use this command, the control panel will request you to enter a range of cells for the data label range. Once you select the data label range, the control panel will ask whether you want the labels centered on the data points or above, below, to the right, or to the left of the data points.

A line chart such as the one showing the Dow Jones averages can make effective use of values as data labels as shown in Figure 14.6.

Options such as data labels, grids, and scaling should be used to enhance a graph and make it easier to understand. They should only be used when they help present data in a clear and accurate manner.

CREATE A STACKED BAR CHART

In this tutorial, you will create a stacked bar chart showing attendance figures at three ski resorts over a three-month period. You will use data from a spreadsheet created in a previous chapter.

Retrieve the file ACT12-3. To create a stacked bar chart using the 1991 figures:

PRESS /

PRESS g (Graph)

PRESS t (Type)

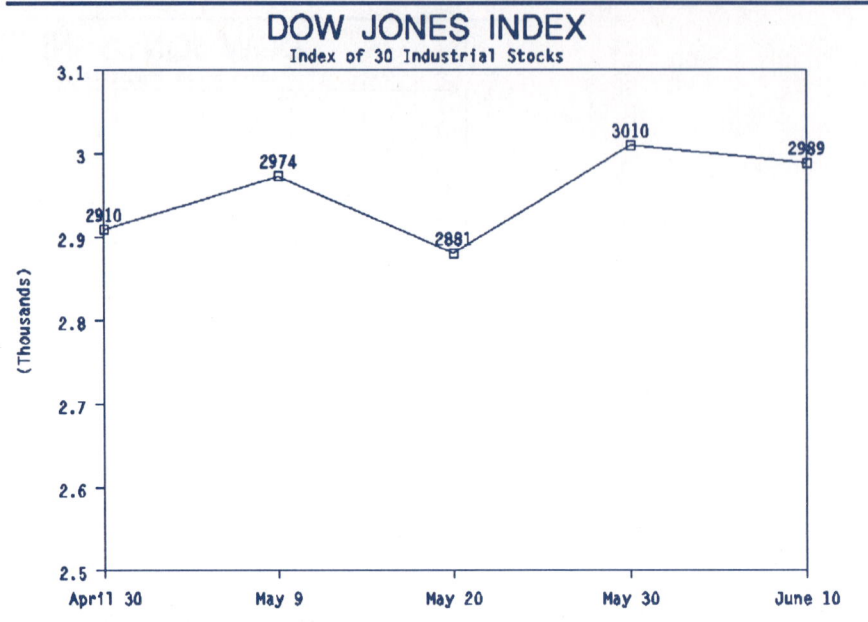

Figure 14.6 ☐ *Line Graph With Data Labels*

To select a stacked bar graph:

P R E S S	s (Stacked-bar)

To select the labels that will be displayed on the X-axis:

P R E S S	x

To select the X-axis range, including January, February, and March, move the cell pointer to B16 and:

P R E S S	. (Period)
P R E S S	→ (2 times)
P R E S S	↵

To indicate the first series of data you want to display:

P R E S S	a

Move the cell pointer to B17.

P R E S S	. (Period)
P R E S S	↓ (2 times)
P R E S S	↵
P R E S S	b

Move the cell pointer to C17:

PRESS   . (Period)
PRESS   ↓ (2 times)
PRESS   ↵
PRESS   c

Move the cell pointer to D17:

PRESS   . (Period)
PRESS   ↓ (2 times)
PRESS   ↵

To view the graph:

PRESS   v (View)

To return to the graph menu:

PRESS   Esc (Esc key or Enter key to return to the graphing menu)

To add titles:

PRESS   o (Options)
PRESS   t (Titles)
PRESS   f (First)
ENTER   High Country Ski Slopes
PRESS   ↵

To enter a second title:

PRESS   t (Titles)
PRESS   s (Second)
ENTER   1991 Attendance Figures
PRESS   ↵
PRESS   q (Quit)

To add the title (In Thousands) on the vertical axis:

PRESS   o (Options)
PRESS   t (Titles)

PRESS   y (Y-axis)
ENTER   (In Thousands)
PRESS   ↵
PRESS   q (Quit)

To view the graph that you created:

PRESS   v (View)

To return to the graph menu:

PRESS   Esc

To add legends,

PRESS   o (Options)
PRESS   l (Legend)
PRESS   a (Set legend for A range)
ENTER   Sun Valley
PRESS   ↵
PRESS   l (Legend)
PRESS   b (Set legend for B range)
ENTER   Keystone
PRESS   ↵
PRESS   l (Legend)
PRESS   c (Set legend for C range)
ENTER   Vail
PRESS   ↵
PRESS   q (Quit)

To view the graph:

PRESS   v (View)

To return to the graph menu:

PRESS   Esc

To change the upper scale:

PRESS   o (Options)

PRESS   s (Scale)

PRESS   y (Y-scale)

PRESS   m (Manual)

PRESS   u (Upper)

The second line of the control panel will display the following:

```
A1: [W12] 'HIGH COUNTRY SKI SLOPES                                    EDIT
Enter upper limit: 0
```

ENTER   250

PRESS   ↵

PRESS   q (Quit)

PRESS   q (Quit)

To view the graph:

PRESS   v (View)

As you view the graph, notice that the upper limit on the Y-scale is 260, even though you entered 250. To determine the upper scale, Lotus 1-2-3 followed the sequence shown on the grid and used the next number above your request.

PRESS   Esc

To name the graph:

PRESS   n (Name)

PRESS   c (Create)

ENTER   ski1

PRESS   ↵

To save the graph on disk for printing:

PRESS   s (Save)

PRESS   ski1

PRESS   ↵

PRESS   Esc (2 times)

To save the graph settings with the file:

PRESS /

PRESS f (File)

PRESS s (Save)

PRESS ↵

PRESS r (Replace)

ACTIVITY 14.1 □ Creating a Stacked Bar Chart

In this activity, you will create a stacked bar chart using a spreadsheet created in the previous chapter. You will chart the changes in sales of clothing from 1989 through 1991.

1. Retrieve the file CENTRE.
2. Cancel all previous graph options using the command **/ Graph Reset Graph Quit**.
3. Choose the type of graph you will create—a stacked bar chart.
4. Select the X-axis labels—1989, 1990, and 1991.
5. Select the series A data range—B20.D20.
6. Select the series B data range—B21.D21.
7. Select the series C data range—B22.D22.
8. Enter a first line title—Centre High School Store.
9. Enter a second line title—Clothing Sales.
10. Enter a Y-axis title—In Dollars.
11. Enter the legends—T-shirts for data range A, Jackets for range B, and Socks for range C.
12. Change the upper scale on the Y-axis scale to 900.
13. View the graph. If needed, make any corrections by reentering titles or data ranges.
14. Name the graph CLOTHING.
15. Save the graph as CLOTHING.
16. Save the spreadsheet file under a new name CLOTHING. Both the graph file and the spreadsheet file will have the same filename, but the filename extensions will be different. The graph file will have a .PIC extension and the spreadsheet file will have a .WK1 extension.
17. Print the graph.

CREATE A LINE GRAPH

In this tutorial, you will create a line graph showing changes in automotive sales over the last four years. You will use data from a spreadsheet used in a previous chapter.

Retrieve the file KRAUSE.

The **/ G**raph **R**eset command cancels all or some of your previous graph specifications. To cancel all previous graph specifications:

PRESS /

PRESS g (Graph)

PRESS r (Reset)

PRESS g (Graph)

PRESS q (Quit)

To create a line graph using only one series of data:

PRESS /

PRESS g (Graph)

PRESS t (Type)

PRESS l (Line)

To select the labels that will be displayed on the X-axis:

PRESS x

To select the X-axis range (Q1, Q2, Q3, and Q4), move the cell pointer to B4 and:

PRESS . (Period)

PRESS → (3 times)

PRESS ↵

To indicate the series of automotive sales data you want to display:

PRESS a

Move the cell pointer to B6.

PRESS . (Period)

PRESS → (3 times)

PRESS ↵

To view the graph,

PRESS	v (View)

To return to the graphing menu:

PRESS	Esc (Esc key or Enter key to return to the graphing menu)

To add titles:

PRESS	o (Options)
PRESS	t (Titles)
PRESS	f (First)
ENTER	Krause Manufacturing
PRESS	↵

To enter a second title:

PRESS	t (Titles)
PRESS	s (Second)
ENTER	Quarterly Sales
PRESS	↵

To enter an X-axis title:

PRESS	t (Titles)
PRESS	x (X-axis)
ENTER	Automotive Sales
PRESS	↵
PRESS	q (Quit)

To view the graph that you created:

PRESS	v (View)

To return to the graph menu:

PRESS	Esc

To set the upper and lower numbers on the scale manually:

PRESS   o (Options)

PRESS   s (Scale)

PRESS   y (Y-axis)

PRESS   m (Manual)

PRESS   l (Lower)

ENTER   1000

PRESS   ↵

To set the upper scale limit:

PRESS   u (Upper)

ENTER   25000

PRESS   ↵

PRESS   q (Quit)

PRESS   q (Quit)

To view the graph:

PRESS   v (View)

To return to the graph menu:

PRESS   Esc

To name the graph:

PRESS   n (Name)

PRESS   c (Create)

ENTER   KRAUSE1

PRESS   ↵

To save the graph on disk for printing:

PRESS   s (Save)

PRESS   KRAUSE1

PRESS   ↵

PRESS   Esc (2 times)

To save the graph settings with the file:

PRESS /

PRESS f (File)

PRESS s (Save)

PRESS ↵

PRESS r (Replace)

ACTIVITY 14.2 □ *Creating a Line Graph*

In this activity, you will create a line graph using the same spreadsheet used in the previous tutorial. You will chart the changes in sales of electrical goods over the four quarters.

1. Retrieve the file KRAUSE.
2. Reset all graph settings.
3. Choose the type of graph you will create—a line graph.
4. Select the series A data range representing electrical sales.
5. Enter a first title—Krause Manufacturing.
6. Enter a second title—Quarterly Sales.
7. Enter an X-axis title—Electrical Goods
8. Change the Y-axis scale to 0 and 20,000.
9. View the graph. If needed, make any corrections by reentering titles or data ranges.
10. Name the graph KRAUSE2.
11. Save the graph under the same name KRAUSE2.
12. Save the file under the name KRAUSE2.

CREATE A MULTIPLE LINE GRAPH

In this tutorial, you will create a multiple line graph using the same spreadsheet file that you used in the previous activity.

Retrieve the file KRAUSE2 if it is not already on your screen. To reset all graph settings:

PRESS /

PRESS g (Graph)

PRESS r (Reset)

PRESS g (Graph)

PRESS q (Quit)

To create a multiple line graph:

PRESS   /

PRESS   g (Graph)

PRESS   t (Type)

PRESS   l (Line)

To select the labels that will be displayed on the X-axis:

PRESS   x

To select the X-axis range (Q1, Q2, Q3, and Q4), move the cell pointer to B4 and:

PRESS   . (Period)

PRESS   → (3 times)

PRESS   ↵

To indicate the first series of data you want to display:

PRESS   a

Move the cell pointer to B6.

PRESS   . (Period)

PRESS   → (3 times)

PRESS   ↵

PRESS   b

Move the cell pointer to B7.

PRESS   . (Period)

PRESS   → (3 times)

PRESS   ↵

PRESS   c

Move the cell pointer to B8.

PRESS   . (Period)

PRESS   → (3 times)

PRESS   ↵

To add titles:

P R E S S   o (Options)
P R E S S   t (Titles)
P R E S S   f (First)
E N T E R   Krause Manufacturing
P R E S S   ⏎

To enter a second title:

P R E S S   t (Titles)
P R E S S   s (Second)
E N T E R   Quarterly Sales for Three Product Lines
P R E S S   ⏎

To add legends:

P R E S S   l (Legend)
P R E S S   a (Set legend for A range)
E N T E R   Automotive
P R E S S   ⏎
P R E S S   l (Legend)
P R E S S   b (Set legend for B range)
E N T E R   Electrical
P R E S S   ⏎
P R E S S   l (Legend)
P R E S S   c (Set legend for C range)
E N T E R   Engineering
P R E S S   ⏎

To add a horizontal grid:

P R E S S   g (Grid)
P R E S S   h (Horizontal)
P R E S S   q (quit)

To view the graph:

P R E S S   v

To return to the graph menu:

PRESS Esc

To name the graph:

PRESS n (Name)
PRESS c (Create)
ENTER KRAUSE3

To save the graph on disk for printing:

PRESS s (Save)
ENTER KRAUSE3
PRESS ↵
PRESS Esc (2 times)

To save the graph settings with the file:

PRESS /
PRESS f (File)
PRESS s (Save)
ENTER KRAUSE3
PRESS ↵

Continue working with the same graph, KRAUSE3. Use the following instructions to remove the horizontal grid and to add data labels.

PRESS /
PRESS g (Graph)
PRESS o (Options)
PRESS g (Grid)
PRESS c (Clear)

To add data labels:

PRESS d (Data labels)
PRESS a (Range A data label)

Move the cell pointer to B6.

PRESS . (Period)
PRESS → (3 times)
PRESS ⏎
PRESS a (Above)

To enter data labels for the series B data:

PRESS b (Range B data label)

Move the cell pointer to B7.

PRESS . (Period)
PRESS → (3 times)
PRESS ⏎
PRESS a (Above)

To enter data labels for the series C data:

PRESS c (Range C data label)

Move the cell pointer to B8.

PRESS . (Period)
PRESS → (3 times)
PRESS ⏎
PRESS a (Above)
PRESS q (Quit)
PRESS q (Quit)

To view the graph:

PRESS v (View)

To return to the graph menu:

PRESS Esc

To name the graph:

> *PRESS* n (Name)
> *PRESS* c (Create)
> *ENTER* KRAUSE4
> *PRESS* ↵

To save thc graph on disk for printing:

> *PRESS* s (Save)
> *ENTER* KRAUSE4
> *PRESS* ↵
> *PRESS* Esc (2 times)

To save the graph settings with the file:

> *PRESS* /
> *PRESS* f (File)
> *PRESS* s (Save)
> *ENTER* KRAUSE4
> *PRESS* ↵

ACTIVITY 14.3 ❑ *Using Scaling and a Grid in a Line Graph*

In this activity, you will create a multiple line graph showing the quantity of different flavors of ice cream sold during the year by an ice cream shop.

1. Retrieve the file DAIRY.
2. Create a multiple line graph using all the data shown in the spreadsheet.
3. Use the months of the year as the X-axis labels.
4. Add appropriate legends.
5. Set the lower scale limit at 0 and the upper scale limit at 22.
6. Add a vertical grid.
7. Name and save the graph as ICECREAM.
8. Save the file as DAIRY.
9. Print the graph.

CHAPTER 14 □ THEORY EXERCISES

True/False ||||||||| Each of the following statements is either True or False. Indicate your choice by circling **T** for a true statement or **F** for a false statement.

1. A stacked bar chart shows the cumulative effect of several sets of data.   1. T   F

2. Legends are not needed in a stacked bar chart.   2. T   F

3. A stacked bar chart is most useful when comparing one bar to another bar rather than when comparing one section of a bar to a similar section in a different bar.   3. T   F

4. Each item within a stacked bar must be related to the other items in the bar.   4. T   F

5. To show trends in sales over a period of time, a line graph is a good choice.   5. T   F

6. A multiple line graph shows several sets of data on the same chart.   6. T   F

7. The term scale refers to the numbers that appear on the Y-axis of all graph types.   7. T   F

8. Only the upper limit of the scale can be set manually.   8. T   F

9. Negatives numbers cannot be included on a scale.   9. T   F

10. To set the lower number on a Y-axis scale to 200, use the command **/ Graph Options Scale Y-Scale Manual Lower 200.**   10. T   F

11. Grid lines are horizontal or vertical lines across a graph that are used to make the values represented by bars or lines easier to understand.   11. T   F

12. Both horizontal and vertical grids should be used in all bar graphs.   12. T   F

13. The command to add data labels is **/ Graph Options Data-Labels.**   13. T   F

14. Since data labels make a graph more accurate, they should be used in every graph created.   14. T   F

Completion **IIIIIIII** For each item below fill in the word (or words) that completes the statement or answers the question.

1. A bar chart that has each bar divided into two or more related parts is called a _____ bar chart.

2. To show changes in car sales over the last six months, either a bar chart or a _____ _____ should be used.

3. Newspapers often show the changes in the Dow Jones Index of industrial stocks on a _____ graph.

4. On a _____ line graph, each line represents a different set of data, and the symbol for the points on each line is different.

5. When using a multiple line graph, _____ are needed to explain what each type of line represents.

6. Manual scaling allows the user to set the _____ limit on the scale and the _____ limit on the scale.

7. When manual scaling is used, both positive and _____ numbers can be used on a scale.

8. The two types of grid lines are _____ lines and _____ lines.

9. If you want to remove grid lines, use the command **/ Graph Options Grid** _____.

10. The purpose of data labels is to help _____

    _____ .

11. Data labels can be centered on the data points or placed above, below, or to the _____ or _____ of the data points.

12. Data labels, grids, and scaling should be used to _____

    _____ .

ACTIVITY 14.4 □   *Using Scaling and Data-Labels in a Line Graph*

In this activity, you will create a multiple line graph showing the increase and/or decrease in three types of wild game birds from 1970-1990.

1. Use the data that follows to create a spreadsheet.

```
A1: 'Wildlife Survey of Game Birds                                              READY


           A         B         C         D         E         F         G         H
 1    Wildlife Survey of Game Birds
 2    1970-1990
 3                 1970      1980      1990
 4
 5    Mallards     95644     87433     74230
 6    Pheasants   140658    103557     85403
 7    Quail       175943    165300    190977
 8
 9
10
```

2. Name the spreadsheet file BIRDS.
3. Create a multiple line graph using all the data in the spreadsheet BIRDS.
4. Include appropriate titles and legends.
5. Change the lower scale limit to 70,000 and the upper scale limit to 200,000.
6. Add data labels indicating the values of all the data points shown on the graph. Use your own judgment to choose the most appropriate placement for those data labels.
7. Name and save the graph as BIRDS.
8. Save the file as BIRDS.
9. Print the graph.

CHAPTER 15

OBJECTIVES

- ☐ Create pie charts
- ☐ Use crosshatchings and color
- ☐ Explode pie slices
- ☐ Create xy graphs
- ☐ Choose appropriate graph types

WHAT IS A PIE CHART?

A **pie chart** is used to compare values that represent parts of a whole. The whole amount is illustrated as a circle, and each slice represents one of the values. While other types of charts can use several ranges of data, a pie chart uses only one range of data, and is less versatile than other types of charts.

Different types of charts have different purposes. Pie charts make it easy to compare each part of the pie to the whole pie. They can be effective in showing budgets, sales, and departmental costs.

Figure 15.1 illustrates a pie chart showing the popularity of computer games based on total sales in a computer store.

Before using a pie chart, consider the type of data being depicted and the types of comparisons you wish to make. They are not effective at showing trends over a period of time. For example, a pie chart would not be a good chart to show changes in temperatures over a month.

WHAT IS AN XY GRAPH?

An **xy graph** shows the relationship between two sets of data by displaying numeric values on both the vertical and horizontal axes. The xy graph allows you to plot the intersection of two pairs of values. The intersections are represented by symbols on the graph.

GROSS SALES FROM COMPUTER GAMES

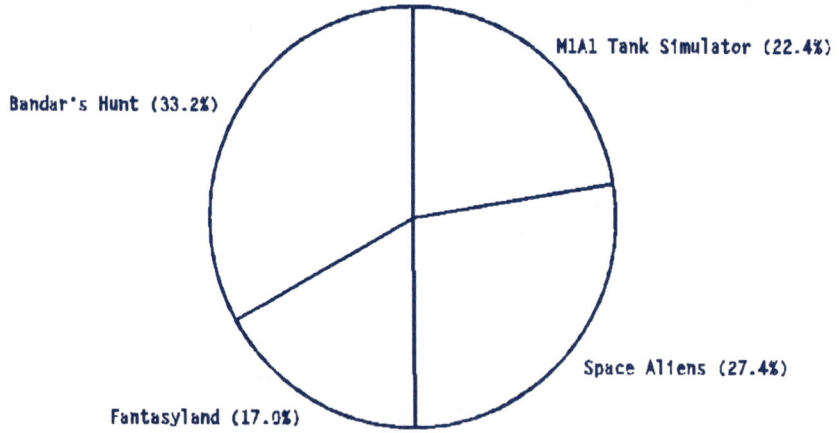

M1A1 Tank Simulator (22.4%)

Bandar's Hunt (33.2%)

Space Aliens (27.4%)

Fantasyland (17.0%)

Figure 15.1 □ *Pie Chart*

Lines that connect the symbols are inserted automatically by 1-2-3. These lines may not help you analyze the data. They can be removed from the graph by invoking the command **/ Graph O**ptions **F**ormat **G**raph **S**ymbols.

Figure 15.2 illustrates an xy graph showing the relationship between the amount of money spent on advertising costs to the amount of sales for each month. It shows that, generally, as more money is spent on advertising, sales increase.

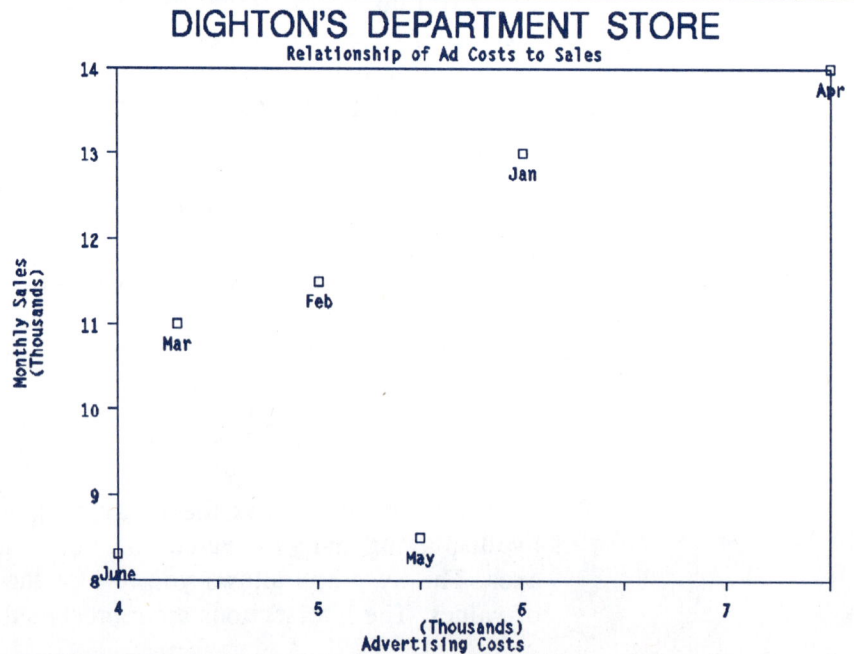

DIGHTON'S DEPARTMENT STORE
Relationship of Ad Costs to Sales

Monthly Sales (Thousands)

Apr

Jan

Feb

Mar

May

June

(Thousands)
Advertising Costs

Figure 15.2 □ *XY Graph*

The previous graph was created from the spreadsheet shown in Figure 15.3. Notice that column B values, Advert. Costs, are used for the X-range and column C values, Sales, are used for data range A. The months of the year are used only as data labels.

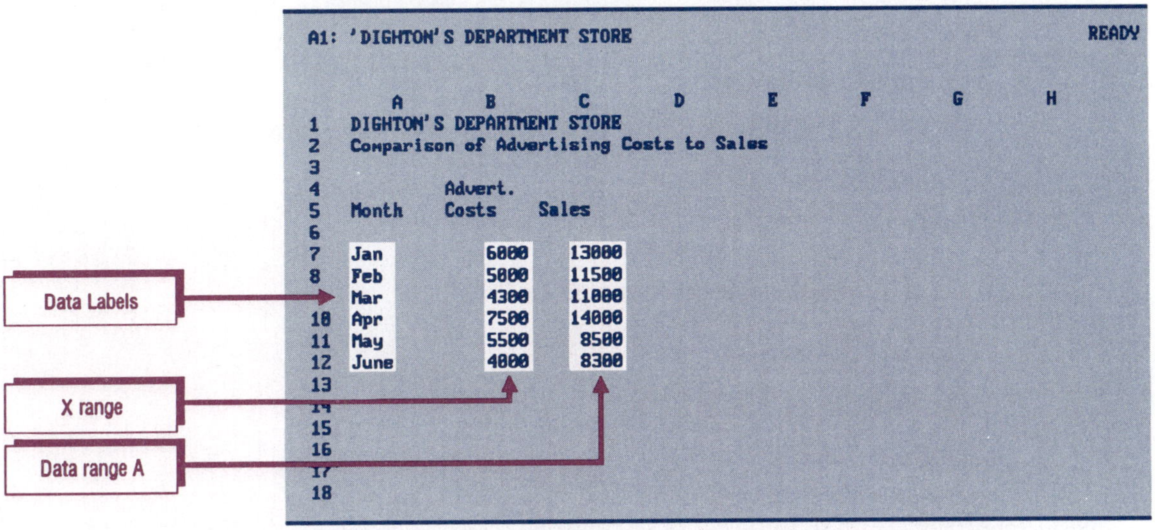

Figure 15.3 ☐ *Data for an XY Graph*

XY graphs show the relationship between two factors and both factors are presented in numeric terms. Therefore, xy graphs have values on both the X-axis and the Y-axis.

CREATE A PIE CHART

In this tutorial, you will create a pie chart showing the number of different types of credit cards being used by consumers.

Retrieve the file CREDITCD. To create a pie chart:

PRESS /

PRESS g (Graph)

PRESS t (Type)

To select a pie chart:

PRESS p (Pie)

To select the labels for the pie chart:

PRESS x

To select the X-axis range including American Express, Mastercard, VISA, Gas, and Dept. Stores, move the cell pointer to A6 and:

PRESS   . (Period)

PRESS   ↓ (4 times)

PRESS   ↵

To indicate the series of data you want to display:

PRESS   a

Move the cell pointer to D6.

PRESS   . (Period)

PRESS   ↓ (4 times)

PRESS   ↵

To view the graph:

PRESS   v (View)

To return to the graph menu:

PRESS   Esc (Esc key or Enter key to return to the graph menu)

To add titles:

PRESS   o (Options)

PRESS   t (Titles)

PRESS   f (First)

ENTER   CREDIT CARD USAGE IN LINCOLN COUNTY

PRESS   ↵

PRESS   q (Quit)

To view the graph that you created:

PRESS   v (View)

To return to the graph menu:

PRESS   Esc

PRESS   q (Quit)

Use Crosshatchings or Color

To add crosshatchings or color to the slides in a pie chart, you must create a B data range on the spreadsheet the same size as the A data range. In the B data range, you enter values from 1-14 in each cell. These values tell the crosshatching patterns or colors. The color each value represents will depend on the monitor you have. If the graphic display on your computer is set for black and white, these values will determine the crosshatching patterns used.

To add crosshatchings or color, begin by creating a B data range. Move the cell pointer to E6.

ENTER	1
PRESS	↓
ENTER	2
PRESS	↓
ENTER	6
PRESS	↓
ENTER	9
PRESS	↓
ENTER	14
PRESS	↵
PRESS	/
PRESS	g (Graph)
PRESS	b (B data range)
ENTER	e6.e10
PRESS	↵
PRESS	v (View)

Each pie slice will be in a different type of crosshatching or color.

PRESS	Esc
PRESS	q (Quit)

Explode a Pie Slice

Exploding one or more pie slices makes that slice or slices stand out from the others. To explode one or more slices in a pie chart, you use a B data range. If no values for crosshatchings or color will be used in the B range, enter 100 in each cell that corresponds to the slice you want to explode. If values for crosshatchings or color are used in the B range, add 100 to the B range values that correspond to the slices you want to explode.

To explode the Visa pie slice and use crosshatching or color, move the cell pointer to E8.

ENTER 106
PRESS ↵

The value 106 was derived by adding 100 to the previous value in E8.
    To view the graph:

PRESS /
PRESS g (Graph)
PRESS v (View)

Look at the graph to see if the Visa pie slice has been exploded.

PRESS Esc

To name the graph:

PRESS n (Name)
PRESS c (Create)
PRESS CREDITCD
PRESS ↵

To save the graph on disk for printing:

PRESS s (Save)
PRESS CREDITCD
PRESS ↵
PRESS Esc

To save the graph settings with the file:

PRESS f (File)
PRESS s (Save)
PRESS ↵
PRESS r (Replace)

ACTIVITY 15.1 ☐ Creating a Pie Chart

In this activity, you will create a pie chart showing the costs and expenses for a clothing store for the first quarter of the year only.

1. Retrieve the file TIMBER.
2. Choose the type of graph you will create—a pie chart.
3. Select the X-axis labels—Salary, Rent, Advertising, and Utilities.
4. Select the series A data range—B8.B11.
5. Enter a first title—TIMBER WOLF CLOTHING, LTD.
6. Enter a second title—Costs and Expenses for the 1st Quarter.
7. View the graph. If needed, make any corrections by reentering titles or data ranges.
8. Name the graph TIMBEREX.
9. Save the graph as TIMBEREX.
10. Save the spreadsheet file under the name TIMBEREX.
11. Print the graph.

CREATE AN XY GRAPH

Retail stores spend enormous amounts of money on advertising, and they want to know whether their advertising campaigns are bringing any results in terms of sales increases.

In this tutorial, you will create an xy graph like the one shown in Figure 15.1. This graph will show the relationship between advertising costs and sales for a department store. The graph will answer the following questions: (1) As more money is spent on advertising, do sales increase, decrease, or stay the same? (2) Should this business spend more or less on advertising in the future?

Retrieve the file ADVSSALE. To create an xy graph:

PRESS /
PRESS g (Graph)
PRESS t (Type)
PRESS x (xy)

To select the X-axis range:

PRESS x

To select B7.B12 as the X-axis range, move the cell pointer to B7 and:

PRESS . (Period)
PRESS ↓ (5 times)
PRESS ↵

To select the data range A:

PRESS a

Move the cell pointer to C7.

PRESS . (Period)
PRESS ↓ (5 times)
PRESS ↵

To add titles:

PRESS o (Options)
PRESS t (Titles)
PRESS f (First)
ENTER DIGHTON'S DEPT. STORE
PRESS ↵

To enter a second title:

PRESS t (Titles)
PRESS s (Second)
ENTER Relationship of Ad Costs to Sales
PRESS ↵

To enter X-axis titles:

PRESS t (Titles)
PRESS x (X-axis)
ENTER Advertising Costs
PRESS ↵

To enter Y-axis titles:

PRESS t (Titles)
PRESS y (Y-axis)

ENTER Monthly Sales

PRESS ↵

PRESS q (Quit)

PRESS v (View)

Notice that the intersecting points of the two sets of data are indicated by symbols, but you do not know which symbols represent which month.

PRESS Esc (Esc key)

To display the months as data labels next to the symbols:

PRESS o (Options)

PRESS d (Data-labels)

PRESS a (Range A)

Move the cell pointer to A7.

PRESS . (Period)

PRESS ↓ (5 times)

PRESS ↵

PRESS b (display labels Below the data points)

PRESS q (Quit)

PRESS q (Quit)

PRESS v (View)

PRESS Esc (Esc key)

In this graph, the lines do not help one analyze or interpret the meaning of the data. To remove the lines from the graph:

PRESS o (Options)

The second and third lines of the control panel will display the following:

```
A1: 'DIGHTON'S DEPARTMENT STORE                                    MENU
Legend  Format  Titles  Grid  Scale  Color  B&W  Data-Labels  Quit
Create legends for data ranges
```

PRESS   f (Format)

The second and third lines of the control panel will display the following:

```
A1: 'DIGHTON'S DEPARTMENT STORE                                    MENU
Graph  A  B  C  D  E  F  Quit
Set format for all ranges
```

PRESS   g (Graph)

The second and third lines of the control panel will display the following:

```
A1: 'DIGHTON'S DEPARTMENT STORE                                    MENU
Lines  Symbols  Both  Neither
Connect data points with lines
```

PRESS   s (display Symbols only)

PRESS   q (Quit)

PRESS   q (Quit)

PRESS   v (View)

On your own, determine whether the graph answers the following questions: (1) As more money was spent on advertising, did sales increase, decrease, or stay the same? (2) Should this company spend more or less on advertising in the future?

PRESS   Esc

To name the graph:

PRESS   n (Name)

PRESS   c (Create)

ENTER   ADVSSALE

PRESS   ↵

To save the graph on disk for printing:

PRESS   s (Save)

ENTER   ADVSSALE

PRESS   ↵

PRESS   Esc (2 times)

To save the graph settings with the file:

PRESS /

PRESS f (File)

PRESS s (Save)

ENTER ↵

PRESS r (Replace)

ACTIVITY 15.2 ☐ *Creating an XY Graph*

In this activity, you will create two xy graphs showing the price of a product and the quantities demanded of it. The degree that changes in demand affect price is called the **elasticity of demand.** This is an economic concept that shows how and why consumer behavior differs for different products as prices changes.

The demand for the product is **inelastic** if changes in demand affect price very little or not at all. This type of product will not show much change in quantity demanded, whether the price rises or falls. Generally, products that are consumed quickly, are inexpensive, or are necessities have inelastic demand. Examples include pencils, salt, and work uniforms.

A product is said to have an **elastic** demand if changes in demand affect price a lot. This type of product will be purchased in greater quantities at lower prices and smaller quantities at higher prices. Products that can be repaired, have good substitutes, or are luxuries have elastic demand. Examples are fur coats, tickets to ball games, and television sets.

First, create an xy graph showing the demand elasticity for apples and then create one showing the demand elasticity for milk.

1. Retrieve the file DEMAND.

2. Select the type of graph—an xy graph.

3. Enter the number of bushels of apples demanded by consumers as the X-axis range—B10.B14.

4. Enter the prices per bushel as the range A data—A10.A14.

5. Enter the first title—VARIATION IN QUANTITY OF APPLES.

6. Enter the second title—DEMANDED AT VARIOUS PRICES.

7. Enter the X-axis title—Bushels.

8. Enter the Y-axis title—Dollars Per Bushel.

9. View the graph. If everything is correct, name and save the graph as—APPLEDEM.

10. Name and save the graph and the file as APPLEDEM.

11. Print the graph.

12. Recall the file APPLEDEM to the screen, if it is not already there. Create a graph showing the demand elasticity for milk using the following instructions.

13. Reset the X data range setting using the command **/ Graph Reset X Quit.**

14. Enter the new X-axis range—the number of gallons of milk consumers buy at various prices.

15. Change the first title to VARIATION IN THE QUANTITY OF MILK.

16. Change the X-axis title to Gallons.

17. Change the Y-axis title to Dollars Per Gallon.

18. View the graph. If everything is correct, name and save the graph MILKDEM.

19. Name and save the graph and the file as MILKDEM.

20. Print the graph.

21. On your own, determine whether the 2 products are elastic or inelastic. The demand curve for an elastic product slopes a good deal from left to right, while that of an inelastic product resembles a vertical line. Before turning this activity in to your instructor, label each graph and indicate whether the product is elastic or inelastic.

ACTIVITY 15.3 □ Creating an XY Graph

In this activity, you will create a simple xy graph showing the relationship between a computer dealer's profits and the number of salespeople employed.

1. Create a spreadsheet using the following data:

XLT, Inc.

Year	Profit (in millions)	No. of Salespeople
1983	62	6,700
1984	63	6,600
1985	64	6,800
1986	65	7,000
1987	68	7,300
1988	69	7,300
1989	70	7,400
1990	60	7,600
1991	58	7,800
1992	55	8,000

2. Use first and second title headings.

3. Place Profits on the X-axis and No. of Sales People on the Y-axis.

4. Include X- and Y-axis titles.

5. Remove the lines on the graph using the command / Graph Options Format Graph Symbols.

6. View the graph. If everything is correct, name and save the graph as XLTPROF.

7. Save the file as XLTPROF.

8. Print the graph.

9. At the bottom of the graph, indicate in writing the relationship between increases or decreases in profit and the increases or decreases in salespeople.

CHAPTER 15 □ THEORY EXERCISES

True/False |||||||| Each of the following statements is either True or False. Indicate your choice by circling **T** for a true statement or **F** for a false statement.

1. A pie chart is used to compare values that represent parts of a whole.   1. T   F

2. A pie chart can use only six ranges of data.   2. T   F

3. Pie charts can be effective in showing departmental sales for the year in five departments in a store.   3. T   F

4. Pie charts can be effective in showing changes in total sales over a period of six months.   4. T   F

5. An xy graph shows the relationship between two sets of data by displaying numeric values on both the vertical and horizontal axes.   5. T   F

6. An xy graph can be used effectively to show the relationship between the number of salespeople employed by a company over a period of five years and the amount of sales during that period.   6. T   F

7. XY graphs have values on only the Y-axis.   7. T   F

8. XY graphs require lines to connect the plotted points on the graph.   8. T   F

9. To remove the lines from a graph, use the command **/ Graph Op**tions **Format Graph Symbols**.   9. T   F

10. XY graphs can be created to show elasticity of demand for products.   10. T   F

Completion |||||||| For each item below fill in the word (or words) that completes the statement or answers the question.

1. To show the relationship between two numeric sets of data, use the _____ chart or graph.

2. To compare values that represent parts of a whole, use a/an _____.

3. A pie chart can use _____ range(s) of data.

4. A pie chart (can or cannot) _____ be used to show changes in oil production over the last three years.

5. To show the relationship between the rate of inflation for the last five years and an automobile manufacturer's revenues over the last five years, use a/an _____ graph or chart.

6. XY graphs show the relationship between _____ factors.

7. Lines can be removed from an xy graph by using the command **/ Graph Options Format Graph** _____.

8. To select values for the Y-axis for data range A, use the command **/ Graph** _____.

9. To change the lower scale on the Y-axis, use the command **/ Graph Options Scale Y-axis Manual** _____.

ACTIVITY 15.4 ☐ *Choosing Appropriate Graph Types*

In this activity, you will create a spreadsheet using the graph data that follows. Then you will create a pie chart, a bar chart, and line graph using the data. Finally, you will select the type of chart that depicts the data in the boldest, most striking manner possible, print a copy of the chart, and turn that chart in to your instructor. Use all graphing features needed to make the data understandable.

Save the PIC file and data file as ACT15-4.

The average patient stay at Marion Memorial Hospital has varied from 6.5 days in 1975, 4 days in 1980, 3.5 days in 1985, and 2.5 days in 1990.

ACTIVITY 15.5 ☐ *Setting Up Graph Data and Choosing Graph Types*

In this activity, you will create a spreadsheet using the data that follows. Then, create a bar chart, a stacked bar chart, and a line graph using the data. Finally, select the type of chart that lets you clearly and easily compare the closing prices of a given stock over three weeks. Turn in a printout of that chart to your instructor. Use all graphing features needed to make the data understandable.

Save the PIC file and data file as ACT15-5.

The closing prices of three stocks at the end of the first week in January are: $18.75, Herington Fabrics; $28.50, Burdick Milling; and $98.25, Kansas City Computers. The closing prices at the end of the second week in January are: $18.50, Herington Fabrics; $30.50, Burdick Milling; and $99.00, Kansas City Computers. The closing prices at the end of the third week in January are: $19.00, Herington Fabrics; $31.00, Burdick Milling; and $100.25, Kansas City Computers.

CYCLE 4
Beginning Database Tutorials and Exercises

CHAPTER 16

Creating and Sorting Databases

OBJECTIVES

- ☐ Create a database
- ☐ Enter field names
- ☐ Enter data in fields
- ☐ Sort using a primary key
- ☐ Sort using primary and secondary keys
- ☐ Sort data in ascending and descending order
- ☐ Print a sorted database

WHAT IS A DATABASE?

A **database** is a collection of related data organized in a way that lets the user find, retrieve, and use the data. The 1-2-3 database function provides a structure for storing data so it can be accessed quickly and easily. Using 1-2-3 to store database information has many advantages. You can run many types of calculations and create graphs, as well as use database functions.

Many types of information can be stored in databases. For example, a business may store employees' names, addresses, department names, and salaries in an employee payroll database. Some businesses with relatively small inventories store inventory information, including catalog numbers, descriptions, and quantities in stock. In schools, an athletic department might use a database to keep track of sports equipment, including volleyball, football, track, and basketball equipment.

WHAT IS THE STRUCTURE OF A DATABASE?

Common databases

A 1-2-3 database is a spreadsheet organized as a group of records and fields. A **record** is all the information about a specific person, product, or item such as all the information about one employee. With 1-2-3, all entries in a single row create an individual record.

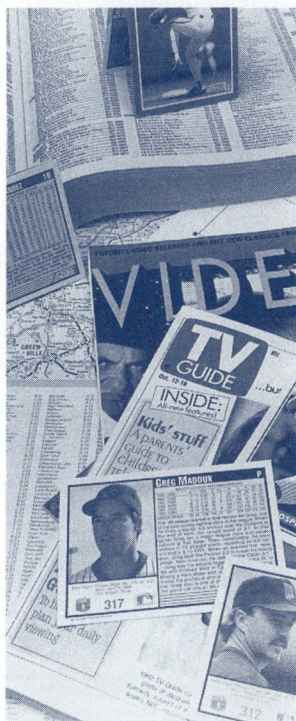

A **field** contains an individual unit of information. The column containing employees' names is an example of a field. A **field name** is a column title. Field names should be short but descriptive. Try to use field names that are no longer than the length of the entries listed under them. Examples of records, field names, and fields are shown in Figure 16.1.

Figure 16.1 ☐ *Database Structure*

WHAT CAN YOU DO WITH A DATABASE?

Lotus 1-2-3 provides several database functions, including sorting and querying the database. For example, suppose a department store keeps track of daily sales in each department and stores the information in a database. With this database, the store manager could rearrange the information alphabetically by department name or determine the departments that sold more than a specified amount each day.

With a database that lists all sales representatives and their sales records for a computer store, you could determine the sales representatives who have fallen below the sales quota for the month. Or you could sort the database in descending numerical order by total sales and determine the top sales representatives.

HOW IS A DATABASE CREATED?

Before entering information in a database, you need to organize the data. You need to determine what information should and should not be included. For example, if you create an employee database for a business, you must determine the types of information you want to include. Do you want to include the employees' names, addresses, and telephone numbers or do you want employees' names only? Do you want to include employees' ages? The fields included in a database depend on how you want to use them in the future.

Order of Data

You need to decide the order you want to enter the data. The field most frequently used to sort, find, or update information is often chosen as the first field. However, there are times when a different, but logical, order is used such as ZIP code in the first field, company name in the second field, street address in the third field, city in the fourth field, and state in the fifth field.

Column Width

You also need to determine the column width for each field. One way to determine column width is to review all the data that will be entered in a particular field, count the number of characters in the longest item, and set the column width based on the longest entry.

To separate one field from another and to make data easier to read, one or two extra characters are sometimes added to column widths. In other cases, field widths are decreased, and data is abbreviated so that more fields can be viewed on the screen at one time.

Many times databases are so extensive it would take too much time to review all the data to determine the column widths needed. Instead, a small sample of information is reviewed, and column widths are determined on the basis of this sample. With 1-2-3, it is very easy to change the field width (column width).

Some of the raw data that will be used to create a database follows:

Richardson, Allen ⟵——— **Field 1**
Account: RTR Corp.   Longest entry = 17 characters
$3,500

Osins, Edgar
Account: Bronson Incorp.
$15,600 ⟵——————— **Field 3**
                                      Longest Entry = 7 characters

Thill, Angel
Account: Hendrickson Steel ⟵— **Field 2**
$14,000   Longest Entry = 17 characters

By analyzing this sample of information, you can determine the field widths. An analysis of this data shows that column A, Field 1, would need a minimum of 17 characters; column B, Field 2, 17 characters; and column C, Field 3, 7 characters. To make the data easier to read, two extra characters will be added to each of these fields.

After adding two characters to each field, the widths of columns A and B will be set at 19 characters and column C at 9 characters.

Consistent Data Entry

You should be very consistent when entering data. When first and last names are used in a single field, usually the last name is entered first, followed by a comma, and then the first name—i.e. Richardson, Allen. By entering the name in this manner, you can sort the Name field alphabetically by last name. All fields containing employee names should have the names entered in the same manner. An alternative is to have two separate fields—a first name field and a last name field.

You should also be consistent when abbreviating words. If you abbreviate the word Corporation, you should choose one abbreviation such as Corp. and use it consistently. Corporation should not be spelled out completely in one record and abbreviated in another record. This is most important when selecting records based on a criterion. If you select a list of records for ABC Corporation, records for ABC Corp. will not be listed.

Prior to entering the data, you should select formats for fields containing values. The format for a field that contains values can be changed at any time by using the procedures you have learned in previous chapters, but preplanning is more effective.

Databases created with 1-2-3 are based on a spreadsheet structure, which makes it very easy to add, delete, or change data, formats, or field widths.

Organizing and Creating a Database

In this tutorial, you will create the structure for a database for a personal collection of books and enter the data. Use the following handwritten list containing book names, types of books, and the year of publication to create the database.

Type	Title	Year
Romance	Caribbean Adventures	1991
Adventure	Under the Ocean	1990
Romance	Shopping Mall Fever	1992
Mystery	Mystery in Albany	1988
Mystery	Buster's Robbers	1987
Sports	Tennis for Teens	1986
Sports	Body Builders	1990
Sports	Basketball Strategy	1991
Adventure	Ride the Waves	1992

In this database, the order of the fields has already been selected for you. The first field will be the type of book; the second field, title; and the third field, year of publication.

To determine the number of characters in the first field, count the number of characters that will be in the longest entry in that field. You will find that Adventure is the longest entry at 9 characters. Add one character to this number to separate the first field from the second field. Move the cell pointer to column A. To set the column width:

PRESS   /

PRESS   w (Worksheet)

PRESS   c (Column)

PRESS   s (Set-width)

ENTER   10

PRESS   ↵

Count the number of characters that will be in the longest entry in the second field, the title field. You will find that Caribbean Adventures is the longest entry, containing 20 characters. Add one character to this number to separate the second field from the third field.

Move the cell pointer to column B. To set the column width:

PRESS   /

PRESS   w (Worksheet)

PRESS   c (Column)

PRESS   s (Set-width)

ENTER   21

PRESS   ↵

Count the number of characters that will be in the longest entry in the third field, the Year of publication field. All of the entries have 4 characters. Add one character to this number.

Move the cell pointer to column C. To set the column width:

PRESS   /

PRESS   w (Worksheet)

PRESS   c (Column)

PRESS   s (Set-width)

ENTER   5

PRESS   ↵

The next step is to select field names. Try to keep field names short but descriptive.

On your own, select a field name for each of the three fields. Move the cell pointer to A1. To enter a field name for the first field:

ENTER   (Use a field name of your choice.)
PRESS   →

Move the cell pointer to B1.

ENTER   (Use a field name of your choice.)
PRESS   →

Move the cell pointer to C1.

ENTER   (Use a field name of your choice.)
PRESS   ⏎

Move the cell pointer to A2. To enter the type of book for the first record:

ENTER   Romance
PRESS   →

To enter the title of the book for the first record:

ENTER   Caribbean Adventures
PRESS   →

To enter the year of publication for the first record:

ENTER   1991
PRESS   ⏎

Move the cell pointer one row down. Using the handwritten information presented earlier, enter the data for the second record in cells A3 through C3. Then, continue entering all of the other records in subsequent rows. To save the database:

PRESS   /
PRESS   f (File)
PRESS   s (Save)
ENTER   books
PRESS   ⏎

ACTIVITY 16.1 ☐ Creating a Database

In this activity, you will create a database showing the gross sales for each sales employee at a car dealership for each quarter of the year. Assume you will want to sort the database alphabetically by employee name at some time in the future. Use the following information to create the database:

EMPLOYEE NAME: Rosalind Hines
1ST QUARTER SALES: $42,500
2ND QUARTER SALES: $64,500
3RD QUARTER SALES: $85,300
4TH QUARTER SALES: $75,995

EMPLOYEE NAME: Harold Garcia
1ST QUARTER SALES: $44,595
2ND QUARTER SALES: $54,500
3RD QUARTER SALES: $44,600
4TH QUARTER SALES: $65,400

EMPLOYEE NAME: Willie Johnson
1ST QUARTER SALES: $12,400
2ND QUARTER SALES: $24,500
3RD QUARTER SALES: $39,300
4TH QUARTER SALES: $29,400

EMPLOYEE NAME: Jim Smith
1ST QUARTER SALES: $8,900
2ND QUARTER SALES: $24,800
3RD QUARTER SALES: $44,400
4TH QUARTER SALES: $64,400

EMPLOYEE NAME: Roger Martin
1ST QUARTER SALES: $65,900
2ND QUARTER SALES: $78,900
3RD QUARTER SALES: $97,500
4TH QUARTER SALES: $86,400

EMPLOYEE NAME: Tammy Chau
1ST QUARTER SALES: $75,400
2ND QUARTER SALES: $65,300
3RD QUARTER SALES: $109,000
4TH QUARTER SALES: $98,400

1. Determine the number of fields you will have in the database and the type of information that will be entered in each field.

2. Determine the column widths for each of the fields. Remember you will need to sort by employee name at some time.

3. Determine and set the format for the fields containing values.

4. Enter a title for the database—JOHN COLE MOTORS in cell A1.

5. Choose a field name for the first field and enter it in A3.

6. Choose field names for the other fields and enter them in row 3 also.

7. Enter the data for the first record in row 4. Enter the employee's name with the last name first, a comma, followed by the first name—i.e. Hines, Rosalind. Then enter her sales for the four quarters of the year.

8. Enter the data for the other records in rows 5-9. Be consistent in the way you enter data in each record. Enter the employee's names the same way in all the records.

9. Save the file as AUTOSALE.

10. Print the entire file including the field names.

HOW IS A DATABASE SORTED?

The initial command to sort a database is / Data Sort. The sort function rearranges records in a database in the order you specify.

To identify the data range you want sorted, use the command / Data Sort Data-Range. Then the control panel will request that you enter the range to be included in the sort. A **data range** includes all of the records within a database, but not field names. The data range needs to be selected only once if the same range will be used for subsequent sorting operations.

In Figure 16.2, notice that all the records are highlighted as part of the data range to be sorted, but the field names (column titles) are not included in the data range.

```
A1: [W19] 'NAME                                                          READY


              A                    B               C          D        E
   1   NAME                 ACCOUNT          SALES
   2   Richardson, Allen    RTR Corp.         3,500
   3   Osins, Edgar         Bronson Incorp.  15,600
   4   Thill, Angel         Hendrickson Steel 14,000
   5   Wilson, Susan        XRT Corp.        13,450
   6   Strong, Leslie       Eastern Pipe Co. 18,350
   7   Perez, Juan          Adams Corp.       4,500
   8   Scott, Leonard       Hines & Bullock  12,600
   9
  10
  11
  12
  13
  14
  15
  16
  17
  18
  19
  20
```

Figure 16.2 ☐ Data Range Highlighted

WHAT IS A PRIMARY KEY?

After you enter the command **/ Data Sort Data-range**, the next step is to identify the first or main field you wish to have sorted, called the **Primary-key**. The command to sort using a primary key is **/ Data Sort Primary**. The primary key is the field that 1-2-3 will use to sort and rearrange the database. The control panel will request you to enter any cell address within the field to be sorted. Do not use the cell address for the field name as a primary key address.

As shown in Figure 16.3, the primary key cell address entered is C2, indicating that the Sales field will be sorted. Actually, any cell address between C2 and C8 could be used as a valid cell address for the sort.

```
C2: (,0) 3500                                          POINT
Primary sort key: C2


         A                    B                C       D       E
 1  NAME                 ACCOUNT           SALES
 2  Richardson, Allen    RTR Corp.          3,500
 3  Osins, Edgar         Bronson Incorp.   15,600
 4  Thill, Angel         Hendrickson Steel 14,000
 5  Wilson, Susan        XRT Corp.         13,450
 6  Strong, Leslie       Eastern Pipe Co.  18,350
 7  Perez, Juan          Adams Corp.        4,500
 8  Scott, Leonard       Hines & Bullock   12,600
 9
10
11
12
13
14
15
```

Figure 16.3 ☐ *Entering a Primary Key*

WHAT IS A SORT ORDER?

After you select the primary key cell address, the control panel will request you to identify the sort order. Sorting can be done in either ascending or descending order. **Ascending order** means the data in the primary field will be arranged either alphabetically from A-Z or numerically from the lowest to the highest value. **Descending order** means the data will be arranged from Z-A or from the highest to the lowest value.

If using a 1-2-3 version prior to Release 2.2, the control panel will display a default setting of either A or D. To select a sort order other than the default, enter either A for ascending order or D for descending order. The sort order shown in Figure 16.4 is ascending order.

```
C2: (,0) [W9] 3500                                              EDIT
Primary sort key: C2                Sort order (A or D): A
```

If using 1-2-3 Release 2.2 or above, a dialog box will appear as follows:

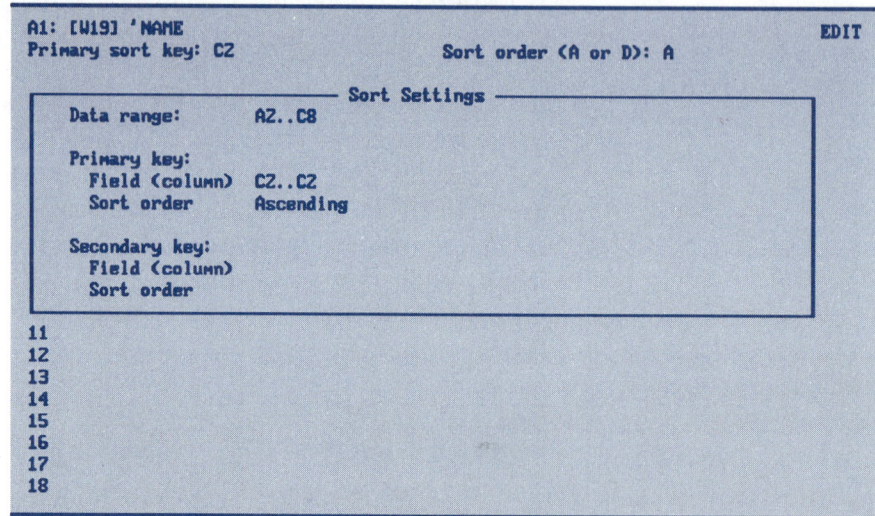

```
A1: [W19] 'NAME                                                                        EDIT
Primary sort key: C2                        Sort order (A or D): A
                          ── Sort Settings ──
      Data range:        A2..C8

      Primary key:
         Field (column)  C2..C2
         Sort order      Ascending

      Secondary key:
         Field (column)
         Sort order

   11
   12
   13
   14
   15
   16
   17
   18
```

To execute a sort procedure, the final command is **G**o. Figure 16.5 shows the sales field sorted numerically in ascending order.

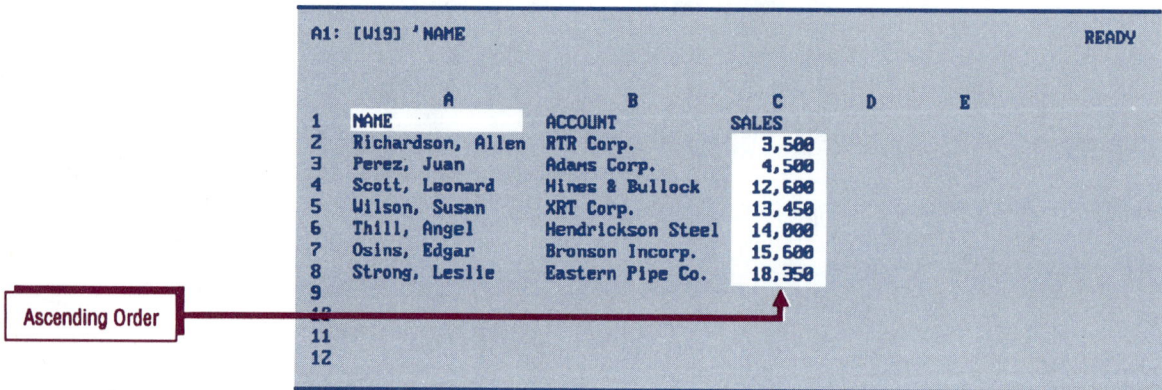

```
A1: [W19] 'NAME                                                                        READY

              A                     B                C        D        E
   1  NAME                    ACCOUNT          SALES
   2  Richardson, Allen       RTR Corp.            3,500
   3  Perez, Juan             Adams Corp.          4,500
   4  Scott, Leonard          Hines & Bullock     12,600
   5  Wilson, Susan           XRT Corp.           13,450
   6  Thill, Angel            Hendrickson Steel   14,000
   7  Osins, Edgar            Bronson Incorp.     15,600
   8  Strong, Leslie          Eastern Pipe Co.    18,350
   9
  10
  11
  12
```

Ascending Order

Figure 16.5 ◻ *Sorted Database*

Sorting a Database Using a Primary Key

In the following tutorial, you will sort the BOOKS database you created in the previous tutorial.

Retrieve the file BOOKS if it is not already displayed on the screen. To sort this database in alphabetical order by type of book:

PRESS /

PRESS d (Data)

The second and third lines of the control panel will display the following:

```
A2: [W10] 'Romance                                                    MENU
Fill  Table  Sort  Query  Distribution  Matrix  Regression  Parse
Fill a range with a sequence of values
        A              B           C        D         E       F      G
```

PRESS　s (Sort)

The second and third lines of the control panel will display the following:

```
A2: [W10] 'Romance                                                    MENU
Data-Range  Primary-Key  Secondary-Key  Reset  Go  Quit
Select records to be sorted
```

To identify the range to be sorted:

PRESS　d (Data-range)

The second line of the control panel will display the following:

```
A2: [W10] 'Romance                                                   POINT
Enter data range: A2

        A              B           C        D         E       F      G
```

The cell address shown will be the cell address of the present location of the cell pointer; therefore, the cell address shown on your screen may not be A1. Remember, the data range should include all the records but not the field names. Move the cell pointer to A2.

PRESS　. (Period)
PRESS　↓ (8 times)
PRESS　→ (2 times)
PRESS　↵

The second and third lines of the control panel will display the following:

```
A2: [W10] 'Romance                                                    MENU
Data-Range  Primary-Key  Secondary-Key  Reset  Go  Quit
Select records to be sorted
```

To select the field to be sorted and the order (ascending or descending) in which it will be sorted:

PRESS　p (Primary-key)

The second line of the control panel will display the following:

```
A2: [W10] 'Romance                                          POINT
Primary sort key: A2

          A           B        C     D      E      F      G
```

The cell address shown will be the cell address of the present location of the cell pointer; therefore, the cell address shown may not be A1.

To sort by type of books, the first field, you must enter a valid cell address within column A (A2-A10).

ENTER a2

PRESS ↵

The second line of the control panel will display the following:

```
A2: [W10] 'Romance                                          EDIT
Primary sort key: A2                   Sort order (A or D): D
```

The sort order, A or D, that is displayed depends on the default that has been set on your software. To be sure that you sort the database in ascending order:

ENTER a (Ascending)

PRESS ↵

The second and third lines of the control panel will display the following:

```
A2: [W10] 'Romance                                          MENU
Data-Range  Primary-Key  Secondary-Key  Reset  Go  Quit
Specify primary order for records
```

To execute the sort:

PRESS g (Go)

View the sorted database on the screen. It has been sorted alphabetically in ascending order by type of book. To save this rearranged database under the name BOOKTYPE:

PRESS /

PRESS f (File)

PRESS   s (Save)

ENTER   booktype

PRESS   ↵

Now that the sorted database has been saved as a file, it can be retrieved or printed at a later date.

ACTIVITY 16.2 ☐ *Sorting a Database*

In this activity, you will sort the database you created in Activity 16.1. First, you will sort it by employee name and then by fourth quarter sales.

1. Retrieve the file AUTOSALE.
2. Enter the **/** D**ata** S**ort** command.
3. Select the primary key to sort the database by employee name.
4. Choose ascending order for the sort procedure.
5. Execute the sort.
6. Print the database including all the titles.
7. Sort the database in descending order based on fourth quarter sales.
8. Save the rearranged database under the filename AUTO4QTR.
9. Print the rearranged database, including all the titles.

ACTIVITY 16.3 ☐ *Sorting a Database by a Primary Key*

In this activity, you will retrieve the file BOOKS and sort it first by title in ascending order and then by year of publication in descending order.

1. Retrieve the file BOOKS.
2. Enter the **/** D**ata** S**ort** command.
3. Select the data range, A2 through C10.
4. Select the primary key, any cell address between B2 and B10.
5. Choose ascending order for the sort procedure.
6. Execute the sort.
7. Store the rearranged data under the filename BOOKTITL.
8. Print the file including the field names and all records.
9. Retrieve the file BOOKS.

10. Sort the file using the year of publication as the primary key field. Select descending order so the newest books will be at the top of the list.

11. Store the rearranged data under the filename BOOKYEAR.

12. Print the file, including the field names and all records.

WHAT IS A SECONDARY KEY?

Previously, you learned to sort a database using one field, called the primary key. 1-2-3 allows you to sort using a primary field and a secondary field, called a **secondary key.** The second field is used only when two or more items in the primary field are identical.

In Figure 16.6, the primary key used for the sort is the Type of book; the secondary key is the book Title. Ascending order was used for both the primary and secondary keys. Several of the items in the primary key are identical. As you can see, the first type of book listed is Adventure. The book titles that are within the adventure category are listed in alphabetic order.

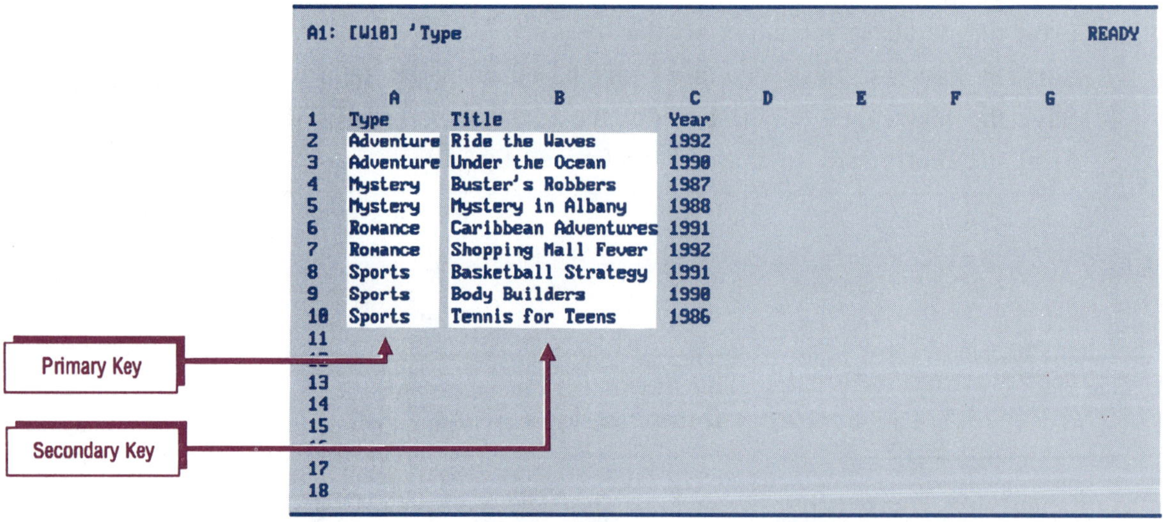

```
A1: [W18] 'Type                                                             READY


         A                  B                 C        D        E        F        G
1    Type          Title               Year
2    Adventure     Ride the Waves      1992
3    Adventure     Under the Ocean     1990
4    Mystery       Buster's Robbers    1987
5    Mystery       Mystery in Albany   1988
6    Romance       Caribbean Adventures 1991
7    Romance       Shopping Mall Fever 1992
8    Sports        Basketball Strategy 1991
9    Sports        Body Builders       1990
10   Sports        Tennis for Teens    1986
11
12
13
14
15
16
17
18
```

Primary Key

Secondary Key

Figure 16.6 □ *Sorted Database*

SORTING A DATABASE USING A PRIMARY AND SECONDARY KEY

In the following tutorial, you will sort a database listing baseball cards, the company issuing the cards, the date cards were issued, and estimated low and high values of the cards. Today many people collect, sell, and trade cards at baseball card shows and stores. The database you will use is one person's estimates of the high and low values for numerous baseball cards based on local selling prices.

Retrieve the file BASECD.

The following instructions will tell you how to sort the file using players' names as the primary key and the year of the card as the secondary key.

To select the data range to sort:

PRESS   /
PRESS   d (Data)
PRESS   s (Sort)

To identify the range to be sorted:

PRESS   d (Data-range)
ENTER   a6.f59
PRESS   ↵

To select the primary field to be sorted and the order (ascending or descending) in which it will be sorted.

PRESS   p (Primary-key)

To do a primary sort by player's name, you must enter a valid cell address within column A that contains the players' names.

ENTER   a6
PRESS   ↵

To sort the primary field in ascending order:

ENTER   a (Ascending)
PRESS   ↵

To select the year of the card as the secondary field to be sorted:

PRESS   s (Secondary-key)

Any cell address in column C between C6 and C59 can be used as the secondary key address. To enter the secondary field address:

ENTER   c6
PRESS   ↵

To sort the secondary field in ascending order:

ENTER   a (Ascending)
PRESS   ↵

To execute the sort:

PRESS   g (Go)

The sort has been completed, but it is difficult to view. Before analyzing the data, set a vertical window.
    Move the cell pointer to any location in column B.

PRESS   /
PRESS   w (Worksheet)
PRESS   w (Windows)
PRESS   v (Vertical)

To move the cell pointer to the right window:

PRESS   F6 (Window key)

To view only columns C-F in the right window:

PRESS   → (4 times)

Now move the cell pointer down column F to determine whether the older cards for such players as George Brett, Reggie Jackson, Willie Mays, and others are more valuable than the newer cards issued for the same players.
    To clear the windows:

PRESS   /
PRESS   w (Worksheet)
PRESS   w (Windows)
PRESS   c (Clear)

To save this sorted list:

PRESS   /
PRESS   f (File)
PRESS   s (Save)

ENTER basevalu

PRESS ↵

ACTIVITY 16.4 ☐ *Sorting with a Primary and Secondary Key*

In this activity, you will retrieve and sort a database that contains a list of record albums in a collection of records from the 1970s. Since 33 rpm records are no longer being marketed, some people are collecting them and hoping they will be treasured antiques in the future.

This database contains fields in columns A-E for record album titles, artists' names, the year the albums were made, the recording company, and the type of album.

You will sort the database using the type of album for the primary sort and artist name for the secondary sort.

1. Retrieve the file RECDINV.
2. Select the data range for the sort operation.
3. For the primary sort, select the Type of Album field and ascending order.
4. For the secondary sort, select the Artist Name field and ascending order.
5. Execute the sort. View the data.
6. Save the file as RECDTYPE.
7. Print the rearranged data, including field names.

C H A P T E R   1 6 □ T H E O R Y   E X E R C I S E S

True/False |||||||| Each of the following statements is either True or False. Indicate your choice by circling **T** for a true statement or **F** for a false statement.

1. A database is a collection of related data organized in a way that lets the user find, retrieve, and use the data.   1. T   F

2. An inventory for a pet shop could be stored as a database.   2. T   F

3. All the information related to a single product or person is an example of a record in a database.   3. T   F

4. In a database, an individual piece of information about a product such as a catalog number for the product is an example of a record.   4. T   F

5. A field name in a database is actually a column title.   5. T   F

6. Field names should be short but descriptive.   6. T   F

7. To execute a sort, the final command you use is **Go**.   7. T   F

8. To save the original database in the order created, you must store the new rearranged list under a different filename.   8. T   F

Use the following database to answer Questions 9-14.

```
A1: [W13] 'Description                                    READY

        A          B     C      D      E       F      G       H
1  Description   Qty.
2  Pet brushes   10
3  Dog leashes   15
4  Flea dip      20
5  Pet shampoo   34
6  Flea collars  22
7
8
9
10
```

9. Each record in the database contains three fields.   9. T   F

10. The field names are Description and Qty.   10. T   F

11. To sort all the records in the database, you should enter A1.B7 as the data range.   11. T   F

12. To sort alphabetically in ascending order by Description, you would enter the cell address A1 as the primary key.   12. T   F

13. To sort by Qty., you could enter any cell address between B2 and B8 as the primary key address.   13. T   F

317

14. To sort by quantity with the highest quantities at the top of the
list, you must sort in descending order.   14. T   F

15. The field selected as the second field to sort is called a secondary key.   15. T   F

16. The secondary key is used for the sort only if two or more re-
cords in the database have primary fields that are identical.   16. T   F

Completion IIIIIIII For each item below, fill in the word (or words) that completes the
statement or answers the question.

1. The **/ Data Sort** command _____ the records in a database in the order that you specify.

2. The data range must be specified (before/after) _____ the **/ Data Sort** command has been invoked.

3. Field names (should/should not) _____ be included in a data range.

4. The field that 1-2-3 will use to sort and rearrange the database is called the

_____ .

5. The primary key address is/is not _____ the cell address of the field name.

6. To arrange information from the largest number to the smallest number within a

field, you should use _____ order.

7. The field most frequently used to sort, find, or update information is often chosen

as the _____ field when creating a database.

8. The _____ _____ for a field should be based on the number of characters

in the longest entry that will be made in that field.

9. To separate one field from another and to make the data easier to read, _____

extra characters are sometimes added to the column widths.

10. The field width (can/cannot) _____ be changed once it has been set.

11. The initial command to select a secondary key is **/ Data Sort** _____ .

12. The second field in a sort operation is only used when _____ or more items

in the primary field are identical.

ACTIVITY 16.5 ☐ *Sorting with Primary and Secondary Keys*

In this activity, you will retrieve the file RECDTYPE created in Activity 16.4 and conduct another sort based on the record artist name and record album titles field.

1. Retrieve the file RECDTYPE.
2. Conduct another sort on the database. For the primary sort, select the record Artist Name field and ascending order.
3. For the secondary sort, select the record album titles field and ascending order.
4. Execute the sort. View the data.
5. Save the file as RECDNAME.
6. Print the rearranged data including field names.

CHAPTER 17

OBJECTIVES

☐ Define input range
☐ Define criterion range
☐ Find records with query command
☐ Use "and" criteria
☐ Use "or" criteria

WHAT IS THE DATA QUERY FIND COMMAND?

The command **/ Data Query Find** lets you search a database and locate particular records that match criteria you specify. For example, you could ask 1-2-3 to search a database listing computer programs and find all the computer programs purchased in 1991. In this case, 1991 is the criterion, and 1-2-3 would locate all the records that match this criterion.

Several steps are involved when using the **/ Data Query Find** command. First, you must set up input and criterion ranges before executing the **Find** command.

Defining the Input Range

The **input range** is the range of the database you want 1-2-3 to search. This range includes all the records and the field names. The initial command to select the input range is **/ Data Query Input**. In Figure 17.1, the range A1 through C11 is the input range.

Setting Up a Criterion Range

The **criterion range** is set up outside the database where information is stored. Information is entered in the criterion range that tells 1-2-3 which records to search for in the database. The initial command to select the criterion range is **/ Data Query Criterion**. Use the following rules for setting up a criterion range:

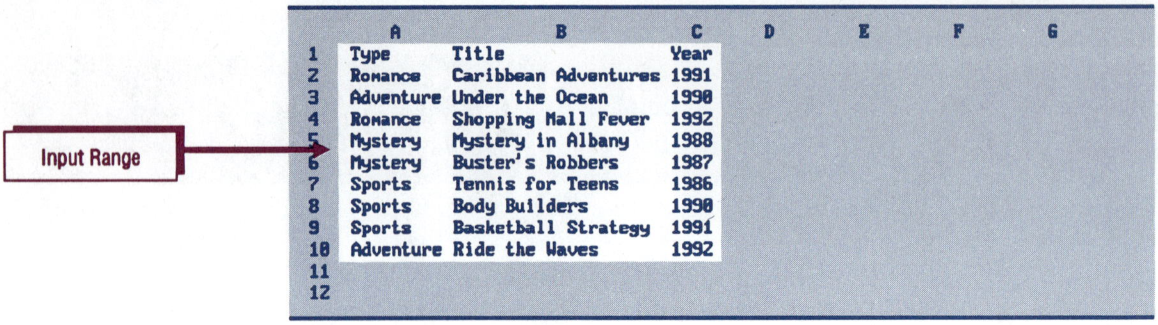

Figure 17.1 □ *Input Range*

1. Choose a blank range in your spreadsheet either below or to the right of your database as your criterion range.

2. The criterion range consists of two or more rows. In the first row of the criterion range, copy one, some or all of the field names used in the database. Each field name must be entered exactly as it appears in the database. You need to copy only the name of the field your criteria will be checking, but copying all of the field names will make it easier to change criteria.

3. Your criterion is entered in the second row (and subsequent rows) of the criterion range. It is entered below the field name to which it relates. This **matching criteria** tells 1-2-3 to find all records that exactly match it.

4. For labels, the criterion must be entered in exactly the same way it was entered in the database. If a word was entered in capital letters in the database, it should be entered in capital letters in the criterion.

5. You can enter several criteria in the same row if you want to search for records that satisfy several criteria. This is called using two or more matching criteria.

The criterion range in Figure 17.2 is the range A13 through C14. The field names have been copied from row 1 to row 13. In this example, the criterion is 1990, meaning you want to find all books published in 1990. This criterion, 1990, has been entered in row 14 under the field name Year.

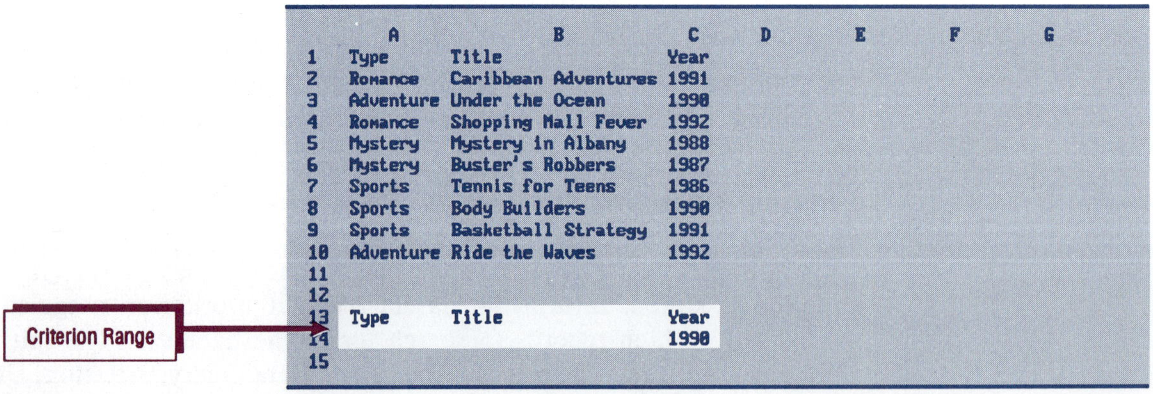

Figure 17.2 □ *Criterion Range*

FINDING RECORDS

The final command to search the database is **/ D**ata **Q**uery **F**ind. After you invoke this command, the first record in the database that matches the criteria will be highlighted. By continuing to press the Down Arrow, you will see other records that match the criteria highlighted.

When the last matching record has been highlighted, the computer will beep. Then, if you wish, press the Up Arrow to look at the matching records again. To return to the query menu, you can press the Enter or Escape keys. To quit the data query operation and return to the READY mode, you can press q.

The first record that matches the criterion, 1990, is highlighted in Figure 17.3. By pressing the Down Arrow key once, you will see the other book published in 1990 highlighted.

First Matching Record →

	A	B	C	D	E	F	G
1	Type	Title	Year				
2	Romance	Caribbean Adventures	1991				
	Adventure	Under the Ocean	1990				
4	Romance	Shopping Mall Fever	1992				
5	Mystery	Mystery in Albany	1988				
6	Mystery	Buster's Robbers	1987				
7	Sports	Tennis for Teens	1986				
8	Sports	Body Builders	1990				
9	Sports	Basketball Strategy	1991				
10	Adventure	Ride the Waves	1992				
11							
12							
13	Type	Title	Year				
14			1990				
15							

Figure 17.3   ☐   *First Matching Record*

Finding Records Using a Single Criterion

In the first section of this tutorial you will search a database to find all the Italian restaurants listed in a database.

Retrieve the file CAFE.

To begin the query process:

PRESS /

PRESS d (Data)

The second and third lines of the control panel will display the following:

```
A4: [W15] 'American                                                    MENU
Fill  Table  Sort  Query  Distribution  Matrix  Regression  Parse
Fill a range with a sequence of values
          A                    B              C          D      E        F        G
```

To query the database:

PRESS   q (Query)

The second line of the control panel will display the following:

```
A4: [W15] 'American                                                    MENU
Input  Criteria  Output  Find  Extract  Unique  Delete  Reset  Quit
Specify range that contains records to search
```

To select Input:

PRESS   i (Input)

The second line of the control panel will display the following:

```
A4: [W15] 'American                                                    POINT
Enter input range: A4
```

The cell address shown in the control panel will depend on the present location of the cell pointer. Do not include the main title, located in A1 in the input range, but do include the field names.
To enter the input range:

ENTER   a3.f19
PRESS   ↵

The second and third lines of the control panel will display the following:

```
A4: [W15] 'American                                                    MENU
Input  Criteria  Output  Find  Extract  Unique  Delete  Reset  Quit
Specify range that contains records to search
```

To select a criterion range:

PRESS   c (Criterion)

The control panel will request you to enter the criterion range. To select two blank rows below the database as the criterion range:

ENTER   a22.f23
PRESS   ↵
PRESS   q (Quit and return to the READY mode)

To copy the field names to row 22 in the criterion range, move the cell pointer to A3:

PRESS /

PRESS c (Copy)

PRESS . (Period)

PRESS → (5 times)

PRESS ↵

To copy the field names to the criterion range, move the cell pointer to A22 and:

PRESS ↵

To view the field names in the criterion range:

PRESS Pg Dn (Page Down key)

To enter the criterion, Italian, move the cell pointer to A23.

ENTER Italian

PRESS ↵

Rows 22 and 23 should appear as shown below:

```
           A           B           C       D    E     F        G
21
22  Type            Name          Avg PriceBrkfst Lunch Dinner
23  Italian
24
25
```

To find all the Italian restaurants in the database:

PRESS /

PRESS d (Data)

PRESS q (Query)

PRESS f (Find)

The first record listing an Italian restaurant will be highlighted on the screen. It is located in row 14.

PRESS ↓

The next Italian restaurant, located in row 16, is highlighted.

PRESS ↓

Note that the computer beeps when you reach the last record in the database that meets your criterion. To view previous records that match the criterion:

PRESS ↑

To escape to the find operation and return to the READY mode.

PRESS Esc
PRESS q (Quit)

In the next section of the tutorial, you will erase the previous criterion and enter criterion that will locate all restaurants that are open for breakfast.
Move the cell pointer to A23. To erase data in A23:

PRESS /
PRESS r (Range)
PRESS e (Erase)
PRESS ↵

Move the cell pointer to D23, under the field name Brkfst. To enter criterion to search the database for all restaurants that serve breakfast:

ENTER Y (Be sure to use a capital letter.)
PRESS ↵

Rows 22 and 23 should appear as follows:

	A	B	C	D	E	F	G
21							
22	Type	Name	Avg Price	Brkfst	Lunch	Dinner	
23				Y			
24							
25							

To execute the search for all restaurants that serve breakfast:

PRESS /
PRESS d (Data)

P R E S S   q (Query)

P R E S S   f (Find)

The first restaurant named in the database that is open for breakfast is Lucie, located in row 8. To view other records that match the criterion:

P R E S S   ↓

A second restaurant in the database, the West End Cafe, is now highlighted.

P R E S S   ↓

The computer will beep, indicating there are no more records that match the criteria.

P R E S S   Esc

P R E S S   q (Quit)

To save the file including the criterion range:

P R E S S   /

P R E S S   f (File)

P R E S S   s (Save)

E N T E R   CAFEBKFS

P R E S S   ↵

ACTIVITY 17.1 ❐ *Finding Records Using One Criterion*

In this activity, you will conduct three queries. In the first query, you will find all albums that are listed as Country records. In the second, you will find all albums that were recorded by Capitol Records. In the third, you will find all albums by John Denver.

1. Retrieve the file RECDINV.
2. Select the input range for the query.
3. Set a two-row criterion range including A32-E33.
4. Copy the field names in A1-E1 to A32-E32.
5. Search the database for all country record albums by entering the criterion, Country, in E33.

6. Enter the command to find the records that match the criterion.

7. Use the Down Arrow key to highlight the records that match the criterion.

8. Escape and return to the READY mode.

9. Save the file as COUNTRY.

10. Print the file, including the criterion range.

11. Erase the criterion entered in E33.

12. Enter criterion to find all albums recorded by the recording company named Capitol.

13. Use the Down Arrow key to highlight the records that match the criterion. Then, escape and return to the READY mode.

14. Save the file as CAPITOL.

15. To save paper, print the criterion range only.

16. Enter criterion to find all the albums recorded by John Denver.

17. Save the file as DENVER.

18. To save paper, print the criterion range only.

Finding Records Using "And" Criteria

As stated previously, you can enter multiple criteria in the same row if you want to search for records that satisfy several criteria. 1-2-3 considers criteria entered in the same row to be linked by the word "and."

To search a database for all books about sports that were published in 1990, the criterion range would be created as shown in Figure 17.4. Sports is entered under the field name Type and 1990 is entered under the field name Year. Both criteria are entered in the same row.

	A	B	C	D	E	F	G
1	Type	Title	Year				
2	Romance	Caribbean Adventures	1991				
3	Adventure	Under the Ocean	1990				
4	Romance	Shopping Mall Fever	1992				
5	Mystery	Mystery in Albany	1988				
6	Mystery	Buster's Robbers	1987				
7	Sports	Tennis for Teens	1986				
8	Sports	Body Builders	1990				
9	Sports	Basketball Strategy	1991				
10	Adventure	Ride the Waves	1992				
11							
12	Type	Title	Year				
13	Sports		1990				
14							
15							
16							

Two Criteria

Figure 17.4 □ "And" Criteria

Finding Records Matching Two Criteria

In this tutorial, you will enter multiple criteria to search a database for all restaurants that serve both lunch and dinner.
Retrieve the file CAFE.
To query the database:

PRESS   /

PRESS   d (Data)

PRESS   q (Query)

To select the input range:

PRESS   i (Input)

ENTER   a3.f19

PRESS   ↵

To select a criterion range:

PRESS   c (Criterion)

ENTER   a22.f23

PRESS   ↵

PRESS   q (Quit and return to the READY mode)

To copy the field names to row 22 in the criterion range, move the cell to A3:

PRESS   /

PRESS   c (Copy)

PRESS   . (Period)

PRESS   → (5 times)

PRESS   ↵

To copy the field names to the criterion range, move the cell pointer to A22 and:

PRESS   ↵

To enter the first criterion, all restaurants that are open for lunch, move the cell pointer to E23 and:

ENTER   Y (Use a capital letter.)

PRESS   ↵

To enter the second criterion listing all restaurants that are open for dinner, move the cell pointer to F23 and:

ENTER   Y (Use a capital letter.)
PRESS   ↵

Rows 22 and 23 should appear as shown below:

	A	B	C	D	E	F	G
21							
22	Type	Name	Avg Price	Brkfst	Lunch	Dinner	
23					Y	Y	
24							
25							
26							

To find the records that match the two criteria:

PRESS   /
PRESS   d (Data)
PRESS   q (Query)
PRESS   f (Find)
PRESS   ↓ (until the computer beeps)

You may have noticed that only one of the restaurants in the database did not match the criteria.
     To escape and return to the READY mode:

PRESS   Esc
PRESS   q (Quit)

To save the file, including the criterion range:

PRESS   /
PRESS   f (File)
PRESS   s (Save)
ENTER   cafel&d
PRESS   ↵

Finding Records Matching Three Criteria

In this tutorial, you will enter three criteria to locate restaurants in a database that serve breakfast, lunch, and dinner.

Retrieve the file CAFEL&D, if it is not on your screen.

To enter criterion to search the database for all restaurants that serve breakfast in addition to lunch and dinner, move the cell pointer to D23 and:

ENTER   Y (Use a capital letter.)
PRESS   ↵

Rows 22 and 23 should appear as follows:

	A	B	C	D	E	F	G
21							
22	Type	Name	Avg Price	Brkfst	Lunch	Dinner	
23				Y	Y	Y	
24							
25							
26							
27							
28							

To execute the search for all restaurants that serve breakfast, lunch, and dinner:

PRESS   /
PRESS   d (Data)
PRESS   q (Query)
PRESS   f (Find)
PRESS   ↓
PRESS   ↓

You will find that only two restaurants listed in the database match the criteria and serve breakfast, lunch, and dinner.

To save the file including the criterion range:

PRESS   /
PRESS   f (File)
PRESS   s (Save)
ENTER   cafebld
PRESS   ↵

ACTIVITY 17.2 ☐ *Using "And" Criteria*

In this activity, you will query a database of record albums and find all albums recorded in 1972 that are considered Pop albums. Then, you will find all albums by Columbia Records that are classified as Country Music albums.

1. Retrieve the file RECDINV.
2. Select the input range for the query.
3. Select a two-row criterion range below the database and copy all field names to the top row in this criterion range.
4. Enter the two criteria, 1972 and Pop, in the appropriate locations in the criterion range.
5. Find the records that match the criteria.
6. Save the file as RECD72.
7. Print the criterion range only.
8. Change the criteria. Find all albums recorded by Columbia that are classified as Country Music albums.
9. Save the file as RECDCOLU.
10. Print the criterion range only.

Finding Records Using "Or" Criteria

You can also find records using "or" criteria. When "or" criteria is used, records must match either the first criterion or the second. Two rules should be followed when setting up the criterion range:

1. Each criterion must be entered in a separate row. If two criteria are entered, two separate rows must be used. If three criteria are entered, three rows must be used.

2. The criterion range must include the field names and all of the criteria.

Figure 17.5 shows the criterion range created to search a database for all books that are either adventure books or were published in 1992.

Figure 17.5 ☐ *"Or" Criteria*

Finding Records Using "Or" Criteria

In this tutorial, you will search a database listing different types of restaurants and locate the ones that are either American or that serve breakfast.

Retrieve the file CAFE.
To query the database:

PRESS /
PRESS d (Data)
PRESS q (Query)

To select Input from the menu:

PRESS i (Input)

To enter the input range to be searched:

ENTER a3.f19
PRESS ↵

To select the criterion range:

PRESS c (Criterion)

To enter a three-row criterion range below the database:

ENTER a22.f24

To escape from the data query menu:

PRESS q (Quit)

To copy the field names from row 3 to row 22, move the cell pointer to A3 and:

PRESS /
PRESS c (Copy)
PRESS . (Period)
PRESS → (5 times)
PRESS ↵

Move the cell pointer to A22.

PRESS ↵

To enter the first criterion, Y, below the field name Brkfst, move the cell pointer to D23 and:

ENTER Y (Use a capital letter.)

PRESS ↵

To enter the second criterion, American, under the field name Type, move the cell pointer to A24.

ENTER American

PRESS ↵

To find the records that match either of the criteria:

PRESS /

PRESS d (Data)

PRESS q (Query)

PRESS f (Find)

The first record that matches either of the criteria will be highlighted.

PRESS ↓

View the second record that matches either of the criteria.

PRESS ↓

View the third record that matches either of the criteria.

PRESS ↓

The computer will beep, indicating there are no more records that match the criteria.

To escape and return to the READY mode:

PRESS Esc

PRESS q (Quit)

To save the file:

PRESS /

PRESS f (File)

PRESS s (Save)

ENTER cafeamer

PRESS ↵

ACTIVITY 17.3 ☐ *Using "Or" Criteria*

In this activity, you will query a database for all records that are classified as either Rock or Disco albums.

1. Retrieve the file RECDINV.
2. Enter the input range.
3. Copy the field names in row 1 to row 32.
4. Enter the first criterion, Rock, in E33.
5. Enter the second criterion, Disco, in E34.
6. Select the criterion range.
7. Find the records that match either criteria.
8. Save the file as RECDR&D.
9. Print the criterion range only, rows 32-34.
10. On your printout, write the names of the albums that match the criteria.

CHAPTER 17 □ THEORY EXERCISES

True/False ||||||||| Each of the following statements is either True or False. Indicate your choice by circling **T** for a true statement or **F** for a false statement.

1. The criterion range is the range of the database that you want 1-2-3 to search.   1. T   F

2. The initial command to select the input range is **/ Data Query Input.**   2. T   F

3. The criterion range is located below or to the right of the database.   3. T   F

4. By copying all of the field names to the criterion range, it is possible to change criteria easily.   4. T   F

5. The criterion is entered in the first row of the criterion range.   5. T   F

6. The criterion must be entered in exactly the same way it was entered in the database.   6. T   F

7. Only two criteria can be searched for at one time.   7. T   F

8. The final command to search the database is **/ Data Query Find.**   8. T   F

9. The Page Up and Page Down keys are used to view the records that match the criteria.   9. T   F

10. The computer will beep when the last matching record has been highlighted.   10. T   F

11. Lotus 1-2-3 considers criteria entered in the same row to be linked by the word "and."   11. T   F

12. When you use "or" criteria, two rows must be in the criterion range.   12. T   F

13. Records must match either the first criterion or the second criterion when "or" criteria is used.   13. T   F

14. When you use "or" criteria to search for two criteria, three rows must be in the criterion range.   14. T   F

Completion |||||||| For each item below, fill in the word (or words) that completes the statement or answers the question.

1. The command to set up an input range for a data query operation is **/ Data Query** _____.

2. The input range includes all the records in the database and the _____ _____.

3. The _____ range is set up outside the database where information is stored.

4. Field names are entered in the first row in the _____ range.

5. An inventory database has been set up with a field named Year in it. To save time creating the database, years were entered as 91 to indicate a 1991 purchase and 92 to indicate a 1992 purchase. To query this database and find all items in the inventory purchased in 1992, _____ should be entered under the field name Year located in the criterion range.

6. When using "or" criteria, each criterion must be entered in a _____ row.

Use the following database to the answer the next questions.

```
A1: [W15] 'Salesperson                                                           READY


            A                B              C         D       E       F
1    Salesperson      Account Name      Sales
2    Eggland          ABC Co.           1,000
3    Burrows          Alco Chemical     2,500
4    Holder           ABC Co.             800
5    Eggland          S&S Pipeline      4,500
6    Burrows          Wisconsin Energy  3,500
7
8    Salesperson      Account Name      Sales
9
10
```

7. The input range in the example should include _____.

8. To search for all records of sales by Eggland, the criterion _____ should be entered in cell _____.

9. To search for all records showing sales made to ABC, you should enter the criterion _____ in cell _____.

10. Assume criterion has been entered in B9 and B10 to search for all records showing sales to either Alco Chemical or S&S Pipeline. What criterion range should be entered? _____

11. To search for all records showing sales by either Holder or Burrows, if Holder is entered in A9, then you should enter Burrows in _____.

12. The criterion range used to find all sales made by either Holder or Burrows will include the range _____.

ACTIVITY 17.4 ☐ Querying a Database

In this activity, you will conduct three queries for records in a database that lists employee information.

1. Retrieve the file EMPL.
2. Select the input range. Select a criterion range located below the database.
3. Enter criteria to search for all the records of part-time, PT, employees. View the records that you find. How many records were found?
4. Enter criteria to search for all the records listing employees in the Management Department, MGT, who are also full-time, FT, employees. View those records. How many records were found?
5. Search for the records of employees who work in either the Legal Department, LEG, or the Research and Development Department, R&D. View those records. How many records were found?
6. Save the file as EMPLDEPT.
7. Print the file, including the database and the final criterion range used. On the printout, write the answers to Questions 3-5.

CYCLE 5
Advanced Database Tutorials and Exercises

CHAPTER

18 Extracting Records □ Using Formula Criteria

CHAPTER 18

OBJECTIVES

□ Define an output range
□ Extract records using an output range
□ Use formula criteria
□ Use partially matching criteria

HOW ARE RECORDS EXTRACTED?

The command to extract records is **/ Data Query Extract**. When this command is executed, 1-2-3 will display all the records meeting the specified criteria. These records will be displayed in an output range located below the criterion range.

Guidelines for Extracting Records

Before the extract command is invoked, you must define an output range on the spreadsheet. When setting up the output range, use the following guidelines:

1. The output range must be in an area of the spreadsheet below the criterion range.
2. Only the first row of the output range is defined as the output range.
3. The field names must be copied into the first row of the output range.

Figure 18.1 shows the input, criterion, and output ranges prior to invoking the command to extract all of the books related to sports.

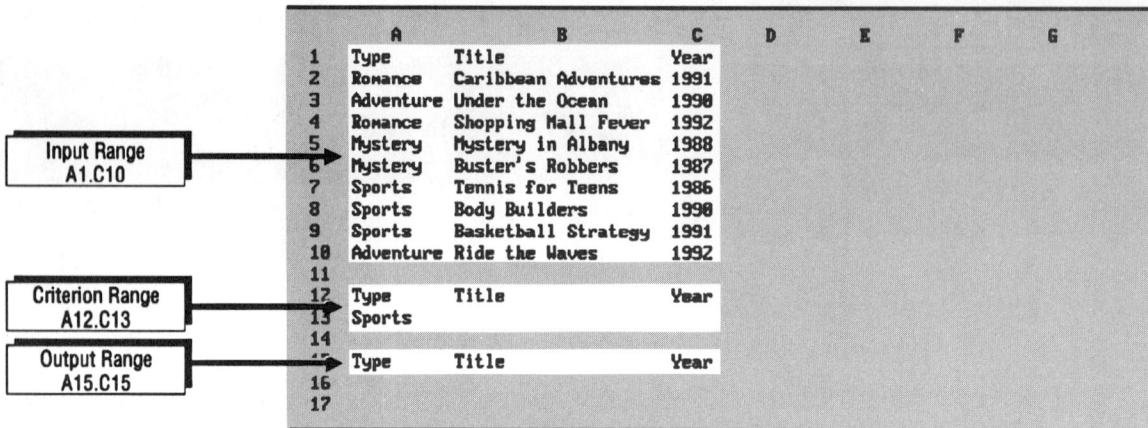

Figure 18.1 □ *Input, Criterion, and Output Ranges*

After you use the command **/ Data Query Extract** to extract all sports books, the output range will display three records as shown in Figure 18.2.

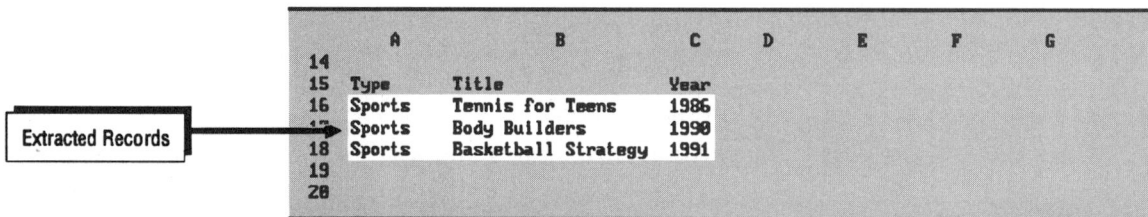

Figure 18.2 □ *Output Range Containing Extracted Records*

The extracted records are displayed under the field names in the output range.

Defining an Output Range and Extracting Records

In this tutorial, you will retrieve the file CAFEBKFS that you created in Chapter 17 and extract all the records that match the criterion—all the restaurants that serve breakfast.

Retrieve the file CAFEBKFS.

To copy the field names from the criterion range to an output range in row 25, move the cell pointer to A22.

PRESS /

PRESS c (Copy)

PRESS . (Period)

PRESS → (5 times)

PRESS ↵

To enter the range to copy to, move the cell pointer to A26 and:

PRESS ↵

To define the field names in row 26 as the output range:

PRESS   /

PRESS   d (Data)

PRESS   q (Query)

PRESS   o (Output)

ENTER   a26.f26

PRESS   ↵

To extract the records:

PRESS   e (Extract)

To return to the READY mode:

PRESS   q (Quit)

If needed, press the down arrow key to view the two records in the output range. These two records match the criterion.

To save the file under a new name:

PRESS   /

PRESS   f (File)

PRESS   s (Save)

ENTER   breakfas

PRESS   ↵

ACTIVITY 18.1   ◻   *Extracting Records*

In this activity, you will retrieve the file EMPLDEPT created in the previous chapter. You will define an output range and extract records of employees in the Management Department who work full-time.

1. Retrieve the file EMPLDEPT.
2. Copy the field names to row 18.
3. Define the output range, including all field names.
4. Extract the records specified in the criterion range.
5. View the four extracted records.
6. Save the file under the name EMPLMGT.
7. Print the output range only—rows 18-22.

WHAT ARE FORMULA CRITERIA?

Previously, the records you located in databases matched the criteria in the criterion range. **Formula criteria** are nonmatching criteria used to locate values. Formula criteria help you locate records with fields less than, equal to, not equal to, or greater than a given value.

For example, using formula criteria, you could find the names of all employees who earn:

- ☐ More than $30,000
- ☐ Less than $30,000
- ☐ Equal to $30,000
- ☐ Greater than or equal to $30,000
- ☐ Less than or equal to $30,000

Symbols Used in Formula Criteria

Six symbols are used in formula criteria. These symbols and their meanings follow:

Symbol	Meaning
=	Equal to
<	Less than
<=	Less than or equal to
>	Greater than
>=	Greater than or equal to
<>	Not equal to

Formula criteria can be entered in any cell in the correct field in the criterion range. A formula criterion is made up of two parts: the first is the cell address of the first field in the database that is related to the criterion, and the second part is the criterion itself.

In Figure 18.3, the formula criterion could be entered in any cell in the correct field in the criterion range. In this example, it is entered in B11 under the field name to which it pertains, Salary. As shown in Figure 18.3, the formula to find all employees whose salaries are greater than or equal to $50,000 is +b2=50000.

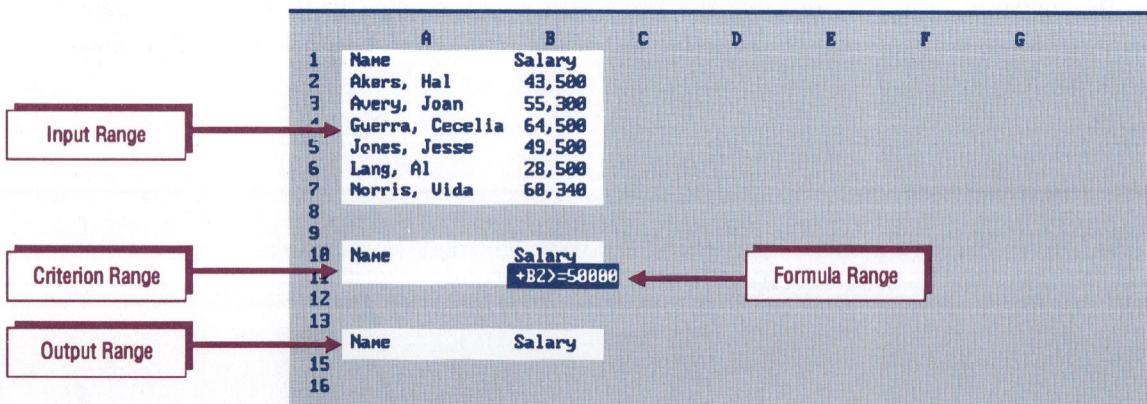

Figure 18.3 ☐ *Formula Criterion*

In Figure 18.3, cell B2 is used in the formula because it is the cell address for the first field in the database related to salary. The symbols >= mean that 1-2-3 will search for all records that include a salary greater than or equal to $50,000.

After you create and enter the formula in cell B11, a zero (0) will appear because cell B2 is not greater than or equal to $50,000. If B2 were greater than or equal to $50,000, a one (1) would appear.

After entering a formula, you can extract the records by executing the command **/ Data Query Extract**. Figure 18.4 shows that three records have been located and extracted to the output range.

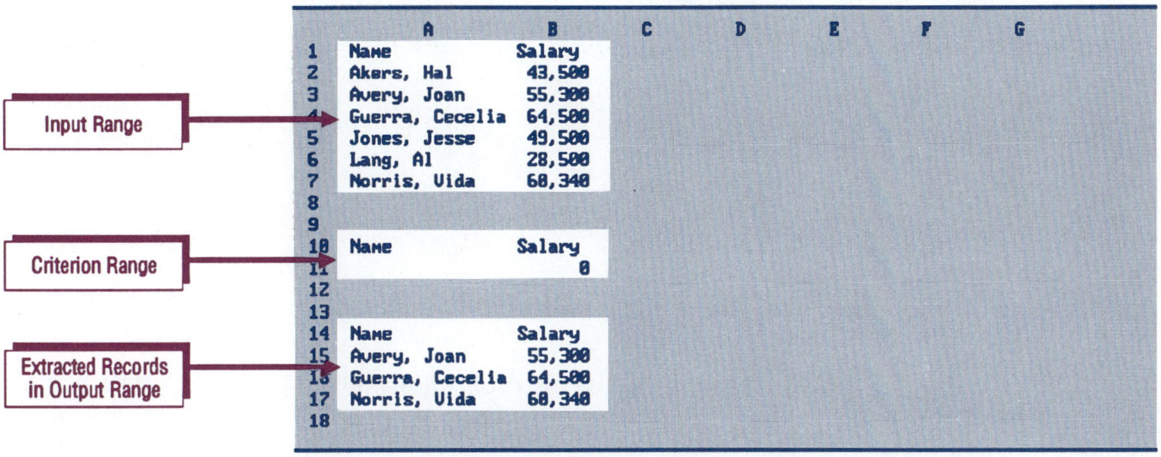

Figure 18.4   □   *Extracted Records in Output Range*

Using Formula Criteria

In this tutorial, you will extract records from a database containing employee information.

Retrieve the file EMPLDEPT created in the previous chapter.

Before you enter a formula criterion, you must erase the criteria entered previously in E16 and E17. To erase these formulas, move the cell pointer to E16 and:

PRESS /

PRESS r (Range)

PRESS e (Erase)

PRESS . (Period)

PRESS ↓

PRESS ↵

Enter the formula under its related field name in the criterion range. Move the cell pointer to G16.

To enter a criterion formula to locate all employees who make $55,000 or less than $55,000:

ENTER   +g2<=55000
PRESS   ↵

A one (1) appears in cell G19 because cell G2 is less than or equal to $55,000.

Next, you will copy the field names to a blank area below the criterion range that will be the first row of the output range. Move the cell pointer to A15 and:

PRESS   /
PRESS   c (Copy)
PRESS   . (Period)
PRESS   → (6 times)
PRESS   ↵

Move the cell pointer to A18 where the output range will begin.

PRESS   ↵

To define the output range including the row with the field names:

PRESS   /
PRESS   d (Data)
PRESS   q (Query)
PRESS   o (Output)
ENTER   a18.g18
PRESS   ↵

Since the input and criterion ranges were defined in the previous chapter, all you need to do now is extract the records. To extract the records:

PRESS   e (Extract)

To return to the READY mode:

PRESS   q (Quit)
PRESS   ↓ (until the 5 extracted records are displayed)

All five records will list employees who earn $55,000 or less.

Now, you will enter several other formula criteria. Move the cell pointer to G16.

To enter a formula to find employees who earn more than $60,000:

ENTER	+g2>60000
PRESS	↵

The Data Query key, F7, will remember the last data query option you used. To save time extracting records:

PRESS	F7 (Data Query key)

Notice that the records in the output range changed immediately. View the six extracted records listing employees who earn more than $60,000.

Next, you will enter a formula to extract a list of employees who earn $76,500 or more. Move the cell pointer to G16.

ENTER	+g2>=76500
PRESS	↵

To extract the records:

PRESS	F7

View the two extracted records of employees who earn $76,500 or more.

In the next part of the tutorial, you will extract the records of employees who have offices on various floors of a building. To erase the previous criterion formula, move the cell pointer to G16 and:

PRESS	/
PRESS	r (Range)
PRESS	e (Erase)
PRESS	↵

Move the cell pointer to C16 before entering the next formula.

To extract the names of all employees whose offices are located on the third floor:

ENTER	+c2=3
PRESS	↵

To extract the records:

PRESS   F7

View the four records displayed in the output range.

The next formula is designed to extract the names of all employees who have offices on any floor except the fourth floor.

Move the cell pointer to C16 and:

ENTER   +c2<>4
PRESS   ↵

To extract the records:

PRESS   F7
PRESS   ↓ (until all extracted records are displayed)

To save the file under a new name:

PRESS   /
PRESS   f (File)
PRESS   s (Save)
ENTER   emplflor
PRESS   ↵

ACTIVITY 18.2   □   *Using Formula Criteria*

In this activity, you will extract records of baseball cards based on their value and the date they were issued.

1. Retrieve the file BSBL.
2. Copy the field names in row 1 to a criterion range beginning in row 57.
3. Copy the field names in row 57 to an output range beginning in row 60.
4. In cell F58, enter a formula that will locate and extract all records of baseball cards valued at $25 or more.
5. Define the input, criterion, and output ranges.
6. Enter the command to extract records.
7. View the extracted records.
8. Save the file as BSBLVALU.
9. Print the output range only.

10. Erase the formula entered in F58.
11. Enter a formula to extract all records of baseball cards that were issued before 1950.
12. Use the Data Query key to extract the records.
13. Save the file as BSBLYEAR.
14. Print the output range only.

WHAT ARE PARTIALLY MATCHING CRITERIA?

Partially matching criteria will allow you to search a database for all items purchased in a certain month or in a certain year. Partially matching criteria are used to search for labels in a database, not values.

Symbols Used in Partially Matching Criteria

Symbols, called **wildcards**, are used in partially matching criteria to replace characters. Two of the symbols used in partially matching criteria are the ? and the *. Examples of each of these symbols and how they can be used follows:

SYMBOL	EXAMPLE
?	A question mark matches or replaces any single character. For example, MA? matches MAY and MAR (March).
*	An asterisk matches or replaces all characters to the end of a label. For example, B* will match any labels that begin with B including Bench and Bookcase.

Partially matching criteria must be entered under the appropriate field name in the criterion range. Be sure to enter characters exactly as they appear in the database. Lowercase letters in the database should be entered as lowercase letters in the criterion; uppercase letters in the database should be entered as uppercase letters in the criterion.

Extracting Records Using Partially Matching Criteria

In this tutorial, you will retrieve a database for a household inventory, including items purchased, date of purchase, and cost. You will use partially matching criteria to locate all tables in the database and then to locate all items purchased in 1991.

Retrieve the file HOUSE.

First, you will create a criterion range by copying the field names from row 1 to row 24. Move the cell pointer to A1.

PRESS   /

PRESS   c (Copy)

PRESS   . (Period)

PRESS   → (2 times)

PRESS   ↵

Move the cell pointer to A24.

PRESS   ↵

To enter a partially matching criteria to locate all tables in the database, move the cell pointer to A25.

ENTER   Table*

PRESS   ↵

Next, you will create an output range by copying the field names from row 24 to row 28. Move the cell pointer to A24.

PRESS   /

PRESS   c (Copy)

PRESS   . (Period)

PRESS   → (2 times)

PRESS   ↵

Move the cell pointer to A28.

PRESS   ↵

To define the input range:

PRESS   /

PRESS   d (Data)

PRESS   q (Query)

PRESS   i (Input)

ENTER   a1.c20

PRESS   ↵

To define the criterion range:

PRESS   c (Criterion)
ENTER   a24.c25
PRESS   ↵

To define the output range:

PRESS   o (Output)
ENTER   a28.c28
PRESS   ↵

To extract the partially matching records:

PRESS   e (Extract)

To return to the READY mode:

PRESS   q (Quit)

To view the extracted records:

PRESS   ↓ (until all 3 records are displayed)

Notice that the criterion extracted all records containing a field that started with the word Table. To save the file:

PRESS   /
PRESS   f (File)
PRESS   s (Save)
ENTER   table
PRESS   ↵

Next, you will enter criterion to locate all items purchased in 1991. Move the cell pointer to A25.
    To erase the criterion entered previously:

PRESS   /
PRESS   r (Range)
PRESS   e (Erase)
PRESS   ↵

To enter the criterion to locate all items purchased any time in 1991, you will replace each character preceding 1991 in the Date Purchased field with a question mark (?). Since each date contains eight characters or spaces before the year, eight question marks will precede 1991.

Move the cell pointer to B25 under the Date Purchased field name.

ENTER ????????1991
PRESS ↵

To extract the records matching the criterion using the query key:

PRESS F7

Notice that two records are displayed in the output range. This means that two items were purchased in 1991.

To save the file:

PRESS /
PRESS f (File)
PRESS s (Save)
ENTER house91
PRESS ↵

ACTIVITY 18.3 ☐ Using Matching Criteria

In this activity, you will use a file created in the previous tutorial. You will extract all items that include the word Sofa at the beginning of the field. Then, you will extract all items purchased during the 1970s.

1. Retrieve the file HOUSE91.
2. Since a criterion range has already been defined, all you need to do is change the criterion within it.
3. Erase the present criterion stored in B25.
4. Enter criterion to extract all items that begin with the word Sofa. Use the * symbol in the criterion.
5. Extract the partially matching records.
6. View the extracted records.

7. Save the file as HOUSESOF.

8. Print the criterion and output ranges only.

9. Erase the previous criterion.

10. Enter criterion that will extract all items purchased in the 1970's.

11. Extract the partially matching records.

12. View the extracted records. Nine records should be listed in the output range.

13. Enter a formula in C38 to determine the total amount spent during the 1970s.

14. Format the value in C38 so it is in the same format as the other values in the COST field.

15. Enter the word TOTAL in B38.

16. Save the file as HOUSE70.

17. Print the criterion range, the output range, and the row containing the total amount spent in the 1970s.

C H A P T E R   1 8 □ *T H E O R Y   E X E R C I S E S*

True/False ‖‖‖‖‖‖‖ Each of the following statements is either True or False. Indicate your choice by circling **T** for a true statement or **F** for a false statement.

1. The command to extract records and display them in an output range is **/ Data Query Extract.**   1. T   F

2. The output range must be in an area of the spreadsheet below the criterion range.   2. T   F

3. At least two rows of the output range must be defined as the output range.   3. T   F

4. Field names are copied into the first row of the output range.   4. T   F

5. Formula criteria use the symbols <= to locate records with fields less than or equal to a certain value.   5. T   F

6. To locate fields with more than $1,000 entered, you would include >1000 in the formula.   6. T   F

7. When +c2<>50 is included in a formula criterion, all records with fields in column C equal to 50 will be located.   7. T   F

8. Formula criteria must be entered in a cell in the appropriate field of the criterion range.   8. T   F

9. The first part of a formula criterion is any cell in the field that pertains to the criterion.   9. T   F

10. The formula criterion +b2=200 will extract all records with fields in column B that contain the value 200.   10. T   F

11. After you create and enter a +b2>300 formula criterion in a cell, a zero (0) appearing in the formula cell address means that the cell address used in the formula, B2, contains a value that is less than or equal to 300.   11. T   F

12. After entering a formula criterion, you can extract records by executing the command **/ Data Query Extract.**   12. T   F

13. Partially matching criteria are used to search for values in a database, not labels.   13. T   F

14. A question mark is used in partially matching criterion to replace one character.   14. T   F

15. An asterisk is used in partially matching criteria to replace all characters to the end of a label.   15. T   F

16. The criterion Office* will locate all records with a field that begins with Office.   16. T   F

17. The criterion S??? will locate all records with a field that begins with S that contain four or more characters.   17. T   F

18. Partially matching criteria must be entered under the appropriate field name in the criterion range.   18.   T   F

Completion ||||||||| For each item below, fill in the word (or words) that completes the statement or answers the question.

1. Before extracting records, you must define three ranges—the input range, the criterion range, and the _____ range.

2. The output range must contain the _____ _____ in the first row.

3. When you define ranges, the criterion range must contain a minimum of at least two rows, and the output range must contain a minimum of _____ row(s).

4. When you enter the formula +a2>200 in the criterion range, all records with data in column A with values _____ _____ 200 will be located.

5. When you enter the formula +c2>=12000 in the criterion range, all records with data in column C with values _____ _____ or _____ _____ 12,000 will be located.

6. When you enter the formula +b2>100 in the criterion range, all records with data in column B with values _____ _____ 100 will be located.

7. After you enter the formula +c2>200 in the criterion range, a one (1) appearing in the formula cell address means that the value in C2 is _____ _____ 200.

8. The command to extract records is **/ Data Query** _____ .

9. When using partially matching criteria, you must enter lowercase letters used in fields in a database as _____ letters in the criterion.

10. A question mark is used in partially matching criteria to replace _____ character(s).

11. The criterion Com* will located all records in a given field with cells that begin with _____.

12. The criterion ????1992 will search for all records in a given field with cells that begin with any _____ characters and end with 1992.

ACTIVITY 18.4 □ *Using Partially Matching and Formula Criteria*

In this activity, you will use matching criteria and formula criteria to locate records in a database. You will use the file HOUSE70 created in Activity 18.3. First, you will search for all lamps costing $50 or more and then you will search for all items purchased in either the 1980s or 1990s.

1. Retrieve the file HOUSE70.
2. Erase the criterion entered previously.
3. Enter a partially matching criteria to search for lamps of all types.
4. Enter a formula criteria to search for all Lamps costing $50 or more.
5. Extract the records. Only one extracted records should be displayed in the output range.
6. Save the file as LAMP.
7. Print only the criterion and the output ranges.
8. Erase the criteria entered previously.
9. Now enter criteria to find all items purchased in either the 1980s or the 1990s.
10. Increase the size of the defined criterion range to include the field names and all the criteria.
11. Extract the files. Twelve records should be displayed.
12. Save the file as 1980-90.
13. Print the criterion and the output ranges only.

CYCLE 6
WYSIWYG Add-In for Release 2.3

CHAPTER
19 WYSIWYG Features of Release 2.3

WYSIWYG Features of Release 2.3

OBJECTIVES

- ❏ Attach an add-in program
- ❏ Use WYSIWYG features
- ❏ Change type styles and type sizes
- ❏ Change the spreadsheet display colors
- ❏ Add a graph to a spreadsheet
- ❏ Use the zoom feature
- ❏ Remove a graph
- ❏ Move a graph
- ❏ Print a graph and spreadsheet together

WHAT IS WYSIWYG?

WYSIWYG is an **add-in** program that comes with 1-2-3 Release 2.3. 1-2-3 add-in programs enhance the standard features of 1-2-3. The WYSIWYG add-in provides features needed for spreadsheet publishing. It allows you to change the style and size of text in a spreadsheet as well as to add a graph to a spreadsheet printout. WYSIWYG stands for what-you-see-is-what-you-get because a spreadsheet or graph shown on the screen will look like what you get when you print it. WYSIWYG features improve the appearance of spreadsheets.

HOW DO YOU USE WYSIWYG?

Before you can use any WYSIWYG commands, you must attach WYSIWYG. The process of attaching WYSIWYG means that the WYSIWYG files are loaded into memory. To attach WYSIWYG, use the command **/ Add-In Attach**. After this command has been invoked, you must select the WYSIWYG.ADN file name from the list shown in the control panel. Finally, you select No-Key. If you wish to assign the WYSIWYG add-in to a key that you can press to display the WYSIWYG menus, see the software instruction manual for further instructions.

Once you attach the WYSIWYG add-in, you can access the special WYSIWYG menus by entering a colon. The WYSIWYG add-in will remain attached until you detach it or exit 1-2-3.

WHAT ARE THE MAIN FEATURES OF WYSIWYG?

The use of **fonts** is one of the main WYSIWYG features. A font is a type style of a certain point size. A point is approximately 1/72 of an inch. Point size determines the height of characters. Swiss 12 point is a font with characters about 1/6th of an inch high; Swiss 24 point has characters twice as high.

By changing the type style and size in a spreadsheet, you can improve the appearance of the spreadsheet. The initial command to change fonts is : Format Font. Then, you will be asked to select one of the fonts listed in the dialog box. Examples of these fonts are shown in Figure 19.1. Finally, you will need to highlight the text that you want to be displayed and printed in the font selected.

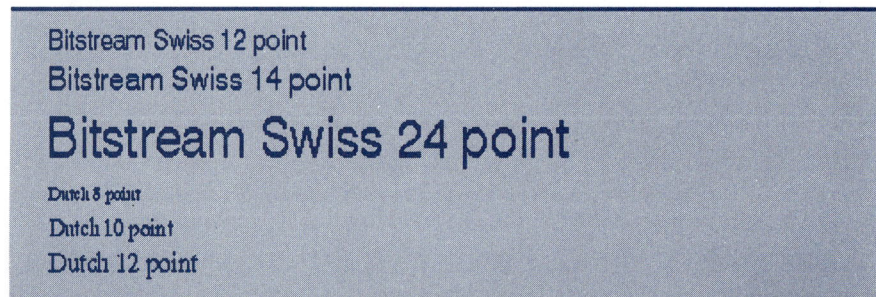

Bitstream Swiss 12 point
Bitstream Swiss 14 point

Bitstream Swiss 24 point

Dutch 8 point
Dutch 10 point
Dutch 12 point

Figure 19.1 □ *Examples of Type Styles and Type Sizes*

Be careful when choosing type styles. Generally, it is best to use the same type style throughout a spreadsheet. Two different type styles in a spreadsheet is the maximum number recommended.

Remember that most text is printed in 10 or 12 point size. Footnotes or notes may be in 8 point size. Be careful that the point size used is large enough to be readable. Titles are usually in 14 point but can be in 24 point as long as the title does not overwhelm the rest of the data in the spreadsheet. When a very large type size makes a spreadsheet title longer than the data under it, a smaller size should be selected.

Figure 19.2 shows an example of a spreadsheet with the main title in Swiss style 14 point, the column headings in Dutch style 12 point, and the other data in Dutch style 10 point.

Other features include the ability to change the colors of the screen display. The background for the spreadsheet, the cell pointer, and even the row and column frame colors can be changed to suit your individual preferences.

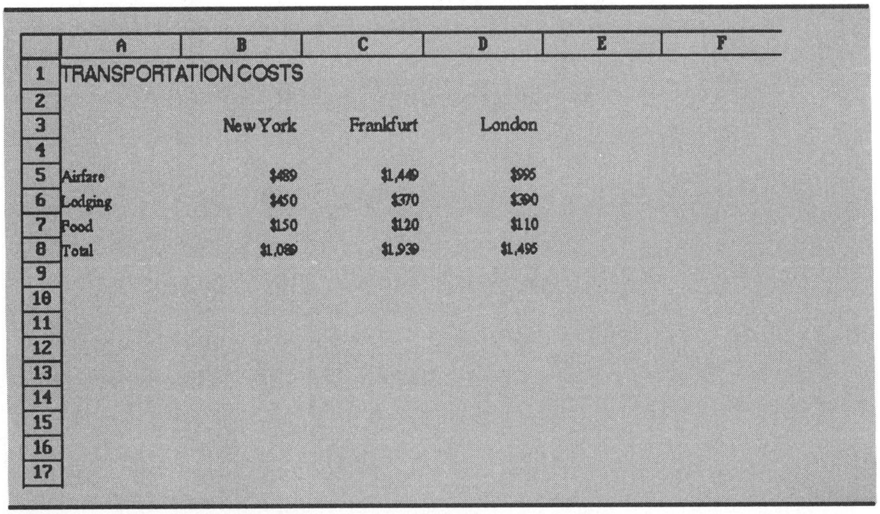

	A	B	C	D	E	F
1	TRANSPORTATION COSTS					
2						
3		New York	Frankfurt	London		
4						
5	Airfare	$489	$1,449	$995		
6	Lodging	$450	$370	$390		
7	Food	$150	$120	$110		
8	Total	$1,089	$1,939	$1,495		
9						
10						
11						
12						
13						
14						
15						
16						
17						

Figure 19.2 ☐ *Fonts Used in a Spreadsheet*

ATTACHING WYSIWYG

Retrieve the file BASECD.
To attach the WYSIWYG add-in:

PRESS /

PRESS a (Add-In)

PRESS a (Attach)

PRESS → (until the WYSIWYG.ADN file name is highlighted)

PRESS ↵

The second and third lines of the control panel will display the following:

```
                                                                    MENU
No-Key  7  8  9  10
Do not assign add-in to a key
               A              B         C         D         E
```

To assign WYSIWYG to no key:

PRESS n (No-Key)

PRESS q (Quit)

The screen will go blank and then the WYSIWYG copyright information will flash across the screen briefly before the original file BASECD reappears.

ACCESSING WYSIWYG MENUS

To move the cell point to A1:

PRESS   Home key

To access the WYSIWYG menus:

ENTER   : (Colon)

The second and third lines of the control panel will display the following:

```
A1: [W21] 'Baseball Card Collection                                    WYSIWYG
Worksheet  Format  Graph  Print  Display  Special  Text  Named-Style  Quit
Column  Row  Page
         |        A        |      B      |     C     |    D    |    E    |
```

USING FONTS

Next, you will change the fonts in some parts of the BASECD file. To change the type style and type size of the main title BASEBALL CARD COLLECTION:

PRESS   f (Format)

The second and third lines of the control panel will display the following:

```
A1: [W21] 'Baseball Card Collection                                    WYSIWYG
Font  Bold  Italics  Underline  Color  Lines  Shade  Reset  Quit
1 2 3 4 5 6 7 8  Replace  Default  Library  Quit
         |        A        |      B      |     C     |    D    |    E    |
```

To select a font:

PRESS   f (Font)

To change the main title to Swiss style in 24 point:

PRESS   3 (3:Bitstream Swiss 24 Point)

The control panel will display the following:

```
A1: [W21] 'Baseball Card Collection                                    POINT
Change the attributes of range: A1..A1

          A              B           C         D         E
```

To accept the range A1..A1:

PRESS ↵

The font will change immediately on the screen. Notice that row 1 increased in size.

To change the column headings to Swiss 14 point, move the cell pointer to A3.

ENTER :
PRESS f (Format)
PRESS f (Font)
ENTER 2 (2:Bitstream Swiss 14 point)

The second line of the control panel will display the following:

```
A3: [W21] 'Player's                                                    POINT
Change the attributes of range: A3..A3

          A              B           C         D         E
```

To highlight the range containing all column headings:

PRESS . (Period)
PRESS ↓
PRESS → (5 times)
PRESS ↵

To emphasize data, it can be printed in bold. To print the values and labels in row 15 in bold, move the cell pointer to A15.

ENTER :
PRESS f (Format)
PRESS b (Bold)
PRESS s (Set)

The second line of the control panel will display the following:

```
A15: [W21] 'Paige, Satchel                                              POINT
Change the attributes of range: A15..A15

       |           A          |      B     |     C     |    D    |     E     |
```

To highlight the information in row 15:

PRESS   . (Period)
PRESS   → (5 times)
PRESS   ↵

The first line of the control panel will display the following;

```
A15: {Bold} [W21] 'Paige, Satchel                                       READY

       |           A          |      B     |     C     |    D    |     E     |
```

To change the background of the file displayed on the screen to red:

ENTER   :
PRESS   d (Display)
PRESS   c (Colors)
PRESS   b (Background)
PRESS   r (Red)

To change the color of the cell pointer to yellow:

PRESS   c (Cell-pointer)
PRESS   y (Yellow)

To change the color used as background for the row numbers and letters:

PRESS   f (Frame)
PRESS   g (Green)
PRESS   q (Quit)
PRESS   q (Quit)

PRINTING IN WYSIWYG

To print a file that has text in fonts, you must use the print command in the WYSIWYG main menu. Remember that some printers cannot print in special fonts while others will print only certain fonts. Try out various fonts to see which ones will work with your printer. To print the spreadsheet BASECD:

E N T E R :

P R E S S p (Print)

A dialog box similar to the one in Figure 19.3 will appear on your screen:

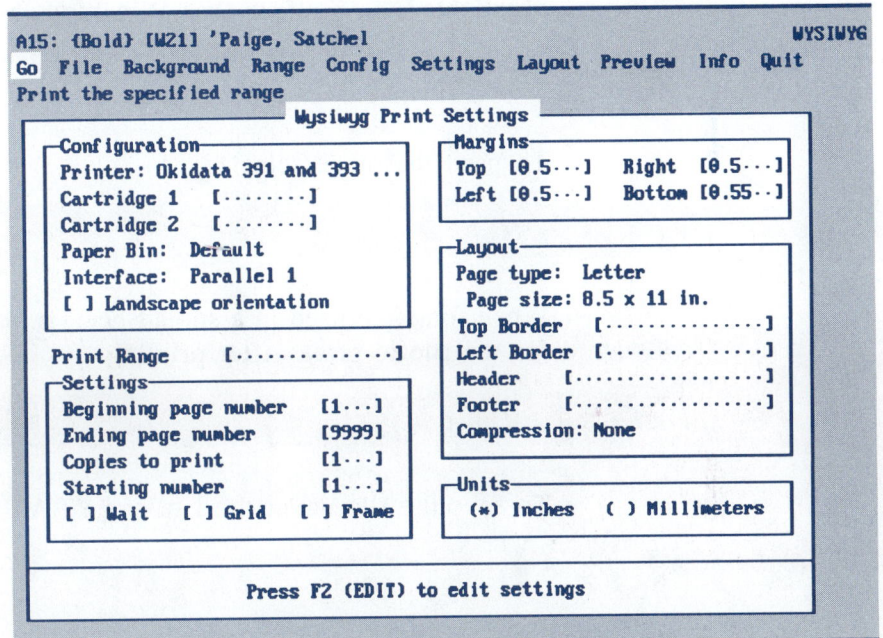

```
A15: {Bold} [W21] 'Paige, Satchel                              WYSIWYG
Go  File  Background  Range  Config  Settings  Layout  Preview  Info  Quit
Print the specified range
                         ┌─ Wysiwyg Print Settings ─┐
    ┌─Configuration──────────────┐  ┌─Margins─────────────────────┐
    │ Printer: Okidata 391 and 393 ... │  │ Top  [0.5···]   Right  [0.5···] │
    │ Cartridge 1    [········]   │  │ Left [0.5···]   Bottom [0.55··] │
    │ Cartridge 2    [········]   │  └─────────────────────────────┘
    │ Paper Bin:  Default        │  ┌─Layout──────────────────────┐
    │ Interface:  Parallel 1     │  │ Page type:  Letter           │
    │ [ ] Landscape orientation  │  │  Page size: 8.5 x 11 in.     │
    └────────────────────────────┘  │ Top Border    [·············] │
                                     │ Left Border   [·············] │
    Print Range     [·············]  │ Header    [·················] │
    ┌─Settings───────────────────┐  │ Footer    [·················] │
    │ Beginning page number  [1···] │  │ Compression: None            │
    │ Ending page number   [9999]  └─────────────────────────────┘
    │ Copies to print      [1···]  ┌─Units───────────────────────┐
    │ Starting number      [1···]  │ (*) Inches    ( ) Millimeters │
    │ [ ] Wait  [ ] Grid  [ ] Frame └─────────────────────────────┘
    └────────────────────────────┘
              Press F2 (EDIT) to edit settings
```

Figure 19.3 □ *Dialog box for WYSIWYG Print Commands*

To access the dialog box:

P R E S S F2 (F2 key)

To change the settings of any of the six main categories, you will enter the highlighted character within that category. To select the printer brand and model:

P R E S S c (Configuration)

P R E S S p (Printer)

A printer list will be overlayed on the WYSIWYG Print Settings Menu. Use the up and down arrow keys to highlight the brand and model of printer you will be using. Then:

PRESS ↵

PRESS Esc

To print the range A1-E20:

PRESS r (Range)

ENTER a1.e20

PRESS ↵

In the bottom right hand corner of the screen the word OK will be highlighted. To confirm that all settings are OK:

PRESS ↵

To print the range selected:

PRESS g (Go)

When fonts are used in a spreadsheet, it may take longer than usual for the file to print. After printing:

PRESS q (Quit)

To save the file under the file name BASECD:

PRESS /

PRESS f (File)

PRESS s (Save)

PRESS ↵

PRESS r (Replace)

ACTIVITY 19.1 ☐ *Using WYSIWYG and Fonts*

In this activity, you will retrieve the file BOOKS, use the WYSIWYG add-in, change the format of the file, the colors of the display, and print the file.

1. Retrieve the file BOOKS.
2. Attach the WYSIWYG.ADN add-in.

3. Change the titles in Row 1 to Bitstream Swiss 24 point.
4. Change the font of rows 2-10 to Bitstream Dutch 12 point.
5. Change the background of the entire file to yellow.
6. Change the frame color to red.
7. Change the cell pointer color to dark-blue.
8. Change the book title SHOPPING MALL FEVER to bold.
9. Print the file from the WYSIWYG menu.
10. Save and name the file as BOOKS.
11. Change the background color to white.
12. Change the frame and cell pointer colors to cyan.

HOW CAN GRAPHS BE ADDED TO SPREADSHEETS?

Another main feature of WYSIWYG is the ability to display and print a graph and spreadsheet together. The graph can be displayed in any size and in any location. The initial command to add a current graph to a spreadsheet is : Graph Add Current. Then you will highlight the range in which you want the graph to be displayed. Remember to make the graph large enough to be readable. Figure 19.4 shows a printout of a spreadsheet with a graph below it.

TRANSPORTATION COSTS

	New York	Frankfurt	London
Airfare	$489	$1,449	$995
Lodging	$450	$370	$390
Food	$150	$120	$110
Total	$1,089	$1,939	$1,495

TRANSPORTATION COSTS

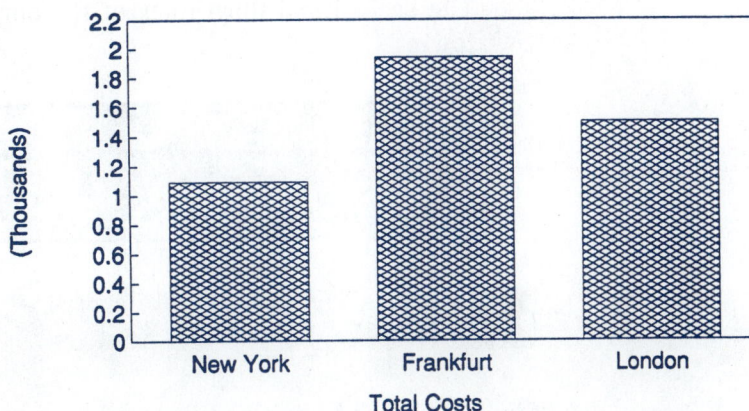

Figure 19.4 ❑ *Spreadsheet and Graph Printout*

A graph that is added to a spreadsheet may be too small to view details in it and check its accuracy. To view a full scale version of the graph, you may use the zoom feature.

You can also edit spreadsheet values and update the graph. If you add a graph to a spreadsheet and then make changes in the spreadsheet data, those changes will update the graph automatically.

ADDING GRAPHS TO SPREADSHEETS

In this tutorial you will retrieve the file DAIRY, view the graph created previously, and add it to the spreadsheet.

Attach the WYSIWYG add-in if it is not already attached by:

PRESS /

PRESS a (Add-In)

PRESS a (Attach)

PRESS → (until the WYSIWYG.ADN file name is highlighted)

PRESS ↵

PRESS n (No-Key)

PRESS q (Quit)

PRESS Home (Home key)

To access the WYSIWYG menus:

ENTER : (Colon)

To add a graph:

PRESS g (Graph)

The second and third lines of the control panel will display the following:

```
A1: 'Dairy Delight Shop                                          WYSIWYG
Add  Remove  Goto  Settings  Move  Zoom  Compute  View  Edit  Quit
Add a graphic to the worksheet
     A        B        C        D        E        F        G
```

PRESS a (Add)

The second and third lines of the control panel will display the following:

```
A1: 'Dairy Delight Shop                                          WYSIWYG
Current  Named  PIC  Metafile  Blank
Add the current graph to the worksheet
    |    A    |    B    |    C    |    D    |    E    |    F    |    G    |
```

PRESS c (Current)

The second line of the control panel will display the following:

```
A1: 'Dairy Delight Shop                                          POINT
Enter the graphic display range: A1
    |    A    |    B    |    C    |    D    |    E    |    F    |    G    |
```

Move the cell pointer to H1.

PRESS . (Period)

PRESS ↓ (9 times)

PRESS → (5 times)

PRESS ↵

PRESS q (Quit)

The graph will appear on the screen beside the spreadsheet.
    To view a full scale display of the graph, move the cell pointer to any location in the graph.

PRESS : (Colon)

PRESS g (Graph)

PRESS z (Zoom)

To accept the cell address displayed in the second line of the control panel:

PRESS ↵

A full scale version of the graph will be displayed.
    To view the spreadsheet and graph:

PRESS Esc

PRESS q (Quit)

REMOVING GRAPHS AND ADDING GRAPHS

After adding a graph to a spreadsheet, you may change your mind and want to remove it. To remove the graph created previously from the screen:

PRESS   Home
PRESS   : (Colon)
PRESS   g (Graph)
PRESS   r (Remove)

The second line of the control panel will display the following:

```
A1: 'Dairy Delight Shop                                        POINT
Select the graphics to remove: A1

      A       B       C       D       E       F       G
```

Move the cell pointer to H1.

PRESS   . (Period)
PRESS   ↓ (9 times)
PRESS   → (5 times)
PRESS   ↵
PRESS   q (Quit)

The graph will disappear from the screen.
   To add the same graph below the spreadsheet data:

PRESS   : (Colon)
PRESS   g (Graph)
PRESS   a (Add)
PRESS   c (Current)

Move the cell pointer to A13.

PRESS   . (Period)
PRESS   ↓ (15 times)
PRESS   → (5 times)
PRESS   ↵
PRESS   q (Quit)

CHANGING VALUES AND UPDATING GRAPHS

When values are changed in a spreadsheet, the graph added to it will be redrawn to reflect those changes if 1-2-3 defaults are set for automatic recalculate. Using the graph created previously, change the sales figures for Pecan Delight Sales for October-December. Be sure that the WYSIWYG add-in is still attached.

Move the cell pointer to F7.

E N T E R   18
P R E S S   ↵

To view the redrawn graph, move the cell pointer to the graph. Check the graph to see if Pecan Delight Sales for October-December is accurate.

PRINTING A GRAPH AND SPREADSHEET

To print a spreadsheet and graph together, you must use the print command in the WYSIWYG main menu. To print the spreadsheet and graph:

E N T E R   :
P R E S S   p (Print)

To access the WYSIWYG Print Settings dialog box:

P R E S S   F2

To change the settings of any of the six main categories, you must enter the highlighted character within that category. Since you selected the printer brand and model in an earlier tutorial, you may not need to again. However, if no printer brand and model is displayed in the dialog box:

P R E S S   c (Configuration)
P R E S S   p (Printer)

Use the up and down arrow keys to highlight the brand and model of printer you will be using.

P R E S S   ↵
P R E S S   Esc (Escape key)

To select the print range A1-F29:

PRESS   r (Range)
ENTER   a1.f29
PRESS   ↵

In the bottom right hand corner of the screen the word OK will be highlighted. To confirm that all settings are OK:

PRESS   ↵

To print the range selected:

PRESS   g (Go)

The spreadsheet and graph should print on one page.

PRESS   q (Quit)

Save the file as DAIRY.

ACTIVITY 19.2 ☐ *Adding and Removing Graphs*

In this activity, you will add a graph to a spreadsheet, use the zoom command to view it, remove the graph and add it in a different location.

1. Retrieve the file BIRDS.
2. Attach the WYSIWYG add-in if it is not already attached.
3. View the graph created previously that depicts the 1991 bird population figures.
4. Remove the data-labels from the graph since they will be too small to read when the graph is added to the spreadsheet.
5. View the graph to be sure the data-labels have been removed.
6. Save and name the graph BIRDS.
7. Add the current graph in the range F1-J12.
8. To see a full scale version of the graph, move the cell pointer to the graph and use the zoom command.
9. Since the graph is too small to be read easily, remove the graph.
10. Add the same graph below the 1991 spreadsheet figures. Select a larger range than was used previously.
11. Print the spreadsheet with the graph directly below it.
12. Save the file as BIRDS.

MOVING GRAPHS

Once a graph has been added to a spreadsheet, it can be moved to a different location. Be sure you know the exact range of the graph before moving it. Otherwise, you may move only one section of the graph or a message may appear saying that the graph cannot be located.

In this tutorial, you will add a graph and then move it to a different location. Add and attach WYSIWYG if you have not already done so.

Retrieve the file CREDITCD and view the graph created previously.

To add the graph below the spreadsheet:

PRESS	: (Colon)
PRESS	g (Graph)
PRESS	a (Add)
PRESS	c (Current)
ENTER	d12.i26
PRESS	↵
PRESS	q (Quit)

To move the graph so that it will be directly below the spreadsheet data:

PRESS	Home
ENTER	: (Colon)
PRESS	g (Graph)
PRESS	m (Move)

The second line of the control panel will display the following:

```
A1: 'CREDIT CARD USAGE                                    POINT
Select the graphic to move: A1

    |   A   |   B   |   C   |   D   |   E   |   F   |   G   |   H   |
```

ENTER	d12.i26
PRESS	↵

The second line of the control panel will display the following:

```
A1: 'CREDIT CARD USAGE                                                POINT
Enter the new top left position: A1

        A       B       C       D       E       F       G       H
```

PRESS ↓ (11 times so the cell pointer is at A12)

PRESS ↵

PRESS q

Using the instructions presented previously, print the spreadsheet and graph on one page using WYSIWYG print commands.
Save the file as CREDITGR.

ACTIVITY 19.3 ☐ *Adding and Moving a Graph*

In this activity, you will add a graph to a spreadsheet and then move it to a different location.

1. Retrieve the file ACT12-3.
2. Press F10 to view the graph created previously. This graph should depict the 1991 attendance figures.
3. Add the graph to the right of the 1991 attendance figures in cells G12-K22.
4. Move the cell pointer to A23 and insert 10 blank rows.
5. Move the graph from G12-K22 to a new top left cell position of A22.
6. Print the 1991 spreadsheet data (titles, headings, and values) and the graph based on the 1991 spreadsheet data.
7. Save the file as SKIGRAPH.

CHAPTER 19 □ THEORY EXERCISES

True/False IIIIIIIII Each of the following statements is either True or False. Indicate your choice by circling **T** for a true statement or **F** for a false statement.

1. WYSIWYG is an add-in program that provides features for spreadsheet publishing. 1. T   F

2. WYSIWYG allows you to change the style of text in a spreadsheet but not the size of text. 2. T   F

3. WYSIWYG stands for what-you-see-is-what-you-get. 3. T   F

4. The WYSIWYG add-in must be attached before the WYSIWYG menus can be accessed. 4. T   F

5. Once WYSIWYG has been attached, the WYSIWYG menus can be accessed by entering a /. 5. T   F

6. The initial command to change styles and sizes of text in a spreadsheet is **: Format Font**. 6. T   F

7. With 1-2-3 Release 2.3, you can select from 12 different type styles and sizes. 7. T   F

8. Generally, it is best to use the same type style throughout a spreadsheet although several different type sizes can be used in it. 8. T   F

9. Spreadsheet titles are usually in 8 point size. 9. T   F

10. Most spreadsheet text is printed in 10 or 12 point size. 10. T   F

11. The **: Format Bold** command allows you to print values and labels in bold. 11. T   F

12. To print a spreadsheet using fonts, you must use the WYSIWYG print menus. 12. T   F

13. The initial command to add a current graph to a spreadsheet is **: Graph Add Current**. 13. T   F

14. After a graph has been added to a spreadsheet, a full scale version of it can be displayed using the Large Scale Feature. 14. T   F

15. The initial command to remove a graph from a spreadsheet is **: Remove Graph**. 15. T   F

16. When values are changed in a spreadsheet, the graph will be updated automatically to reflect those changes if 1-2-3 defaults are set for automatic recalc. 16. T   F

17. To move a graph, you must know the exact range of the graph. 17. T   F

Completion ||||||||| For each item below, fill in the word (or words) that completes the statement or answers the question.

1. WYSIWYG is a/an _____ program that comes with 1-2-3 Release 2.3.

2. WYSIWYG commands allow you to change the style and _____ of text in a spreadsheet as well as adding a graph to a spreadsheet printout.

3. WYSIWYG stands for _____.

4. The initial command to attach WYSIWYG is **/** _____ _____.

5. The initial command to change styles and sizes of spreadsheet text is : Format _____.

6. Most spreadsheet text is printed in _____ or _____ point.

7. Titles in spreadsheets are often printed in _____ point but may be printed in 24 point depending on the size of the spreadsheet.

8. The command to change the background color displayed on the screen to red is : _____ Colors Background Red.

9. To print a spreadsheet using fonts, you must use the _____ print menus.

10. The initial command to add a current graph to a spreadsheet is : Graph Add _____.

11. The initial command to remove a graph from a spreadsheet is : Graph _____.

12. After the command : Graph Move has been entered, you must select (one cell or the entire graph range) _____ to be moved.

ACTIVITY 19.4 ❐ *Reviewing WYSIWYG Features*

In this activity, you will create a spreadsheet and a graph, use fonts in the spreadsheet and add the graph below the spreadsheet.

1. Create a spreadsheet using the following data.

```
PHOENIX MOVIE PRODUCTIONS, INC.
MOVIE REVENUES


Type            1990        1991        1992

Adventure      489,000   1,729,000   2,100,000
Comedy       1,149,000   1,400,000   1,689,000
Romance      2,400,000   1,999,000   1,732,000
```

2. Create a bar chart using the spreadsheet data. Use 1990, 1991, and 1992 as X-axis labels. Use appropriate first and second titles and legends.

3. Save and name the graph PHOENIX. Save the file as PHOENIX.

4. Change the font in the two titles to Swiss 14 point.

5. Change the font in the rest of the spreadsheet to Swiss 12 point.

6. Add the PHOENIX graph below the spreadsheet.

7. Change the format of the value 2,400,000 in the spreadsheet to bold.

8. Print the spreadsheet and graph on the same page.

9. Save the file as PHOENIX.

INDEX

LOTUS 1-2-3 TUTORIAL AND APPLICATIONS

For use with Lotus 1-2-3, Releases 2.0, 2.01, 2.2 and 2.3

Nancy Groneman

Keyboard Commands

Command	Function
ESC	Cancels current entry
←	Backspace
PG UP	Moves screen up one page (20 lines)
PG DN	Moves screen down one page (20 lines)
TAB	Moves screen right one page
SHIFT-TAB	Moves screen left one page
HOME	Moves cursor to cell A1
END	Moves cursor to end of active area (used with arrow keys)
END-HOME	Moves cursor to lower right corner of worksheet
NUM LOCK	Uses numbers from the keypad
PRT SC	Printout of computer screen
"	Right aligns labels
'	Left aligns labels
^	Centers labels
\	Repeats label
F1	Help
F2	Edit cell contents
F5	Moves cursor to specific cell address
F6	Moves cursor between windows
F7	Repeats most recent data query
F9	Forces recalculation of spreadsheet
F10	Displays most recent active graph

WYSIWYG MENU COMMANDS

WYSIWYG is an add-in program that can be used with Version 2.3 of 1-2-3. WYSIWYG must be added in and invoked before the commands can be used. The WYSIWYG menu is used by pressing the : (Colon) key. The following is a list of common WYSIWYG commands. Many commands contain additional subcommands that will display on the control panel.

:Worksheet

:WC	Sets width of column
:WR	Sets width of row
:WP	Inserts and deletes vertical and horizontal page breaks

:Format

:FF	Changes fonts for selected range
:FB	Adds or deletes boldface in range
:FI	Adds or deletes italics in range
:FU	Adds or deletes underlines in range
:FC	Selects color for background, text, and negative numbers in range
:FL	Adds or deletes lines, outlines 3-D effects, etc.
:FS	Adds or deletes shading in range
:FR	Resets all formats
:FQ	Exits to WYSIWYG menu

:Graph

:GA	Adds graph to range in worksheet
:GR	Clears graphic range from worksheet
:GG	Moves cell pointer to graph in worksheet
:GS	Affects appearance of graphs in worksheet
:GM	Moves graph to different range
:GZ	Displays full screen version of selected graph
:GC	Recalculates graph displayed on worksheet

:Print

:P	Accesses the various print commands in WYSIWYG

/Add-In (for use with Version 2.3 only)

/AA	Loads specific add-in program into memory
/AD	Removes add-in program from memory
/AI	Activates attached add-in program
/AC	Removes all add-in programs from memory
/AQ	Exits add-in menu

/Quit

/Q	Exits 1-2-3; returns to DOS prompt

@FUNCTION COMMANDS

@ Functions are shortcuts formulas for 1-2-3. All the functions begin with the @ symbol.

@AVG	Average value of list
@COUNT	Counts nonblank cells in list
@MAX	Maximum value in list
@MIN	Minimum value in list
@PMT	Payment required to repay loan
@SUM	Sum of list of values

MACRO KEYSTROKES

Macros are series of keystrokes stored for later use. Macros are invoked with a two-keystroke sequence: \ (backslash) and a letter. The following list includes common commands included in macros.

{UP}	Moves cursor up one cell
{DOWN}	Moves cursor down one cell
{RIGHT}	Moves cursor to the right one cell
{LEFT}	Moves cursor to the left one cell
{PGUP}	Moves cursor up one page (20 lines)
{PGDN}	Moves cursor down one page (20 lines)
{HOME}	Moves cursor to A1
~	Enter key
{DEL}	Deletes
{EDIT}	Places you in edit mode (F2)
{GOTO}	Moves cursor to specified location
{ESC}	Escape
{BS}	Backspace
{CALC}	Recalculates worksheet
{GRAPH}	Displays current graph

SOUTH WESTERN PUBLISHING CO.

Lotus® 1-2-3® is a registered trademark of Lotus Development Corporation.

1-2-3 COMMANDS

To use 1-2-3 commands, press the / (Slash) key. Move the pointer to the proper command or select the first letter of the command. The following is a list of common commands. Many commands contain additional subcommands that will display in the control panel.

/ Worksheet

/WGFF	Global fixed format
/WGFC	Global currency format
/WGF,	Global comma format
/WGFG	Global general format
/WGFP	Global percent format
/WGFD	Global date format
/WGFT	Global text format
/WGFH	Global hidden format
/WIC	Inserts a column
/WIR	Inserts a row
/WDC	Deletes a column
/WDR	Deletes a row
/WCS	Sets width of column
/WCR	Resets width of column
/WCH	Hides a column
/WCD	Displays a hidden column
/WE	Erases a worksheet from screen
/WTB	Freezes horizontal and vertical titles
/WTH	Freezes horizontal titles
/WTV	Freezes vertical titles
/WTC	Clears frozen titles
/WWH	Splits screen horizontally
/WWV	Splits screen vertically
/WWS	Synchronized scrolling of windows
/WWU	Unsynchronized scrolling of windows
/WWC	Clears windows
/WS	Displays worksheet settings
/WP	Creates a page break when printing
/WLR	Range for recording macro in LEARN mode (versions 2.2 and above)
/WLC	Cancels learn range
/WLE	Clears contents of learn range without canceling range

/Range

/RFF	Fixed format of range
/RFC	Currency format of range
/RF,	Comma format of range
/RFG	General format of range
/RFP	Percent format of range
/RFD	Date format of range
/RFT	Text format of range
/RFH	Hide a range of data
/RFR	Redisplays hidden range
/RLL	Left aligns labels in range
/RLR	Right aligns labels in range
/RLC	Centers labels in range
/RE	Erases a range
/RNC	Creates a range name
/RND	Deletes range name
/RJ	Rearranges labels is specified range
/RP	Protects range
/RU	Unprotects range

/Copy

/C	Copies a cell or range of cells

/Move

/M	Moves a cell or range of cells

/File

/FR	Retrieves a file
/FS	Saves a file
/FC	Combines a file or named range with current file
/FE	Erases files from disk
/FL	Displays list of files
/FI	Imports text from another file
/FD	Changes default directory

/Print

/PP	Prints file on a printer
/PF	Prints to a file
/PPR	Sets range to be printed
/PPL	Line feed
/PPP	Page feed
/PPO	Sets printer options (header, footer, margins, borders, etc.)
/PPC	Resets printer options
/PPA	Tells printer paper is positioned at top of page
/PPG	Begins printing
/PPQ	Exits print menu

/Graph

/GT	Sets type of graph (line, pie, bar, etc.)
/GX	Sets X-axis labels
/GA	Sets first data set on graph
/GB	Sets second data set on graph
/GR	Resets graph settings
/GV	Views current graph
/GS	Saves graph file (.PIC) for later printing
/GO	Sets graph options (legend, format, titles, etc.)
/GN	Names graphs to display later
/GQ	Exits graph menu

/Data

/DF	Fills range of sequential values
/DS	Rearranges data in order specified
/DQI	Identifies range of data to be queried
/DQC	Sets up criteria range defining query
/DQO	Sets up range to place output of query
/DQF	Highlights records meeting criteria
/DQE	Places records meeting criteria in output range
/DQD	Deletes records in input range that match criteria
/DQR	Clears settings for input, criteria, and output ranges

/System

/S	Exit to DOS; 1-2-3 remains in memory